Building Dreams
My Heart Belongs to Israel
A Memoir
by
Efraim Margolin

1950 Golda Meir's visit to Beer Sheva

Beer Sheva 1950

Beer Sheva 1994

From the Russian pogroms and murder to the Palestine frontier to building the cities and society of a new nation, this is a sweeping memoir of persecution, poverty, struggle, smuggling, war, determination, independence and hope.

It is the story of the Jewish people in the last century.

Most of all, it is a love story: the love between a man and a woman, and their love for Israel.

Building Dreams

My Heart Belongs To Israel

A Memoir

By Efraim Margolin

8

ACKNOWLEDGEMENT

I wish to thank Timothy Harper who started me on my memoir and for several years, patiently guided me in writing my book, leaving my voice in my memoir to be judged by the readers.

www.timharper.com

To Joanne Weck, who edited my book, understanding my wish to have the voice heard in my memoir. Her suggestions and advice helped me in my final stages of my writing.

www.joanneweck.com

In memory of Nancy Nierer, my personal secretary, who for 15 years diligently worked for me, typing my handwritten manuscript into her computer and helped me arrange the chapters in order. I miss her dearly and I am sorry that she could not see my book in print.

I want to thank Maj. Gen. Amos Lapidot, Commander of Israel Air Force (Ret.), who assisted me in acquiring the Aerial Photo of Beer Sheva.

To Esther Gaber, Librarian at Elyachar Central Library – Technion Israel Institute of Technology, who diligently searched and provided me with the background of Bosmat High School which I attended in 1934.

To David Bardin, my appreciation for providing me with his mother's Elastius Brooklyn Family history, who helped Dr. Shlomo Bardin attain his ambitious dreams.

I greatly appreciate the assistance of Mr. Jehoshua Rapaport, CFO of Solel-Boheh, who helped me gather the information on the activities of Solel-Boneh in Abadan, Iran and Baharien Island.

Thanks to the Mayor of Beer Sheva Rubik Danilovich, who was kind to provide me with his handsome latest photo.

Many thanks to Mrs. Hannah Kuhn, Special Projects Coordinator of Brandeis-Bardin Campus - American Jewish University, who helped me gather the information about Dr. Shlomo Bardin early years in Israel.

Table of Contents

Prologue	PROLOGUE	15
Chapter One	THE EARLY YEARS	
	1921, Immigrating To Israel	19
	Beth Habocharim Housing Center, Jerusalem 1922	25
	The Kindergarten	31
	Moving To Geola – School	33
	Mekor Chaim, 1929 Arab Riots	35
	Moving To Schneller	43
	Summer In The Kibbutz With My Uncle Moshe	44
	Chapter 1 Photos	50-51
Chapter Two	GROWING UP	
	Haifa – Technical School	52
	Moving To Dr. Bardin's Home	56
	My Friend Yakov Lior	62
	Jerusalem 1940 – Entering The Job Market	67
	Chapter 2 Photos	71-73
Chapter Three	ABADAN, IRAN: WITH THE ANGLO IRANIAN OIL COMPANY	
	First Year	74
	Second Year	89
	Chapter 3 Photos	93-96
Chapter Four	BAHARIEN ISLANDS	
	Airport Construction	97
	Baharien Kitchen	99
	Swimming	103
	Pearl Diving	105
	Transferring Money	107
	Chapter 4 Photos	109-110
Chapter Five	AMERICA	
	Traveling To The United States To Study	111
	War in Israel, Recruited In The U.S., And Getting Married	114
	Smuggling Torpedo Boats	124
	Buying A Steam Boat	135
	Chapter 5 Photos	139-141
Chapter Six	BEER SHEVA	
	Back to Israel	142
	Beer Sheva	147
	Chapter 6 Photos	168-172

Chapter Seven	SETTLING IN AMERICA	
	Returning To America, Adjusting To A New Life	173
	American Technion Society, New Job	180
	Starting My Own Company And Going Bust	188
	Looking For A New Job, Personnel Agency	194
	Chapter 7 Photos	204
Chapter Eight	DEVELOPING MY OWN BUSINESS	
	Starting My Own Personal Agency	205
	My Bookkeeper Sidney	210
	Stealing My Hard-Earned Money	211
	Romance In The Office	217
	The Mugging	224
	John Clark, His Life and Death	228
	Joe Schwartz and Sons	230
	Losing My Father	232
	Moving To A New Apartment	234
	Chapter 8 Photos	238-240
Chapter Nine	SARAH CALDWELL: THE METHODIST ZIONIST; DEVELOPING OPERA	
	Living With Opera With Sarah Caldwell	241
	Traveling To The Philippines Through Japan	250
	Opera In The Philippines	253
	Visit To Hawaii	259
	Sarah Caldwell And The Opera In Israel	261
	Opera Workshop In Israel	267
	Visit With Sarah Caldwell To London	271
	American Israel Opera Foundation	275
	Sarah Caldwell's Auditions In Santa Fe	284
	Sarah Caldwell's Visit To Seattle, WA	286
	Back To Santa Fe	289
	Sarah's Last Days	290
	Chapter 9 Photos	293-300
Chapter Ten	ISRAEL ADVENTURES	
	Developing New Business With Israel	301
	Next Visit To Israel	302
	New Ventures With Israel	304
Addendum	ADDENDUM	
	My Mother's Funeral And Rabbi Pollak	313
	Bernice Korsavitzky Fisher	318
	Our Forest In Israel	322
SELECTED PHOTOS		325-337
INDEX		339-353

PROLOGUE

I walk down the steps of the Broadway bus and look at my watch. It is 8:40 a.m. on a Monday morning in Manhattan, and I am on my way to the dentist on 116th Street. Twenty minutes early, I think with a little shudder. How can I kill the next twenty minutes? I hate being early, because I do not like to waste time. Every moment is precious, and I want to use it in the best way possible. I surely am not going to window-shop or sit on a bench biding my time.

Suddenly, with a shock of recognition, I realize that I am standing right by the ornate entrance of Columbia University. It has been fifty-seven years since the first time I walked through that big Iron Gate. I am drawn through that gate, as though by a magnet's force. Looking around, I am stunned to see that everything seems very much the same. The walk is still paved with cobblestones, and here is the same path leading into Columbia Square. My heart begins pounding. All of this is so familiar, as though I have been here only yesterday. True, the students are dressed differently from the way they were in the 1940s. Back then, all the men wore jackets and even ties. The women wore dark-colored suits, and no one would go out without a hat. Yet, the expressions on these young people's faces are unchanged. They all seem very involved with their own thoughts, their own problems. Some are laughing and teasing their friends, but still they have that intense, inward look. I hear several different languages being spoken too, and I wonder whether those students from far-away lands are feeling the way I did when I came to New York City in 1946, wondering if I was good enough to compete, to make it in the greatest university in the greatest city in the world.

I glance at the squat stone building to my left, and recall that the Industrial Engineering Department was on the second floor. I have the feeling that, if I could look in the window, Professor Rotensrich would be standing as always in his shirtsleeves, writing on the blackboard in big block letters. I realize with a start that the poor man must be long dead. How can this be?

I walk further along the cobblestone path. On the left, Low Library rises up as always – a majestic building with stairs stretching along its entire length. And here in front is the large statue of Alma

Mater, facing out toward the square. How many times had I met a friend, or a date, there, or sat on the steps comparing lecture notes with a classmate? It all comes back in a rush, memories I have not encountered in years, memories I had thought were long buried. The blossoming trees in spring along College Walk... the sound of the steam pipes that clanked during class...and the library! That dusty smell of countless books, the thought of all that knowledge under one roof, an idea that had exhilarated me. I turn right toward that place, Butler Library, where I had spent countless hours absorbed in my reading. I long to walk through those big doors again, but they are closed; it is too early. I feel an almost visceral rush of disappointment.

It seems very strange to me that this place has been waiting here, almost as though in a time capsule, for me to return, for all these years... and yet I live only 15 blocks away! Where have I been for all those years?

I stand now facing the whole courtyard, leaning against a low stone wall, and an eerie feeling fills me. It seems impossible that over half a century has passed since I first stood in this same spot. I remember the wonderment and anxiety I felt then, thinking how fortunate I was to have reached this point in my life. For me, the child of poor Jewish immigrants to Israel, to be attending this renowned university! It was a dream come true. I had been filled with great excitement, great expectations, yet I was worried about whether I could do well here. My English was not good, and I did not know if my education so far was up to standard. What would the future bring me? All I knew was that I was willing to work hard, very hard, and I did.

Now, here I am again, the same person really. Despite all I have accomplished, I think, my yearning for greater things has not diminished. Why am I unhappy? It seems that I can never reach my elusive, evasive dreams. All my life I have been striving, driven by an unknown force that never lets me go. In my 80s, I feel that there is still so much that I must do. There are still worlds to conquer, and so little time left to do it. Maybe, I think, my new project, writing my memoir, will bring me peace. My life has been full of different kinds of adventures in many different places. What a challenging undertaking that will be!

Suddenly I realize that I have been standing, lost in thought, for over 20 minutes, and now I am late for my dental appointment. I will have to make an excuse, just like a student late for class! How ironic, when I was always on time for class during all my years. My mind is still reeling as I retrace my steps back to 116th and Broadway.

For the rest of the day – in the dentist's chair, on the bus, in my office, and at home with my wife Florence – my mind is not really on what I am doing. Instead it swoops back and forth, moving from past to present, trying to make sense of it all. The passage of time, I realize, is one thing that we human beings can never really understand. Time can move slowly or quickly, and just when we feel we have some control of the present, the past comes back to shake up our sense of reality. It seems to mock us: Who do you think you are, anyway? What gives you the chutzpah to believe that you can make a difference in this wide, wide universe?

Although I do not mention it to Florence or anyone else, the truth is that this impromptu visit to my past has knocked me flat. I have to begin from the beginning now, trying to figure out who I am, and what had made me this way. It is puzzlement. Where to start?

Most of my life I have felt alone with my inner self, never expecting to be helped by others. My drive has come completely from within. Somehow, my feelings of insecurity have driven me to be independent, wanting to take care of my family and myself single-handedly.

My mind is always busy, constantly looking for new ideas and solutions. True, I have done a lot, yet no matter what I have attained, I have never been completely satisfied. I have always been disappointed with my own performance, and have had no peace of mind. Even when I succeed, I feel that there is nothing really to be proud of, because it is only a small percentage of what I have to do.

Success is a relative thing. My drive is not for money, but fortunately, my goals have been practical ones, so in the end money has followed. Still, this seems like nothing compared to what others have achieved. I feel humiliated and jealous of those who have tasted more success, feeling that I am so limited in intelligence, energy, and ability.

I am always driven to be better, faster, and more efficient. This applies to anything and everything. Whether I am shining my shoes, washing dishes, or settling a business deal, I like to be organized, scheduled, and prompt. Yet somehow, I never have enough time to do what I want to do. When I reach a goal, I feel unhappy because it should have been reached better and faster, and I feel empty – so I am not proud of it. When I fail, I go through agony and a painful period of unhappiness. Yet, this does not stop me in the long run. I go on searching. I plow ahead, always worried sick about possible failure.

So, I am unfulfilled and needing something, but what? I perhaps can at least be satisfied with the writing of my life story. I am beginning to sense that it is my involvement with other people, my feelings of compassion and my desire to help others – which have their roots in my own hardships – that have made my life meaningful. How fortunate I am to be able to share the results of my success! I am proud of one thing: proud of all the people I have helped over the years, both in my business and in my personal life. I get more pleasure from giving than does anyone who receives anything from me. Perhaps this in the end is what keeps me going; perhaps this is the secret I can reveal by telling this tale.

CHAPTER ONE

THE EARLY YEARS

1921, Immigrating To Israel

My mother, Esther, was eighteen and my father, Chaim, barely twenty-two years old when I was born in a small village in the Ukraine, not far from Kiev. It was 1920, and the Soviet Union was a new nation. Still, the violence was not over in many parts of the vast republic that was being stitched together by force. In the Ukraine, which had been annexed by Russia in the Eighteenth century, the Russian Revolution had led to a series of pogroms. As they held power in turn, the Red Army, the White Army, the German Army, and finally the new Communist government initiated or allowed massacres of entire Jewish communities. Some groups wanted to kill Jews because of the loyalty of Jewish businessmen and aristocrats to the czar. Others wanted to kill Jews because they thought we were all loyal to Russia, or later to the new Soviet state, rather than to an independent Ukraine. Much of the killing and destruction was carried out by barely organized mobs of ignorant Russian or Ukrainian peasants who simply hated Jews.

Both my father's and my mother's families were middle-class. My father worked for Baron Ginsberg, a Ukrainian-Jewish businessman who had been elevated to nobility. Following in the footsteps of his father and grandfather, my father became a bookkeeper for the baron's sugar beet farms and factories, which provided sugar not only for Russia, but also for much of Eastern Europe. The baron's political loyalty and the substantial taxes and tributes he paid to the czar – from the profits of his many businesses and landholdings – had served him well, but in 1919, Baron Ginsberg's property was seized, and he and his family fled to France.

My parents had not grown up thinking that they would help to settle Israel. They had had no plan beyond working and raising a family in the village where their people had lived for generations. That changed when the pogroms reached us. Our village was attacked by Cossacks, who were less interested in any political philosophy than in killing anyone who was out of favor with the government of the moment. In 1920, it was the new Communist government that saw Jewish people as capitalists who had to be driven out. The Cossacks, with their history of bloodthirsty military loyalty, were happy to oblige. Riding on horseback, wielding long sabers and firing rifles, the Cossacks swept through the Ukraine, killing and driving out Jews and setting our homes and businesses on fire.

Both of my father's parents, and my mother's mother, were killed. My father and his two older brothers fled the burning village ahead of the Cossacks, with my mother and me. I was a year old, a mere babe in arms. My father had cousins in Romania, almost 400 miles to the west. Our family decided to follow the railroad tracks toward Romania. We would hide from the Cossacks, who were also heading west, and catch trains whenever and wherever we could.

After traveling for miles the first day, we took shelter at an abandoned farm near a railroad station. My father told my mother to sleep with me in the farmhouse. She wanted my father to stay with us there, but he refused; he told her he would spend the night with his brothers in the stable. He and his brothers, with their dark hair and complexions, looked Jewish; my mother was blonde, blue-eyed, and fair-skinned, like a Russian girl. If she were caught with my father and his brothers, he said, she would probably be killed with them. She and I would be safer sleeping separately.

Four heavily-armed Cossacks arrived at the farm just before dawn. They banged on the door, awakening my mother and startling me into hysterical tears. Terrified as she was, she had the presence of mind to come up with a story that saved our lives. She was a poor Russian girl, she sobbed, and she was alone in the world. Her husband had been killed by a group of Jews in the next village, and she was on her way east to stay with relatives. If she had not been comforting a crying baby, the Cossacks might have raped her. But they took pity on us and left.

My mother trembled as she looked out of the window into the farmyard. She prayed that the horsemen would simply ride on; but they burst through the doors of the stable, weapons drawn. She could not see what was happening, but she heard shouts, followed by the sound of the

Cossacks galloping away. Then there was silence. Perhaps, she thought my father and uncles were back on the railroad tracks, running west.

She waited an agonizing hour, then two. Finally, she could not stand it any longer; she had to go look for my father. She opened the farmhouse door and walked out into the farmyard with me in her arms. There she saw a sight so horrible that she could have fainted: my father was staggering toward her, almost unrecognizable, covered in blood. My mother was a very strong and sensible young woman. She knew what she had to do, and she did it. After laying me gently on an old mattress in the house, she got water from the pump in the farmyard, tore strips from her underskirts, and cleaned and bandaged my father's wounds. Without her there, he would surely have died from the deep saber cuts on his head, shoulders and arms. He had lost a lot of blood and he was stunned; but slowly, he managed to tell my mother what had happened.

He said he had been the last of the three brothers to run from the Cossacks. He had stood his ground, hoping to defend me and my mother, diverting the attackers so that his brothers had managed to slip away. But he had quickly decided that his wife and child would be safer if all three of them fled, leading the Cossacks away from us. He made a run for it. But as soon as they could remount, the horsemen had quickly caught up with him, and begun hacking at him with their swords. He saw his brothers, a few yards ahead, turn and come back to help; then he lost consciousness. When he awoke, the Cossacks were gone and his brothers were nowhere to be seen. Frantically, he searched for them, afraid to cry out. Then he found them laying a short way from the tracks in a wooded area. He was horrified; they had been beheaded.

My father wept uncontrollably. They must go back and bury his brothers, he said over and over. My mother tried to talk him out of it, but he insisted. He was a mild-mannered office worker, short and wiry, but he was a lot tougher and stronger than he looked. Together, he and my mother returned to the stable, retrieved our small bag of cheese and crusts of bread, and found a rusty old shovel. Then they headed back down the tracks.

My father did not want my mother to see her mutilated brothers-in-law; even though he was very weak, he insisted on burying them, in two shallow graves, by himself. By the time he was finished, he was too tired and it was too late in the day to continue our journey.

They carried me back to the farmhouse and spent a restless night there. Both of my parents cried a great deal throughout that night, but for the first time – as they told me years later – I slept right through without making a sound.

The next day, my parents moved cautiously west on the railroad tracks, keeping an eye out for Cossacks. There were still some Jews in the next village, shopkeepers who had managed to hide from the raiders on the previous day. They were quickly packing up their belongings to leave, but they stopped and risked their lives to help my parents. They took my mother and father in, fed them, and changed the dressings on my father's wounds. When they heard what had happened to my uncles, the villagers agreed that they must be not be left in shallow graves on unconsecrated land. My father was feverish and exhausted; the men told him to rest, but he insisted on going with them. Leaving my mother and me in the village, half a dozen men walked back, carrying my father on a small horse-drawn wagon. They dug up the bodies, put them on the wagon, and pushed it to the small Jewish cemetery, where they gave my uncles a proper religious burial.

My parents and I spent that night in the village. The next morning we waited for the once-daily train. Only by bribing the conductor were my parents able to get tickets to the Romanian border.

Late that night, as guards boarded to check the passengers' papers, my parents slipped off the back of the train, and walked toward the River Volga. They could see the tiny, distant lights of Romania on the far shore, at least a couple of miles away. How could they get across?

Suddenly a light approached. My mother and father drew back in terror, seeing no escape, but the man holding the light did not demand to see their papers. Instead, he pointed to a small rowboat tethered to a tree by the shore. For a fee, he said, he would ferry them across the river.

My parents had only a little money left, but they gave it to this stranger. What choice did they have? My mother carefully hid her last remaining jewelry: her wedding ring, a bracelet from her grandmother, and a necklace that had belonged to her mother.

The smuggler led us down a muddy bank where several other men were waiting with the boat. They warned my mother to keep me quiet or else, and we set off across the river.

Years later, my parents told me how I had almost gotten us all killed. It was a cold, windy night, and the waves on the water were rough. I awoke and began wailing. I was still being breastfed, but the stress of our journey was drying up my mother's milk. I was hungry as well as exhausted.

One of the smugglers swore at my mother, "Shut that brat up or I'll throw him overboard!" Despite her attempts to comfort me, I kept screaming. One of the men made a grab for me, but my mother was too quick for him. She jumped up and took me to the back of the boat, making the whole craft rock dangerously. Meanwhile, the smugglers decided to take advantage of the situation. They told my father that, since they were taking a big risk with us on board, we would have to pay double. Otherwise, they said, they would turn around and take us right back to Russia.

My mother was afraid that my father, even in his weakened condition, was angry enough to try to fight the smugglers. Where would we be then she thought. Before he could make a move, she stripped off her jewelry and handed it to the men. But even that was not enough; they demanded all the money we had. When my parents finally carried me off the boat onto Romanian soil, it was the middle of the night, but they were met by our cousin who knew the spot where the smugglers' boats docked.

Our cousin was a wealthy lumber mill owner with large tracts of forested land in Romania. He lived in a large house with my father's sister Rosa, a brilliant businesswoman who managed several hundred workers in the forest as well as in the lumber mill and yard. We stayed with these relatives for several months, during which time my father recovered from his injuries enough to work for them and save up some money.

Our cousins wanted my father to stay in Romania, but my parents decided that they had had enough. They had never been especially political in their lives, but the pogroms had changed all that. Being persecuted, seeing their families killed, and being chased out of the only homeland they knew – all because they were Jewish – had transformed my parents into Zionists. They wanted to live far away from Russia, and they felt strongly about settling in Israel as pioneers of the new Jewish homeland.

nothing to help her. I was a self-centered little boy, always involved in my own activities, my own world. She adored me, and spoiled me as much as she could.

The money my father earned was just enough to pay our rent; there was very little left over for food. Then one day he became ill, and could not work for a month.

My mother decided that she had to take matters into her own capable hands: at least until my father was healed, she would have to support the family. She had learned to sew as a young girl in the Ukraine, so she began spreading word in the neighborhood that she was a seamstress. Women began bringing her their sewing, and before long she was making enough money to pay the rent and buy a little food.

After my father was able to return to work, things were better because my mother continued to earn this extra income. I grew up hearing this tale of perseverance by my parents, and it strongly influenced my life.

My father worked on the road for two years. By then he spoke some Hebrew, and he started to look for a new job. He heard of a man by the name of Aushiskin who worked for an organization called the Jewish National Fund (in Hebrew, Keren Hakeimet Leisrael). They had an office in town, he was told. My father remembered a man by that name: could it be the same person? For a number of years, Aushiskin had come through my parents' village in Russia, raising money to buy land in Israel. Aushiskin had once stayed at Baron Ginsberg's home, and my father had gotten to know him well.

My father was nervous about approaching this man for a job, but after a great deal of mental preparation and my mother's coaxing, my father went to see him at his small two-room office in Jerusalem. Aushiskin recognized my father immediately.

"What are you doing here?" he exclaimed. He, of course, had not known whether or not my father had escaped the violence in Russia, and he was thrilled to see him. He listened spellbound as my father told him our family's tale: the deaths of so many, including his brothers, our flight to Romania and eventually to Israel.

"I know how capable an accountant you are," Aushiskin said, "but unfortunately we don't need an accountant right now. The only job I could offer you would be cleaning the office and doing odd jobs."

Menial as this labor was, it was infinitely better than road-building, and my father accepted at once. He came home in triumph, and my mother cried for hours because she was so happy.

My father was very proud of his new job, and he loved to go to work. While we lived in Beth Habocharim, he walked one and a half hours each way -- carrying a lunch he had prepared himself, dressed in his best suit and a tie, with shoes shined as brightly as a mirror. (He always wore salamander shoes made in Germany because, he said, they could take his long walk without wear and tear and always kept their shine.) He never missed a day's work for the next forty years. In time he became head of the accounting department, and eventually retired as assistant controller of Keren Keimet Leisrael.

Strong bonds soon developed between our family and the other Russian-speaking families in Beth Habocharim. In the room next to ours lived the Wachtels, who were also newcomers to Israel. As luck would have it, they had a son, Jackie, who was just a year younger than I. Great friendships developed between my mother and Mrs. Wachtel, and between me and Jackie. He and I became inseparable; I was happy to be like an older brother to him.

The Wachtel family had come from England. Jackie's mother was a very well-educated woman, a university graduate; her husband was a Polish man who had immigrated to Britain, where they had met. Her family was originally Russian, and so she knew something of that language, as well as Polish and English.

Mrs. Wachtel was a very energetic woman. She was active in the Zionist Women's Organization, and an excellent organizer and a fiery orator, always working for one cause or another. Mr. Wachtel was just the opposite: he was a quiet man with no particular profession. Mrs. Wachtel decided to get a job for her husband. Since she was a British citizen, she decided to approach the British Administration, which was in charge of Israel at the time. She wrote to the British High Commissioner requesting a meeting, and was soon summoned. Mrs. Wachtel was not intimidated by anything or anybody – certainly not by a mere High Commissioner! Sipping tea in his ornate Jerusalem offices, she confided in him about her husband's situation.

"And, if I may ask, Madam, what is Mr. Wachtel's profession?" The British High Commissioner inquired.

quickly, and they sometimes became annoyed as I babbled on – they could not understand a word. "Speak Russian Efraim, good Russian!" my mother would chide me.

In kindergarten, I was also introduced to wonderful new foods: cocoa with milk and sugar, and fresh bread with yellow Australian butter. I had never had anything like that at home; to this day I can feel those special tastes in my mouth.

I was a very active child, always getting cuts and bruises on my elbows and knees, which never stopped me. But one day something more serious happened. In the middle of the schoolyard there was a wooden pole about six feet tall. All the boys tried to climb this pole; we would dare each other, and nobody would refuse a dare. Every time someone tried this feat, all the kids gathered around, cheering; but the pole was quite slippery and no one could get to the top. Each boy in turn would slip down, red-faced, as the other children pointed and laughed. After this happened to me a few times, I became determined to climb the pole all the way up. Through trial and error, I learned the best way to position my hands for the best grip. I learned how to shift my weight if I began to slide then regain my balance and move higher and higher.

One day, I succeeded. I reached the top of the pole to the cheers of the entire kindergarten; even some of the teachers were watching, and they clapped and yelled, "Hooray, Efraim!" I had never been so proud, but I had a rude awakening. As I slid down the pole with a flourish, I felt a searing pain in my leg. A protruding nail had ripped a big slash in my thigh, and I hit the ground with blood spurting everywhere. I did not really understand what had happened, but I noticed the faces of the other kids turn from laughter to horror in an instant.

The next thing I was aware of was waking up in the hospital with my mother holding my hand. I had needed a dozen stitches, and I have the scar to this day.

As the holiday of Purim approached, the teachers gave us notes to take home to our mothers. The idea was that we would all be dressed up for the occasion. My mother had never before celebrated Purim; she knew nothing about Haman, Esther or Achashverosh, so she decided to make me into a cat. I have no idea how she managed to do it, but somehow she bought a few yards of plush black material. I thought the whole thing was silly and I protested. But she insisted, "Efraim, all the other children will have costumes! It will be fun, you'll see!" She made me stand very still as she carefully cut the material to fit me.

The next morning I woke up with dread. I did not want to be a cat at all! But nonetheless, after breakfast my mother sewed the material so tightly around me that I could barely walk to school. The material was very scratchy and it cut into my skin. Even Jackie had to laugh, and I noticed that he was not dressed as any animal; he was just wearing his best clothes and a little hat. By the time we reached kindergarten I felt thoroughly miserable. We children had to parade in front of the entire school, singing and dancing.

I was mortified but, thanks to my mother's artistry, I was the hit of the show. I still have a picture of me in my cat outfit. Everyone made a big fuss over me, but still I could not wait to get away. When long last I arrived home, my mother cut the seams and let me free. This experience began a terrible fear of enclosed spaces – claustrophobia – that has never left me.

Moving To Geola -- School

Our family was growing; I now had a new baby sister. Strangely enough, I have no memory of her birth. In any case, our one room in Beth Habocharim was feeling rather crowded. With my father now earning a better income, we were able to afford a larger space.

We moved to a two-room apartment in Geola, not far from Beth Habocharim and still a long way from my father's office. Geola was a clean, small Jewish neighborhood.

Most of our neighbors were new immigrants, from many different countries, and many of them spoke a mixture of Hebrew and their own country's language. Everyone in the neighborhood was poor and had to work hard to support their growing families. Food was scarce at that time; fresh fruit was very expensive, and we rarely saw an egg. Bread comprised a large part of the local diet, but no one complained. Everybody was happy just to be there – to be part of the growing Jewish community in Israel. (An interesting footnote is that there were few cows in the country, so the tiny amount of local butter and milk produced by the Tnuva, a collective organization of kibbutzim, was very expensive. The only thing that was imported into Israel at that time was yellow Australian butter, and it was a very big treat. The Arab population used oil, not butter.)

After I graduated from kindergarten, I began attending the Tachkimony public school, an all-boys' institution next door to an Ethiopian church. It was a crowded, run-down school with rickety old desks and chairs, situated in a dusty, dirty yard. The church compound was protected by a high wall and very mysterious to us kids; we saw black-skinned people coming and going, and our imaginations filled in the rest.

At school, the older kids liked to frighten the little ones, so they made up stories about children being kidnapped and disappearing forever behind those high walls. I had never seen a black person before and I did not understand that it was normal for people to have different skin colors. This, coupled with the Ethiopians' unusual clothing, was enough to convince us kids that, in fact, they were perfectly capable of spiriting us away, and we all were terrified. None of us would walk in the narrow alley next to the church compound.

My mother recruited our next-door neighbor, who also attended the Tachkimony School, to go with me to and from school. It was over half an hour's walk, but I felt safe as long as he was with me. I had no sense at the time of the irony of my situation. Earlier I had played a similar role in Jackie's life, as the protective older boy, but now I needed this same service myself. However, this neighbor did not help out willingly – in fact he considered me a pest, and I probably was one. He would have preferred to walk to school alone.

I loved school, playing in the yard with other kids and making new friends. My favorite school subjects were history, the Bible, geography, and some mathematics. I only did well in history and geography, though. I did not like English and poetry, and through the years I was generally a low-average student. By this time my Hebrew was good and I spoke that language most of the time to my parents, even though they still spoke Russian to each other.

Mr. Ilani, the school principal, was an older, short and heavyset man who always wore a hat. Although I did not realize it at the time, Tachkimony was a religious school. I had grown up so far without any knowledge of observant Jewish life; my parents were completely non-religious. Despite this, I did not feel uncomfortable with this sort of education. As a matter of fact, I enjoyed studying the Bible and the history of the Jewish people. Learning about my ancestors became very important to me.

Our school grew, and soon it needed larger quarters. When I was in the second grade, it moved to a new, much larger building near the Schneller German compound. The new school was a beautiful place. It had two floors, several buildings, and a large, clean yard. I remember how pleasant it was to have brand new chairs and tables, plenty of space to move around in, and a large, paved schoolyard where we could play. The new facility was also much closer to home.

Most of the children in my school were from poor families, but there were some rich kids. We all brought our lunches with us, and for the first time I became aware of inequality. Most of us never had fresh fruit, but I could not help noticing that the rich boys had apples for lunch. I was very envious of them. For years, I wondered how an apple might taste.

In the compound was a small store that sold candy and other sweets. One of the popular items was small cups of sweet hot rice extract with cinnamon sprinkled on top. I always watched hungrily as the rich kids sipped this drink; all the rest of us children milled around them, wishing that we could afford it too.

During all my years in that school, I may have had three or four cups altogether, which I paid for after saving my milims for months. It was a delicious drink, and I still remember the taste fondly.

Mekor Chaim, 1929 Arab Riots

In 1926, after my brother was born (an event that I also do not remember) my father decided that we needed a house. Our two-room apartment was very crowded, and we three children were driving my mother crazy. For reasons unknown to me, my father elected to build our house in a small village called Mekor Chaim, about five miles south of Jerusalem. Most of the residents there were ultra-orthodox Jews, Haredim, who were new immigrants. I believe that my father probably chose this village because the land there was inexpensive. He bought an empty lot between two large houses.

The village, which was new, had been named after Rabbi Ha'im Cohen of Brisk, Lithuania. It was in the southern part of Jerusalem, about three kilometers from the old city, near the railway on its western side. The initiative had been a private one by the Hach'sha'rat Ha'ye'shuv company, which sold lots individually to the settlers. Hach'sha'rat Ha'ye'shuv had bought these lands from Keren Ka'yemet Le'Israel after World War I. In addition, the company had bought more property from the nearby Greek Orthodox Church. The neighborhood was modern for its time, with running water and toilets.

Mekor Chaim, at the time we moved there, consisted of about twenty houses, ten on each side of the road. A narrow path led up a hill to a nearby Arab village, Beit Safafa. The Arabs were generally friendly neighbors at that time, but at night they stole anything that was left outside. Eventually the people of our village organized a night watch schedule, and the stealing stopped. The night watchman's only protection was a whistle and a wooden stick, and I always worried about my father when he was on watch.

Mekor Chaim's settlers built the houses themselves, and most were simple, one-story structures. Apparently the settlers had some vague idea that they could cultivate the land. Perhaps they had been sold this idea by the land company, but in fact these were mostly urban people with absolutely no experience in agricultural work. They had not the slightest idea how to grow things under the best of conditions, and this was an arid area without sufficient irrigation. I do not remember ever seeing any gardens or even trees in the neighborhood.

Quite soon after it was built, the neighborhood began to suffer economically, because the residents' families were large and good jobs were hard to come by.

To the left of our property was a long, ten-room house with a very large veranda, occupied by a family with four children. The owner worked in the city. The children were much older than I, and I do not remember much about them. The building had been intended as a tuberculosis sanitarium, but almost no patients came to stay there. However, just in case, my mother always warned me to stay far away from that house.

Behind the village was the railroad line that ran from Jerusalem to Jaffa. We kids all ran to the tracks when we heard a whistle; it was a big thrill to see the enormous train engines and all the cars up close. It made me think about faraway places and wonder where the rail cars had been, and where all the people were heading.

To the right of our property was a beautiful large house, which was occupied only by a husband and wife. The wife was relatively young, beautiful and always beautifully dressed. She was said to have been a singer in her youth. It was whispered around the village that she took two baths every day, which was quite scandalous because water was in short supply and therefore unbelievably expensive. I once overheard my mother telling my father that while this neighbor's husband was working in town, she often had a male friend visiting her. For some reason this intrigued me; perhaps it was the tone of voice my mother used when talking about it, but I could not stop wondering what was going on in that house.

I was so curious that I once investigated at great risk to myself: I stacked four cement blocks below one of the windows and tried to look in. If I had been caught by my neighbor, her friend, my mother or any adult in the community, I would have been in big trouble, and I am still amazed that I took the chance. But I had to know more. Unfortunately, heavy metal-plated shutters blocked my view, and the house kept its secrets.

I already knew where babies came from – this I had learned from the other boys. But of course I did not really understand the details. I suppose it is built into children to have sexual curiosity. In any case, without knowing what I was looking for exactly, I always kept my eyes open listened to adult conversations and tried to puzzle these things out.

A few years later, when I spent the summer at a kibbutz, I was to add more mysterious evidence to this ongoing investigation.

Across the road from us in Mekor Chaim was a small house, home to a religious family with four boys and a girl. They were very poor. The mother ran a tiny grocery store containing very little merchandise: there were only four shelves with various cans, cigarettes and sometimes fresh vegetables. I was friendly with these children and often visited this house. It was always a chaotic mess. The beds were never made; clothes and household items were strewn all over the floor, which was always filthy; there seemed to be no closets or cabinets to store anything. Chickens were everywhere: on the tables and chairs, in the kitchen, and on the beds. There was even a sheep wandering in and out. Needless to say, the place had a peculiar smell.

All the kids in that family wore dirty, torn clothes – rags, really – and they seemed to have very little to eat. My mother sent them packages of food from time to time. I remember that they had no schedule for meals, and just ate when they were hungry. Nevertheless, they attended synagogue regularly, twice every day.

Once when I was visiting these friends, I saw them gobbling white bread spread with olive oil, topped with sugar. I had some myself, and I liked it. Back home, I asked my mother to give me white bread spread with olive oil and sugar. She looked at me in amazement, asking, "Where did you get that great idea?" I told her how much I liked this special treat. She explained, "Those poor kids have no other food to eat; you are lucky to have real food," then sent me over with another care package for them. This was the first time I really understood what being poor meant. I thought a lot about it, and this experience left a big impression on me.

Many years later, I learned that three of those boys had become famous medical doctors; the other boy was a lawyer, and the daughter, a history professor. Maybe if I had eaten more bread with olive oil and sugar, I thought, I would have been more of a success in life!

Our family had adopted a small dog, which we found as a puppy. We named him Navchan, which means "Barker" in Hebrew – for obvious reasons. He was a real mutt, with an ugly personality, and barked at everyone and everything. Although he loved to hang around us kids, he never wanted to be petted. He constantly ran after cars, biting at the tires. Once he was hit by a car, and for a while it seemed as though he would die. Even after he recovered, he did not lose his car chasing habit. Eventually, however, he began to enjoy running and barking at passing trains. It only took a moment of being too close to the train wheels and that was the end of him. Notwithstanding his miserable personality, we kids gave him a proper funeral, burying him next to the railroad tracks. My brother and sister were heartbroken and did not stop crying for a week, but my mother and I did not really miss Navchan.

For some reason I do not have clear memories of my sister and brother at that time. My sister, Mira, is three years younger than I and my brother, Maza, is five years younger. All I remember is that they trailed after me when I wanted to be left alone with friends of my own age. My sister never seemed happy -- she was always crying -- and my brother always seemed to want something of me. I was too self-centered to want to help them in any way or to make an effort to be a considerate big brother.

When I was not in school, I was very busy: running with a metal wheel in front of me, building little houses from wood to crawl into, and looking for all kinds of mechanical junk. Gears, wheels, bolts, nuts – they all interested me. One of my greatest feats was with an old ball bearing brace that I found. For months, I threw heavy rocks at the bearing until it came apart, and then I had beautiful shiny steel balls to play with. I was very proud of this accomplishment.

I remember that I once found an old broken bicycle. Half of the handlebars were missing, and the tires were full of holes. I repaired the inner tubes somehow, stuck a short broomstick into the broken handlebar, and biked downhill. Of course, after a short time, one of the inner tubes blew up and I had to abandon this pastime. But this began my love of bicycles and even led to my owning a motorcycle years later.

From Mekor Chaim, it was about two and a half miles to my school. The bus that I took every day was driven by Michael, a handsome young Yemenite who was always singing. It was a long drive, taking us an hour each way, and Michael was always very friendly to us kids. Years later, I heard of a scandal involving him and a beautiful young German woman who lived in Mekor Chaim with her much older husband. She fell in love with Michael, who was much younger than she, and left her husband to live with him in Jerusalem. That was a shocking event, especially since she was not Jewish and he was a dark-skinned Jew. I believe that at that time (around 1927); Israelis were somewhat against "color mixing." After a year, I heard, Michael had left the German woman; her husband forgave her and she came back to live in Mekor Chaim. Of course, as a child I was unaware that all this was going on. This woman's husband was killed and their house was burned down in the Arab attacks of 1929. She eventually returned to Germany.

was running over my head. A nurse washed my head and face and made sure that I was all right, while another nurse took care of Mrs. Baranoff's hand.

I had been lucky. If her hand had not been over my head, and if I had stuck my head over the windowsill one inch, I would have been hit by a bullet in the head. I was quite shaken, and my mother was hysterical. This was the second time I had narrowly escaped death; the first time was on the river crossing to Rumania, and there was to be a third time – yet far in the future – when I was nearly killed by a robber in New York.

During that night, several homes at the outskirts of the village were burned, and we all knew that the next morning the Arabs would attack in force.

In the morning, the Haganah men surrounded the safe house with sandbags. My father, with his pistol, guarded the women and children inside. Across the street was the synagogue, a large, tall building with a flat roof. One of the Haganah men, armed with the rifle, was in command of a group of men on that roof. He had once been a captain in the Russian army, and was a crack shot.

When the Arabs attacked, the first house they reached was the Baranoffs'. Mr. Baranoff with his pistol was no match for them. They cut his throat and his two arms, and burned the house, leaving his corpse just outside. The mob then crossed the railroad tracks, moving towards the center of the village, on the way burning several other homes – including that of the old German and his wife.

Thousands of Arabs were now walking toward the synagogue. At the front of the mob was the Muktar, head of the village, whom we all knew well. The Russian officer on the synagogue roof told his men to hold their fire. When the mob was just 100 meters away, the Russian aimed at the Muktar and hit him in the head, seriously wounding him. The attackers, seeing this, halted in their tracks. They picked up their fallen leader and fled. One shot had won the battle.

Later that evening, at long last, the British Army arrived to protect us. Expecting more attacks, they loaded the children and women on trucks and drove us to a hotel next to the old city walls. My father and the other Haganah men stayed behind to protect the remaining homes, which were saved from burning.

From the windows of the hotel where we were safely ensconced, we could see the walls of the old city of Jerusalem and the Tower of David. The hotel's rooms were crowded with women and children; we all slept on the stone floors without enough blankets and we shivered with the cold.

All through those terrifying nights, I had nightmares about blood pouring over my ear. One night I fell asleep with my face on the floor and in the morning, one side of my face was paralyzed. I could not move my jaw. I was rushed to the French Hospital, next door to the hotel, where they treated me with electric shocks. It was painful, and the medicine that they applied to my face was very strong. For many years, I woke up at night with the smell of that ointment in my nostrils.

Many Jews were killed by the Arabs during the 1929 attacks. More than 50 were massacred in Hebron alone, and on the way to Jerusalem, 10 members of a family were killed – only one child, Macklef, survived. Years later this child became the Chief General of the Israeli Army. But no more attacks were mounted by the Beit Safafa Arabs, and in fact a peace treaty was eventually negotiated with them. This treaty was a history-making one, very unusual, and it held throughout the troubles of the 1930s and 1940s, up until the War of Independence.

Moving to Schneller

After the raid, my father decided that it was too dangerous for us to return to Mekor Chaim. My father sold the house and found a small first-floor apartment for us in the Schneller neighborhood of Jerusalem, near Beth Habocharim. My family lost contact with all our Mekor Chaim friends. Some time later we heard that Mr. Baranoff had been buried in a Christian cemetery in Jerusalem. Only then did we realize that the Baranoff family was Christian. "We should have known," my parents said, "that no Jew would ever work as a locomotive driver in Zaristic anti-Semitic Russia." We also heard that Mrs. Baranoff and her daughter had returned to their family in Russia.

Next to our new home was the familiar high wall surrounding the German compound; I never did learn who lived there. But I liked the neighborhood. My school was just a short walk from our apartment, and that was quite a change from the long bus drive from Mekor Chaim every morning. Next door to our building was a small store where we bought most of our food. I was a frequent visitor there. That store kept our neighborhood alive; most of our purchases were made on credit. Each sale was recorded in a small book by the storekeeper, and at the end of the month my father paid him. When we did not have enough money we always got an extension of payment. Our credit was good, and eventually all the bills were paid.

I found new companions in the neighborhood. One of them, who became my closest friend, was Avraham Dinaborg, whose father ran a haberdashery store on the Jaffa Road. His family was also from Russia, and they became close to my parents. Avraham and I were inseparable. Avrham's mother was in ill health, and his grandmother ran the household. He had a sister who was several years older; she was a musician, and they had a gramophone. I remember very well one visit to their home during which Avraham played a Mozart recording for me. This was the first time I had ever heard this type of music. It was a new sensation and I was fascinated. At home we never listened much to music, except for some Russian or Israeli songs. From time to time after this, when I went to visit Avraham, he played classical records and we sat together listening. Thinking back, I cannot remember exactly what Avraham and I talked about during all these hours and days, but I enjoyed his company and his presence enriched my life.

Summer In The Kibbutz with My Uncle Moshe

My grandmother on my mother's side had eleven brothers and sisters. One of her younger brothers was named Moshe Krogliak. He was the first in our family to immigrate to Israel, in 1917. He managed, somehow, to get a stipend to study at Mikve Israel, the first agricultural school in the country.

Moshe was a slim young man who wore heavy wire-rim glasses. He was a committed Zionist and a pioneer. In those years there was a great discussion going on about what form of social and political structure the new Israel should take. Should it be communism, or socialism, or should capitalism be established? This was the sort of question that was being hotly debated in the country, and Moshe joined in with enthusiasm.

After his graduation, he joined a new kibbutz, Ginigar, in Emek Israel, not far from Nazareth. When I was seven years old, I spent the summer with Uncle Moshe and his lovely wife, Esther. This was a wonderful experience for me, which expanded my horizons and encouraged my independence.

Esther was the sister of Ruth Hachoen, who was the treasurer of the largest construction company in Israel, Solel-Boneh. Her husband was David Hachoen, one of the founders of Solel-Boneh. Of course I knew nothing of that at my age; I only knew the thrill of being in a completely different environment, and having the freedom, away from my parents, to try to understand and test myself against a new world.

The kibbutz was perched on rugged, rocky hills, with breathtaking views over the Israel Valley with its rich, dark brown soil. On the barren slopes, trees were being planted, paid for by the Jewish National Fund; work crews went out daily to perform this strenuous task. Down in the valley, we could see the Nahalal Settlement. Uncle Moshe explained to me that Nahalal was a moshav, which is different from a kibbutz. It was a cooperative, but each family had its own separate home; the houses all radiated out like the spokes of a wheel around a big recreation and storage area in the center. Beyond the houses, and stretching out to the rim of the "wheel," were fields of lush green alfalfa and vegetables. Trees were planted between the moshav and our kibbutz. As I later learned, at first the kibbutz' only income had come from planting the trees. Later they had gotten a loan and were able to buy a tractor and supplies, so they could plant the land.

Everyone on the kibbutz lived in small wooden huts perched on the side of the hill. Moshe and Esther had just one room, which contained only their bed, a shelf with a few books, a small table, a chair and a kerosene lamp. The floor was wooden and creaky. A bed was set up for me across the room from their bed, but only about four feet of space separated us.

The nights were very, very dark. It was terribly hot that summer, and there was no fan. I often lay awake worrying that wild animals or Arab marauders might come in, because the door and the windows were left wide open for ventilation.

Late at night, I would hear Moshe and Esther talking in low tones. There was a quality to their voices that I had not heard before, but I could not puzzle out what it was. Then suddenly, all would become silent. Their bed would begin to creak, louder and louder. I would strain to look through the darkness, desperate to know what was happening, but I could never see a thing. Despite my terrific curiosity, I could never bring myself to ask my uncle about these noises; somehow I must have sensed that it was not for me to know, and in fact I did not discover the answer until quite a few years later.

But when I woke up, all this did not matter, because my days at the kibbutz were filled with exciting activities. The mornings were cool and pleasant and, after spraying my face with water from an outside tap, I would walk with my uncle up the hill to the main dining room. There, most of the other kibbutzniks were already eating vegetables, cottage cheese, fresh warm bread with margarine, and hot tea. This brought back to me memories of the exciting new tastes I had experienced in kindergarten. Unfortunately, at the kibbutz, there was no cocoa! But I loved dunking bread in my tea and listening to the adults talk, full of energy and plans for their future.

After breakfast, the men and women divided into groups – some went to plant trees, others took the tractor to the fields. There was not a strict division of labor by gender, but I noticed that the tree planters were mostly men, while the field work was mainly done by women.

I was completely free to roam around and do as I pleased. One of the first things that intrigued me at the kibbutz was the big watchdog, Shomer. He was chained to a pole and barked most of the time. My uncle had warned me not to get close to him, because he was said to be vicious. Nevertheless, I decided to try. One morning I went to the kitchen when no one else was around, the breakfast dishes had all been washed and preparations had not yet started for lunch. I opened the big metal can where food scraps were thrown, and spooned some leftover bread and cheese onto a plate. Then I approached Shomer, but he would not let me get near. So I went back to the kitchen, borrowed a broom and with that, pushed the plate right up to the dog's nose. He gobbled up the scraps in an instant.

After that I brought food to Shomer several times a day, slowly getting closer and closer. I made sure that no one saw me do this. After three days, this fierce creature would wag his tail when he saw me coming, and soon he was letting me pet him. When I was sure that we were fast friends, I told my Uncle Moshe. Of course, he did not believe me, and I had to prove it by walking right up and petting Shomer as though he were a little lap dog. My uncle was very proud; he told all the other members of the Kibbutz, and they congratulated me for my perseverance.

My next adventure was as a mule driver. The kibbutz had two mules and an old carriage with wooden wheels. There were also a few cows, and every morning, fresh milk was taken in the carriage to a central collection center in the small town of Afula. A kibbutznik named Chaim was in charge of the mules, and I began to spend time with him, helping him to harness up and to clean the carriage. It was not long until, as I had hoped, Chaim invited me to go with him on his morning rounds. This soon became a daily pleasure.

The center of activity in Afula was a general store, where the nearby kibbutzim got their groceries. In addition to a constant stream of customers loading and unloading supplies, there was often a heated political discussion going on there. People sat at rough wooden tables, drinking tea or Turkish coffee and talking in loud voices. I did not really understand what was being said, but I felt proud all the same to be part of this adult world. As I later learned, such discussions were a big part of Israel's development.

After unloading the milk and picking up supplies, Chaim and I would be on our way, so as to arrive home before noon. Most of the roads were unpaved, and when it rained they became heavy with mud. Then the carriage was constantly getting stuck; shouting at the mules and using the whip were the only ways to make any progress.

I was intrigued by the way Chaim handled the carriage, and after I had ridden for some days by his side, he put the reins into my hands and told me to drive. It felt strange at first; the mules seemed to want to go in two directions at once, or to go nowhere at all. But, with practice, I learned to keep them moving at a steady pace, to shout almost as loudly as Chaim, and to crack the whip when necessary.

A few days later it poured overnight, and the next morning the roads were a sea of mud. We could hardly see the way ahead through a steady drizzle, but Chaim and I set out with the mules. On our return trip he handed me the reins as always. I could feel the mules straining as the thick, sticky mud sucked at the carriage wheels. I shouted until I was hoarse, we lurched along, and we arrived back at the kibbutz in good time.

After I had proved myself in this way, the job of assistant mule driver was mine for the rest of the summer, and I felt very important and almost grown up.

The kibbutz was about two hours' walk from the city of Nazareth. One hot summer Saturday morning, my uncle asked me if I wanted to go there with him, as he had some business to attend there. Of course I was eager to go, and I jumped with excitement. We filled our bottles with water and walked up the hill until we got to the main road, then walked for two hours to Nazareth, a big Arab town with many stores and restaurants.

At the time the Arabs were very friendly and we never felt in danger. We had a great lunch at an Arab restaurant, Techina Chomos: pita bread, olives, salad and grilled kabobs.

My uncle went to visit the office of the registry. After his long meeting over Turkish coffee was over, we started back to the kibbutz. At the market we saw watermelons for sale, and we decided to buy one and bring it back. The melon we chose was large and heavy. My uncle put it in a string basket, and we started home at about two o'clock in the afternoon. The sun was overhead and merciless. Every mile or two we stopped to rest and drink some of our water. We were both perspiring profusely, and the melon was getting heavier and heavier as we walked.

Finally Uncle Moshe reached his limit. He simply could not carry the melon one step further. "Rafa, I'm afraid we're going to have to forget about this," he said with an embarrassed grimace. (Rafa was a nickname given to me as a young child.) But it seemed a shame to just leave this delicious fruit by the side of the road, so he cut the melon in half with his pocket knife, and removed the contents of one half. I watched as he squeezed the beautiful red flesh until the empty half was full of juice. We drank as much as we could and filled our water bottles with the juice, before walking the rest of the way home. This event remained a secret between my uncle and me; I never breathed a word about it to anyone. I must have sensed my uncle's embarrassment, because he was the sort of man who did not like to admit ever making a mistake. I admired my uncle, and as I grew older, this must have influenced my idea of what a man should be.

At the end of the summer I returned to Jerusalem with wonderful memories. A year later, I heard that Esther had given birth to a beautiful baby girl whom they named Neta. Then several months later came a terrible shock: Esther had committed suicide. Was it postpartum depression, as we now call it? No one understood the reasons, but Moshe was devastated. Neta grew up in the kibbutz without her mother. One of Esther's closest friends, Dina, adopted Neta with my uncle's consent. I never knew exactly what the relationship was between Dina and my Uncle Moshe, but it seemed to be close. Neta had a very good relationship with her father, even though she always lived with Dina.

Years later, my uncle married Esterka, another member of the kibbutz, and they had two sons. It was to be some years before I became close again with Moshe and his family. When I lived with my wife Florence in Haifa, we often visited his kibbutz, only thirty minutes' drive away. Florence and Esterka became close friends.

Before my uncle's remarriage, some sort of ideological confrontation among the members had caused the kibbutz to split up. One group, of which my uncle was part, left to start another kibbutz, Ramat Yochanan, near Haifa. Moshe, in time, became Director of Education for the kibbutz movement, and Esterka worked on the kibbutz and raised their two sons. Moshe's daughter Neta eventually became head of the vegetable fields; this was an important job because vegetables were one of the largest sources of income for the kibbutz.

Chapter 1 - The Early Years

My Sister, Me and My Parents

In the Kindergarten
Watering the Garden

Purim Masquerading, Dressed as a Black Cat
Stretched out on the Carpet

Chapter 1 – The Early Years

Tachkimony Elementary School Jerusalem

Family Picture

Our House in Mekor Chaim

CHAPTER TWO

GROWING UP

Haifa - Technical School

Ever since I was a young child, I have always been attracted to mechanical things. My earliest recollection of this was the first time I went with my mother to the bazaar in the old city in Jerusalem to buy fruits and vegetables. I must have been seven or eight years old. All along the narrow corridors were cobblestone streets with shops on either side displaying hanging dresses, scarves, and open sacks of nuts and sweets. The shook (bazaar) was divided into sections with leather, clothing, brass, utensils, and meat hanging on hooks. Donkeys carrying cans of water trotted in between the crowds. Near the wall along the street sat old Arab beggars, both men and women.

Also sitting against the wall, were old women with small baskets full of all kinds of pieces of metal, empty bottles, old combs, brass nails, and numerous old used rusty razor blades. There were so many blades that I walked over to look at this great collection. When I told my mother that I wanted to buy some, she asked me what I needed them for. I explained to her that if I had enough of them, I could place them into a cork with a pin set in the center to build a little motor. Intrigued, she bought me some of these metal odds and ends. When I came home, I immediately got busy building a little rotating generator. I got it to turn pretty fast, as I blew air close to the rotating blades.

It was obvious that I was mechanically inclined from an early age. When the German zeppelin visited Israel, I remember seeing it fly close overhead. I found it very exciting. After witnessing it go by, I told my mother that I wanted to build my own model of the zeppelin. I found a large sheet of cardboard, cut part of it into strips, bent it into a roll, and then cut the ends to form a cone. Once I had created the shape, I glued the front and back sections with some egg yolk, placed a small box on the bottom of the structure, and cut out holes to make windows. When I brought it to school, I won first prize in art for my zeppelin.

I was always collecting old rusted gears, wheels, and other metal junk in our backyard. On top of this big pile of material, I remember building a cardboard box with wings. I used to sit inside of it and fantasize that I was flying a plane.

By the time I was fourteen, I had graduated from the eighth grade and was ready to go to high school. I told my father that I wanted to go to a technical school. The school in Haifa, at the Technion Engineering University, had just opened a year earlier. It was called Bet Sefer Miktzue Tichoni (Technion High School), often called "Bosmat" for short. I do not remember how I had found out about the school, but I was determined to go there. My father's salary was hardly sufficient to support our family. However, seeing how set I was on going to Haifa, he decided to take out a loan to finance my studies there. After corresponding with the school, I was accepted. My father and I traveled to Haifa so that I could register for my classes. He paid the whole year's worth of my tuition in advance and helped me look for a boarding house.

The school recommended a woman called Mrs. Schwartz. She was a widow who lived in town who had two large rooms with four beds in each of them. They were all small, narrow army beds with hard mattresses. There were two large windows and a few nails in the wall above each bed to hang any clothing. Most other belongings had to be kept in a valise under the bed.

The idea of living away from home on my own for the first time was extremely exciting. I chose the bed closest to the window. My father made arrangements with Mrs. Schwartz to provide me with three meals a day, and with that settled, he returned to Jerusalem. The next day, three more students, all from the same class in school, joined us in Mrs. Schwartz's home: Yakov from Ranana, Yezhak from Talpiot in Jerusalem, and Moshe, also from Jerusalem.

Mrs. Schwartz, who had two children of her own, made her living from the income she made housing us eight boys. She saved as much as she could on the food she fed us. We discovered that breakfast was half a banana with a spoon of sour cream, a slice of bread with no butter, and a glass of hot tea. That was all. For lunch, she prepared a small sandwich with one slice of cheese for each of us. In the evening, we were usually give a bowl of watery vegetable soup, a slice of bread, and half of a banana for dessert. During the years I lived at Mrs. Schwartz's boarding house, the menu changed very little. Whenever my parents checked in to ask me how it was going and how Mrs. Schwartz was treating me, I never mentioned the starvation diet she had put us on, because I was afraid that they would take me out of school and make me come back to Jerusalem. In time, all of us boys adjusted to our meager diet and supplemented it with inexpensive nuts and fruits, which we bought in the street. By eating all of those nuts, we were giving ourselves the protein that our growing bodies needed but lacked on Mrs. Schwartz's diet. Years later, I wondered whether I could have been taller if I had been given a proper diet back then when I was fourteen. But somehow, besides being hungry, it never bothered us too much.

We were all very happy in school and excited to be living in such a beautiful city. Haifa was built on the slopes of Mount Carmel facing the harbor. During most of the year, the weather was very pleasant. It was somewhat hot during the summer and rainy, but not too cold during the winter, so I loved living in Haifa.

Because our school was a technical high school, we spent half of the day learning specialized trades such as mechanical fitting, welding, forging, and repair. The other half of the day was spent learning general high school studies. In total, we usually spent seven to eight hours in school every day. I loved working in the shop and learning how to use hand tools, hand files, and different kinds of machine shop equipment. My dream of becoming a mechanic and working with my hands was coming true.

Our teachers were first class professionals and very involved in teaching young students. I looked forward to going to school every day. I especially loved the workshop because it was the subject I excelled in, and I also enjoyed engineering, drafting, and physics. But I was not so thrilled with my general studies. I abhorred going to English class. I simply could not see myself studying another language; I just did not see the purpose in it. Ironically, years later I realized I had to learn English if I wanted to progress and fulfill my dream of becoming an engineer. Nevertheless, writing in English today is still my nemesis.

In the morning, we spent four hours learning general studies. After lunch, we changed into our working clothes and spent three to four more hours in the workshop. As soon as we finished in the shop, we showered, cleaned up, and went down to our pension for our meager meal. After that, we walked over to the main street, bought some nuts and fruits, and spent the next two hours walking, looking at the girls who were flirting at a distance.

In the evening, we spent half an hour to an hour on our homework. As there were no desks in our room, we usually spread our books and papers over our beds and worked there. The four of us had a great time together and a strong friendship developed between us, which continued for the rest of our lives.

Haifa was divided into three main sections. In the downtown area was the port, where there were always ships loading and unloading goods from all over the world. Most of the stevedores were Jewish immigrants from the town of Saloniki in Greece. Whenever I went there, I always smell aromas of coffee and spices surrounding the port. Nearby was the Arab section of town, which consisted of old stone houses and small narrow streets. Alongside the street next to the port, there were small stores spread throughout. Further west, past the port there was a swimming pool close to the ocean. It was the only swimming pool in town and we went there every Saturday during the summer.

Next, further up, there was a stretch of row houses called the German colony. Early German immigrants who had settled in Palestine during the Turks Occupation had made these well-built houses that were surrounded by trees and beautiful gardens full of flowers.

Further up the side of the Carmel Mountain was Hadar Hacarmel. Its main street was called Hertzel Street and all along it were various kinds of stores and restaurants. There was a movie house, which we never went into because it was too expensive, and there was one large building with a clock tower on top of it. Because we did not have watches, we always made our meeting place a set time at the watchtower. Thinking back, I do not know how we managed to always be on time when we had to get to school or meet friends without watches.

The Technion University and the Technion High School were next to the main street, Hertzel Street, near the Ariali School, which was a wealthy high school next to Technion. Our technical high school was the poor working class school. All of the rich kids in Haifa went to the Ariali School, so we never mingled with them. We wore working clothes, while they were always dressed in casual outfits. Our school was all-boys while theirs was co-ed.

Shower time, after the school day was done, was one of the best parts of the day. During the winter and summer, we only had cold water, but we spent a lot of time running around and playing on the slippery floor. Each of us had a storage space for his clothes. We never washed our working pants and, in time, they got so stiff with grease and oil that they could stand up on their own. We considered this as a symbol of professionalism.

Our teachers were young professional mechanics and fitters themselves, so they were always very committed and attentive to our needs. I, for one, could not wait to get to my workspace and tools each day. When I was there, I enjoyed myself so much that the time passed by quickly. I was one of the top students in the shop, and I got along very well with my teachers. All I wanted was to be a first class mechanic, so I focused solely on that. I did not realize that all of my other studies were just as important if I wanted to complete my education in the years to come. I learned of my shortcomings the hard way and ended up spending the rest of my life trying to catch up and improve my general education. However, there was no denying that my first love was being in the workshop.

Moving To Dr. Bardin's Home

At the end of my first happy year in school, my father dropped a bombshell: he told me that he could not afford to keep sending me to Haifa. Financially, he just could not support me any longer. But I did not feel betrayed or angry. I just felt sorry for my father, and cheered myself up by thinking that instead of school; I might go to work in a shop in Haifa.

I went to the principal of the school, Dr. Bardin, to tell him that I was going to have to leave school, and I asked if he could recommend a place in Haifa where I might find work. He told me that he might have an idea for me, and that he would talk to me some more about it the next day.

The following day I went to his office. He invited me to his home on Mount Carmel to meet his wife. I was bewildered. I had no idea what he was thinking, and accepted his request. Dr. Bardin took me on a bus, and we rode out to Mount Carmel. The section of town on top of Mount Carmel was one of the most beautiful places I had seen in the country: there were the most gorgeous homes and apartments, which were surrounded by lovely old trees. Most of the homes were facing the blue Mediterranean Sea. From the top of the mountain, you can overlook the port of Haifa where ships were unloading their goods. It was a breathtaking view.

Dr. Bardin's house was on the edge of the mountain. It was surrounded by beautiful trees and gardens, and there was a large terrace along the side of the house. At the entrance, he introduced me to his wife, Ruth. She was a tall gentle woman with dark curly hair who spoke Hebrew with a heavy American accent. I entered the apartment and was in shock. There were large paneled walls, wooden floors with exquisite carpets, shelves full of books, large sofas, and ornate wooden chairs. I had never visited such an opulent home or apartment before. They invited me to sit down on the sofa. Ruth brought out some cold drinks, and we all sat down. I still did not understand what all of this was about.

Mrs. Bardin inquired about my family. She asked me who my father was, and I told them that he worked as an accountant with the Jewish National Fund in Jerusalem. I told them how my parents had come from Russia, and that I had a brother and sister.

Dr. Bardin looked at me and then explained his idea to me. He told me that rather than me leaving school, he and Ruth had an alternative for me. They needed help in their home taking care of their two children at night, preparing breakfast in the morning, and washing the dishes in the evening. At night, when they went out, they needed someone to be home to watch over their two sons. In exchange for this service, I could live in their home and they would take care of my tuition.

I was in overwhelmed by their generosity. Living at my principal's home would be an extraordinary situation for any fifteen-year-old kid, especially if it meant living in such a palace. I told them that I would gladly accept their offer and that I would let my parents know. I added that I was ready to move into their house at any time.

My parents, of course, were ecstatic. A week later, I brought my little valise with all my worldly goods, which consisted of a few undershirts, underpants, socks, shirts, shorts, a sweater, and a jacket. I really did not need anything more. They moved me into the bedroom with the two boys. At that time, the boys were only two and three years old. The bed they gave me was small, but comfortable, and I got a closet to store my clothes. Next to the room was a beautifully tiled bathroom with a shower and large bath. It was the first time I had ever seen such a bathroom. It was all new and sparkling clean.

There were four other large rooms in the house: a bedroom for Dr. Bardin and Ruth, which faced the sea, a guest room, a children's room, and a spacious living room with a large terrace. In addition, there were two other bathrooms, an eat-in kitchen, and dining room. There were closets all around the house. Most windows faced the blue Mediterranean Sea or the gardens around the house.

Mrs. Bardin explained my duties to me. First, I had to take care of the children at night, especially whenever she and Dr. Bardin were out. Secondly, I had to prepare breakfast every morning. Breakfast duties consisted of setting the table with butter, jam, cheese, and oranges, placing the hot rolls that arrived at the house every morning out on the table, and boiling an egg for each person. This was the first time I had ever boiled an egg. Dr. Bardin was very particular about how he liked his egg to be. Part of it had to be soft and the other half had to be hard. Every morning, I worried if I had made them well, exactly as he liked them, and watched the time carefully to make sure the eggs were not too hard or too soft. Each time Dr. Bardin broke open his egg, my heart pounded loudly in my chest. He never missed the opportunity to remark on what he thought about his egg. He complimented me when it was right, and remarked about it when it was not. My third duty was washing the dishes. After dinner, I had to put the children to bed. After I had done that, I had the evening free to prepare my homework.

Every morning as I walked with Dr. Bardin to school, he talked about the news and gave me some lesson on history, science, or something else that was, generally interesting.

My school days changed dramatically. The other students including all of my old friends abandoned me. They thought I would tell Dr. Bardin about them and snitch if they acted up; but in fact, during the period of time that I lived with him, Dr. Bardin never once asked me about the kids in school. I missed my friends, but my new life with the

Bardins was compensation for me. I did not mind my duties at their home very much. Mrs. Bardin helped me with my homework, and my grades improved considerably.

There were always many visitors coming to their home: teachers, friends, artists, and musicians. On many occasions, they hosted concerts at their home. I was introduced to a new sophisticated life. While living with the Bardins, I saw that there was much more to attain in life than what my parents had to give me. I liked my new surroundings. Life was quite different from what it had been living with Mrs. Schwartz in her pension downtown. However, I missed my friends, who were now cruel to me and avoided me every time I tried to approach them.

Ruth Bardin was a gentle, soft-spoken American woman. She was also a serious and talented artist who was always sculpting and painting. She spent much of her spare time on her beautiful veranda facing the sea, working on her artistic projects. Mrs. Bardin loved Dr. Bardin deeply. She always wanted to serve him herself. I remember one time, I wanted to polish Dr. Bardin's shoes, but she told me that she wanted to do it herself. I was embarrassed in a way. In my family, my mother also loved my father, but he would have never have let her polish his shoes.

Although I enjoyed living in such fine surroundings, I never felt at ease with the Bardins. I tried to be perfect in my duties. I was never late in the morning, and most mornings in the winter, I would get up when it was still dark to start my day. I liked my breakfast, especially the hot rolls and butter. However, I never ate more than one roll at the meal, although I could have eaten half a dozen. I thought that it was not proper to eat too much. The same was true of the Cadbury chocolate they kept in the drawer in the kitchen. I loved this chocolate, but I ate only one bar a week. I did not want them to think that I would eat something without their knowledge. In fact, I later realized the Bardins had never begrudged me anything; it was only in my mind.

Likewise, I was very careful not to be late in the morning. It happened once that I woke up when it was still dark, and I heard Dr. Bardin and Ruth already in the living room. I dressed in a hurry and rushed to the living room, apologizing for being late. They looked at me in amazement. Then I realized that the time was only 11:00 at night! I had thought that it was already morning and I was late for breakfast.

Ruth Bardin came from a very distinguished Jewish family. She was born in Brooklyn in 1906, and she had two younger sisters and a brother. Her father Ralph Jonas was a lawyer and a banker, a philatelist, a country leader, and a patron of the arts. He and his brother Nathan S. Jonas founded the Manufacturers Trust Company of Brooklyn and controlled it until the stock market crash of 1929. Ralph Jonas also founded the Brooklyn Chamber of Commerce, Brooklyn Jewish Hospital, the Brooklyn Ethical Culture Society, and Long Island University, and he helped persuade the state government to open Brooklyn College. He was an active Democrat, and served on the New York City Board of Higher Education.

Dr. Shlomo Bardin was born as Shlomo Bardinstein in the Russian city of Zhitomir on Dec. 3, 1898. Raised in a religious Zionist environment, speaking Russian, Yiddish, and Hebrew, he arrived in Palestine in 1918. To further his education he spent time in Denmark and at London University, supporting himself by teaching Hebrew. In 1928, he traveled to the U.S. to study at Columbia University Teachers College for his Master's and Ph.D.

While Bardin was working towards his higher degrees at Columbia University Teachers College, Ruth had been one of his Hebrew students. She was a Zionist and wanted to master Hebrew. Ruth helped Shlomo to edit his Ph.D. thesis, which was eventually published by the Bloch Publishing Co. Ruth and Shlomo fell in love and they got married in 1930. Bardin's plan had always been to return to Palestine after completing his studies. Ruth was also eager to move to Palestine, and in order to have a vocation, she learned the craft of foot-loom weaving, which she could teach to young girls in Palestine. She had already mastered painting and sculpture.

Bardin dreamed of starting a technical high school in Israel, which would combine high school studies with technical education. He was introduced to some of Ruth's family and influential friends, including Louis Brandeis. All these connections enabled Bardin to raise the money for his school project.

In Israel, Prof. Kaplasky, president of Technion Israel Institute of Engineering, was searching for funds to open such a technical high school under the Technion umbrella. With $10,000 (a large sum of money in those days), Bardin's plan for the Technion High School was approved and by 1933 was opened and named Bosmat, with Shlomo Bardin as the principal.

When I entered the school, it was the second year of its existence. In 1939, Dr. Bardin and Ruth left for the United States because of the forthcoming war. He was never forgiven for leaving: when I visited the school in later years, I found no trace of his name in the school. His successor, Dr. Aharony, a teacher who became the principal, had a school building named after him, but there was nothing for Dr. Bardin, the founder.

When Dr. Bardin and Ruth left for the United States, I found myself without a home. I had just finished my third year in school and I wanted to continue. One of my friends in class told me that his uncle, who had a bakery not far from our school, was looking for a tutor for his children. Since I had experience in taking care of Dr. Bardin's children, I applied for the job, and instead of pay, arranged to work for room and board. The two boys were eight and ten years old, nice kids who were no trouble to teach and supervise. Unfortunately, the bakery had small living quarters and the only place for my bed was just a few feet away from the bakery furnace. Each morning at four o'clock in the morning, they started the furnace and the bread making, and of course, I could not sleep. In the winter, it was nice and warm; however, in the summer it was unbearably hot. But the food was good, and they fed me well. The smell of the fresh bread was wonderful and I could eat as many fresh, crispy rolls as I wanted. I was happy and content. My school friends gradually accepted me again, now that I was no longer a threat to them since there was no chance that I could snitch on them to Dr. Bardin. They never believed me when I told them that Dr. Bardin never asked me about any of the kids. I joined the young Makabi group and had a very active social life. We had dancing parties, went swimming in groups, made forays downtown in Haifa, and looked forward to working as young professionals.

My Friend Yakov Lior

Yakov Lior was one of my three roommates at Mrs. Schwartz' boarding house and one of my closest friends at Technion High School. Yakov was born Yakov Lichnstein. Yakov's father changed his family name when they immigrated to Palestine. He was born in 1921 in Kfar Saba, a small town north of Tel Aviv. His father built a large wooden home on a large piece of land for Yakov and his four sisters. His father was a farmer and a mechanic who owned several large tractors, which he operated all over Israel. He had a very gruff voice and sounded like a commanding general. Whatever he said went. In 1934, Yakov was accepted to the technical high school in Haifa. Yakov was a very active boy, tall and handsome and was very well liked, especially by the girls.

From an early age starting in Kfar Saba, Yakov was a member of the Haganah, a Jewish paramilitary organization, which later became the core of the Israel Defense Forces. There was always a great secret about him. Many nights he was missing from his room, arriving back in the early morning, sleeping four hours, and then going to school for the day. He always fell asleep in class. We knew that he was working secretly in the underground shop at the high school, manufacturing hand grenades and mortars. At that time, the British did not permit the Jews to have arms, and anyone caught making, carrying, or hiding arms could be jailed for many years. We were very careful never to mention or talk about what Yakov was doing.

Yakov was a very good mechanic. He excelled in the machine shop and was one of the best students. In the fall, Yakov would disappear from class for six to eight weeks. His father needed him to drive the tractor: plowing the fields, working on a construction site, or building a road. In fact, he started working on the tractor at the age of eleven. He also learned how to drive a car when he was nine, and always helped his father on his farm. When he was at home, his mother and four sisters spoiled him, waiting on him hand and foot. He was hard working and the darling of the female members of his family. But his father treated him exactly the opposite: he exploited Yakov as a working member of his family.

Yakov knew how to repair an automobile or tractor. His charm was irresistible and he always had the nicest looking girls. We were jealous of his success. Once during the summer vacation he invited me to spend four weeks with him on his farm. I was very excited for the opportunity. During the visit, I hardly had the chance to speak to his father, but his four sisters treated me as a member of the family. Each morning before the sun rose, Yakov and I got on the tractor and drove to a Kibbutz to plow the land. Yakov drove and I sat next to him. But when his father was not around, Yakov let me drive the giant Caterpillar tractor. He also started teaching me how to drive the old Ford car on the farm.

In school, we were both studying automobile mechanics as part of our technical studies, and of course, Yakov was very much the head of the class. The teacher was a young American automotive engineer who was working in the U.S. with the General Motors factory. I do not think that he was Jewish. He came to Israel as a visitor, fell in love with a young Kibbutz girl, left his wife and children in the States, and moved to live with his girlfriend on the Kibbutz. In time, his Kibbutz girlfriend had a baby. He was tall and very handsome and spoke mostly English. He taught us to play basketball, which was an unknown game at the time in Palestine. I lost contact with our American teacher. I heard that he returned to the U.S. during the war, but I do not know if he returned with or without his child and his Kibbutz lover.

As brilliant as Yakov was, he also had a mischievous, reckless streak. I remember one evening in Haifa after school, three of us were roaming the streets looking at girls, and we came to the parking area next to the movie theater, where several cars and motorcycles were parked. Yakov said that he could start a motorcycle and take a ride to Mount Carmel while the owner was in the movie theater. He asked me to ride with him. I thought that he was crazy: if he were caught he would go to jail, but that did not discourage him. He started the motorcycle and rode by himself up to Mount Carmel. Half an hour later he came back and parked the bike, and no one found out about his theft. He sure was lucky and brave. If he had been caught, in addition to spending time in jail, he probably would have been thrown out of school.

At our graduation, Yakov was missing; his father needed him on the farm and he missed the ceremony as well as receiving his graduation certificate. Years later, when he was the plant manager of one of the largest arms manufacturing companies in Israel, employing over 1,000 workers and many graduate engineers of Technion, he was invited to receive his high school graduation certificate.

Over the years, I lost contact with Yakov. He was always active in the Haganah, buying and smuggling arms to Palestine and helping to build underground arms factories in several Kibbutzim. After the establishment of the state of Israel in 1948, he became the manager of several arms factories, including a 2,000-man factory that manufactured Uzi submachine guns. From time to time, I heard about Yakov's successes. I, too, moved around, working on various construction projects in Israel, Abadan in Persia, and Baharien Island, and studying in the U.S.

I met Yakov and his family again twenty years later, in 1960 in New York. By that time, I had settled there, and Yakov and his two young children had moved to the city temporarily. Yakov had a job as head of the purchasing office for the government of Israel, buying arms and equipment for the Israeli defense industries and the armed forces. By that time, I was married and had a son, and was working as the technical director of the American Technion Society. Yakov lived two blocks away from our apartment on West End Avenue. Even after a 20-year separation, when we met again nothing had changed between us. We renewed our friendship as if we had last seen each other the previous day, not twenty years before. Sara, his wife, was a lovely, quiet, gentle woman who took care of her two children, while Yakov was frequently away on business. The children, one girl and one boy, were going to school in the neighborhood, but they were very wild and rambunctious, always fighting with each other. My son David was the opposite, quiet and introverted. We did not see Yakov often, because we were active in different circles, but from time to time, we met with Yakov and Sara for old time's sake. I never lost my warm feeling for him. He had a very charismatic personality, which made me envious, and his success with women never changed from childhood on. He had a girlfriend in every town he traveled to. Sara, his wife, knew about his gallivanting, but she seemed unperturbed by his short-lived romances.

While Yakov was sent to the U.S. to head the purchasing of the Israel Defense Industries Equipment and Machinery, he traveled continuously all around the country, and the purchases he was involved in were very secret. During his stay in the U.S., he bought out complete manufacturing factories producing armaments and heavy machines to build mortars, cannons, and machine guns. He had been involved in this industry since he was in high school in Haifa. After four years in the U.S., he returned to Israel and bought an apartment with the money his father left him and his sisters.

Again, I lost contact with him for several years. Once in a while, when he was visiting the U.S. with Sara, we would meet for lunch or dinner and hear from them the news from Israel. I heard from friends who visited Israel that he was appointed to manage one of the largest defense manufacturing facilities in the country. It had over 2,000 workers and was located near Tel Aviv, and he was proud to employ many of his old friends who were students with him at Technion High School in Haifa. Through the years, he became one of the top executive managers in the Israel Defense Industries. On many occasions, he was sent for special secret assignments in various parts of the world. I was simultaneously proud of being his friend yet jealous of the fact that he had had greater success than I had. Although I too managed large projects in Abadan and Baharien with thousands of workers working for me, I still felt that Yakov had reached higher accomplishments than I had, and it bothered me through the years.

But Yakov's success came at a price. The continuous pressures and responsibilities took their toll on his heart, and he went for a serious heart operation. He recuperated for a short time, but then there was a need for a general manager for the largest cannon manufacturing plant in the north of Israel. The workers' union was rebelling and the plant was losing money. Yakov set out to improve the conditions of the workers. He set up additional facilities in the plant for the manufacture of American Farber aluminum pots and pans, and the factory was on its way to recovery. After that, he was called again for a mission in Germany, and while he was in his hotel, he had a heart attack and died. Florence, my wife, and I mourned his death for a long time.

Looking back, I realize I really loved Yakov. He was a simple, honest person who never showed his greatness. You would never guess that this simple fellow was one of the most important defense industry leaders. I miss him with all my heart.

Sara Lior died a short time before Yakov. She was sick for a long time with diabetes and had become partially blind. I remember on one occasion when we visited Israel, Sara took us in Yakov's chauffeured car for a visit to Jerusalem, to Beer Sheva, and to Yakov's factory in the town of Yokinoam in the north of Israel. We visited the factory and we saw Farber pots & pans and special couscous pots. My wife asked Sara where she could buy one. Sara just did not answer. Later that week, as we were packing our baggage at midnight for the flight back home, Sara and Yakov arrived with a very large box. It was a gift from Sara to Florence: a new Farber couscous pot. It was a real lovely gesture.

After Sara left, I asked Florence how she could take this large box into the plane. I suggested sending it as baggage. Florence insisted on taking it with her. I left Florence with the box. She carried it to the exit gate by herself. The steward saw Florence with this box and came to her rescue. He offered to help her and to place the box in the plane, and so it was imported to New York. Ten years later the couscous pot is still in our kitchen pantry, and to this day, it has never been used to make couscous.

On the same trip, while Sara had Yakov's car with a chauffeur, we went to Beer Sheva to visit my friend Avigdor, with whom I had worked in Baharien and in Beer Sheva. He had a little house -- one of the houses I had built years back. His wife offered us coffee and cake. We noticed that she was not well. She had a touch of Alzheimer's disease. Avigdor also did not look too well. I was sorry to see Avigdor in such a condition. However, we had a good time reminiscing about old times. Two years later, when I visited Israel again, I met Avigdor again in my hotel. His Alzheimer had worsened, and we had a difficult time communicating with him. It broke my heart to see him in this condition. He died two years later and I miss him. He is always in my memory, and I always remember him how helpful and considerate he was to me in Baharien and Beer Sheva. He was indirectly my boss and great friend.

Jerusalem 1940 - Entering the Job Market

After graduation, I went back home to Jerusalem. My parents were very happy to have me home. I joined the workers' union, and left the house very early in the morning with a sandwich in my lunch box to sit at the union's office, waiting to be sent to my first job. My turn came and I was sent to a small iron shop for a welder's job. There were only six men in the shop. An electric welding machine was stationed outside and I was given the sheet metal parts to weld together. I started the machine, placed the welding rod in the handle, and started to weld. But the welding rod kept getting stuck, and whatever I did, adjusting the power, did not help. All I had learned in school could not help me. After watching me struggling for a half an hour, the manager of the shop told me to quit and go home. I was humiliated by the fact that my schooling had not made me a good welder.

I went home with my lunch box. My mother was surprised to see me home early, but told me not to worry, other jobs would be forthcoming.

The next day I went again to the union office early in the morning and they sent me to another metal shop. It was a small shop with six benches, and the job was to saw angle irons for window frames by hand. There were five men cutting. I was given one of the benches, a saw, and a pile of angle irons, and started to saw. The guy next to me was sawing like a machine. I thought that I could do the same, so I started cutting. After three hours I had to slow down, but I kept going all day for eight hours. The pain in my elbow was killing me. I came home, hardly ate, and went to sleep. The next morning I forced myself to keep cutting the angle irons, but I could not compete with the next guy, who kept cutting with the same speed all day. As much as the pay was piecework, I could not do as much as was expected of me. My hands and elbows were so sore I could hardly move them.

After five days I had to quit. My morale was very low. In school I was first in my class and I thought I could conquer the world, but here I could not even keep up with a man who had never gone to school. I was very upset. Thinking of the life I had in Dr. Bardin's home, I knew I wanted a better life than working in a dirty little shop for the rest of my life. I concluded that I must have an education, but how. My parents could not support me, and I had to work and make a living.

So I registered with The British Institute of Engineering School attached to London University, which was a correspondence school in Jerusalem. I decided that I could work during the day and study at night. My stumbling block was my deficiency in the English language. At school I had never thought that I needed to know English, but now my future depended on just that. So I struggled to read and write in English each day after work. My best hours were in the morning. I trained myself to get up each day at 3:00 a.m. and study till 6:00 a.m. I did this on and off for six years, carrying my books and papers with me wherever I went to work. Since I had trained in high school to become both a fitter and an auto mechanic, but I had failed as a fitter, I decided to try to get work as an auto mechanic in a garage.

Again I went to the union office and I was sent for a job as a garage mechanic with a large trucking company called Hovala ("transport"), which transported potash from the Dead Sea to Jerusalem. I was interviewed by the chief mechanic and the manager of the garage and was accepted. The trucking company was owned by four partners who started out as owners of a mule carriage business and over the years graduated to become owners of the trucking company. They were an illiterate, rough bunch. The manager of the garage was Zeev Katzenelson, a very short heavyset man who had studied mechanics with a trucking manufacturing company in the U.S. He had a good education, ran his shop with an iron hand, and knew how to work with the rough and tough owners.

All of the heavy trucks were parked outside the garage on an empty lot. The garage was a wooden structure with a corrugated steel roof and electric wires with light bulbs hanging from the ceiling and outside on poles. Most of the repair work was done inside the garage, but miscellaneous repairs and the greasing work was done outside on unpaved surfaces. The work started at 4:00 a.m., when we started up the trucks. The spark plugs had to be heated up on a gas stove, then the truck placed in gear would be pulled by a tractor, and that was how the truck would start. There were about twenty such trucks to be started every morning, and I was one of the mechanics running the hot plugs from the stove to the trucks. When it rained, the mud was up to our knees. Since it was still dark out, there were light bulbs hanging on poles around the yard. My next job was greasing the trucks' undercarriage. This was done by hand. The greaser would lie down on a wooden platform and move it under the various parts of the truck. On rainy days I was sloshing in mud. The foreman in charge of the greasing did not like me, and most of the time I was busy greasing rather than using my skills as a mechanic.

After I had spent about five months greasing, Zeev, the chief mechanic who knew of my schooling and was very friendly with me, told me that I was wasting my time in his garage. He said that this was not a working place for an educated mechanic, and he suggested that I should apply for a mechanic's job with the British Army auto repair shops. I applied, and the test that they gave me was a breeze. My studying at night with the correspondence school had helped me with my English. Soon I was working in an auto repair shop, in a storefront on the main road to Jerusalem.

I loved being an auto mechanic. I knew more than the young British soldiers who were running the repair shop. The salary was good, the shop was clean, and talking with the soldiers was very helpful in improving my English. The work was easy and close to my home, and I had more time to spend on my studies.

After I had been working there for about six months, the battalion was moved to the Hebron area, south of Jerusalem. I was asked to move with them, so I did. My living quarters were in an old Arab house with heavy walls, damp and cold. It was pleasant in the summer, but freezing in the winter. Sharing the room with me were five Jewish drivers who worked for the British Army with their own trucks. Our beds were placed along the walls. In the center of the room was a large table and chairs, and a kerosene lamp lighted the room. We had our meals three times a day in the mess hall with the soldiers, and we civilians had a good relationship with them. The food was good, and in the garage we did not have much work, so we played basketball many hours of the day. At night, the Jewish truck drivers played cards. Sometimes they played for twenty-four hours without stopping: drinking, smoking and playing. It happened that one of the drivers lost his truck in one of the games, so the next day he was driving his former truck, which now had a new owner.

At the time, the Arabs were rioting around the country and it was dangerous to travel between the main cities. Convoys were organized and the British Army with their armed trucks guarded the convoys. The brigade I worked for was assigned to patrol the convoys, and I was assigned as a mechanic to travel with them. Most of the time, I sat in the armed truck observing the convoy. Fortunately we were not attacked, and it was just an interesting adventure.

During my time in Hebron I spent a great deal of time on my studies and progressed with my English and auto mechanic knowledge. My English was improving every day. I developed a great friendship with the young British soldiers I worked with and for the first time in my life, I felt secure working with foreigners. I was becoming a first class mechanic, and that made me feel very good and happy.

Chapter 2 – Growing Up

Bosmat Technical High School
First Class 1933

In my greasy working clothes

Visiting the school – 50 years later

Dr. Bardin, his wife Ruth,
And sons, David and Hillel

Chapter 2 – Growing Up

British Armed Truck

Convoy on the road to Jerusalem

With the British Soldiers
Maintenance Division

Army Trucks Parking Lot
in Hebron

Chapter 2 – Growing Up

With the Army truck Convoy

Going Swimming

Just relaxing in Hebron

CHAPTER THREE
ABADAN, IRAN:
WITH THE ANGLO IRANIAN OIL COMPANY

First Year

During the Second World War, Persia with its producing oil fields was one of the most strategic areas for the British Empire. The Germans were conquering much of Europe, moving to Russia, and in North Africa, the Germans were moving towards Egypt. The Persian oil supply with its giant refinery in Abadan was the lifeblood for the British in both the Middle East and India. But in 1943, there was a shortage of engineers and technicians for the oil refinery, so the search was on in Palestine, and specifically in the Jewish population, for such technicians.

For many years, technical education and engineering played an important part in developing the Jewish settlements. Small industry was flourishing. Farming was spreading over the land in small villages and Kibbutzim. Illegal Jewish immigration had brought in many educated professionals who were integrating into Israel's industrial growing economy, and so there was a pool of good technical manpower available.

The largest Jewish contractor in the Middle East was the company Solel-Boneh, whose charismatic director, David Hachoen, had grown up in Palestine during the Ottoman Turkish occupation and had a very good relationship with the British Authority. The British needed engineers and technicians for their refinery in Abadan, Persia, and contacted the Jewish Agency, which governed Jewish affairs under the British government. The agency appointed Hachoen to negotiate a contract for Solel-Boneh to provide the engineers and technicians to the refinery.

At that time, I was working as a foreman with the British trucks maintenance depot. This was my first job as a supervisor of about twenty-five mechanics, mostly Arabs and Armenians. I loved the job and the salary. I also loved to supervise and manage people and was in training to become the shop superintendent.

I was living in Haifa at the time, sharing a room with a friend who was a fellow graduate of my class at Technical High School. He was working as an auto mechanic in the police department garage. He was a real Rumanian wise guy, always on the lookout for ways to make money outside of his regular job, and he had a continuous stream of girlfriends coming to our room. On many occasions, I found myself shut out of the room for part of the night because he had a girlfriend with him.

And that was not the only problem: I found out after a while that each day he stole new engine bearings from his shop and rolled them in his shirtsleeves. No one had yet found out, but I was getting very upset and worried. Aside from not being able to rest after work in my room because of his constant liaisons, I was afraid of trouble arising from his criminal activity. It was getting to me. As soon as I found another room, I left, and for a while I did not want to meet with him because if he was caught stealing, my association with him could have gotten me in trouble as well. I could not afford to lose my job.

David Hachoen heard of my success with the British maintenance depot and called me for a meeting in his company's headquarters in Haifa. He told me about the great opportunity of working in Persia as a manager of a construction equipment depot in the largest refinery in the world, The Anglo Persian Oil Company Refinery. The contract was for two years and the salary was triple my present salary, plus all living, food and travel expenses included. Geographically I knew where Persia was, and I thought that it sounded like a great adventure to work outside Palestine for the first time in my life. I signed the contract enthusiastically.

Several weeks later, I was called again to meet other selected professionals, each a specialist in a different area: electrical, hydraulic machining, air conditioning, piping, and pumps. My specialty was the construction machinery. Two others in this group were also graduates of my technical school in Haifa, but I did not know them personally.

I was 22 years old and I was very excited about my new career. David Hachoen told us that we were the first group of professionals going to the refinery and that if the management of the refinery found that our work met their expectations, an additional 300 professionals from Palestine would follow us later. We were supplied with a list of personal effects we should bring along: short pants, light sleeveless shirts, a lot of underwear, and a white suit, white shirt, tie and white shoes. I had never worn a white suit before and I wondered why I needed one now.

The night before our departure, we gathered in a hotel in Haifa. All eight of us had a nice dinner together and started to get acquainted with each other. Early the next morning we were loaded into a small bus going north. That evening we arrived at our first stop: the town of Damascus in Syria. It was a beautiful town. We were put up in a luxury hotel where bellhops brought our luggage to our rooms and took our shoes to be shined. We were very impressed with the high-class service.

The next morning we were loaded onto a different bus, which looked like a truck with heavy truck wheels and was quite dusty outside. Our luggage was tied up on the roof of the bus and water bottles were distributed to each of us. Once the bus was filled with mostly Arab passengers, we took off.

Driving through Damascus, we saw a lot of palm trees and greenery, which looked very picturesque. However, after about an hour, we started driving through high, rocky mountains, and after that, there was nothing but an endless view of desert sand. There was no road. The bus drove across flat desert land, and fine powdered sand blew against the closed windows, engulfing us. The heat was close to 100 degrees. We placed our handkerchiefs over our mouths and noses and could hardly breathe.

As we rode in the back of the bus, we could see a tremendous column of dust rising high in the sky, and wondered what it was. After a while, we noticed another bus driving parallel to us, about a half a mile away, which also had a tremendous column of dust enveloping it. We realized then what was happening to our bus.

Without a road, we drove on the flat endless sandy desert floor, with no turns or curves. We drove for 24 hours straight with only two stops for refueling and using the bathroom. Every cavity in our body was filled with fine dust. During the stop, they used a broom to remove the dust from the bus floor and under the seats. We ate the sandwiches we had with us and thirstily drank the water in our bottles.

Finally, at about nine o'clock the next evening, we arrived in Baghdad. We were exhausted. Through the dusty windows, we could hardly see the town. However, once we got off the bus we were overwhelmed. The hotel was a palace: beautiful inlaid colored stones all around the great big entrances, marble floors, water fountains all around. We were ushered inside the best hotel in Baghdad.

This was the first five star hotel I had ever visited, and I was deeply impressed. We decided that for the occasion we would put on our white jackets. We were paired up, two to a room, and each room had a window facing the bridge and river. We took hot showers, polished our shoes, and went down to the dining room.

For our party they had set up a separate table with a shiny white tablecloth and silver utensils. I could not understand why I had three forks, three knives, two spoons, and a tablespoon around my double plate with a beautiful golden design. There were two glasses at the side of each plate and a red and white napkin was inverted in a silver ring. Behind each chair stood a red-turbaned waiter in a red and white suit. We all looked at each other, wondering how we could handle this fancy dinner without embarrassment.

We were served salad, then soup, and then steak with vegetables. Red and white wine was served and the dessert was fruit and ice cream. Each time we finished using the knife and fork they were removed by the waiters behind us.

At the end of the meal, they brought to each of us a silver cup filled with liquid and another plate with a warm wet napkin on top. We looked at each other and wondered whether it was an additional dessert. We talked among ourselves in Hebrew, wondering how to handle this watery dessert. I looked around for a clue. Sitting at the next table were two British officers, and we waited to see what they would do with the last serving. To our astonishment, we saw that they did not eat or drink from the cup. They just dipped one finger in the water and used the wet napkin to clean their mustache and mouth, then dried their hand with the napkin. So we did the same. That was my first full served dinner at the first class dining room in a five-star Baghdad hotel. The best part was that all this was paid for by the Anglo Persian Oil Company.

The next morning we drove across the river. Several hours later, we arrived in Abadan, which is next to the Euphrates River. The weather was hot and humid, much different from Palestine in the summer. There was an acid smell in the air and a low hanging cloud over the town. This was the "refinery weather." We were driven past the giant refinery, with its high concrete fence surrounding its perimeter, and then drove about a mile on an asphalt road through beautiful well-kept gardens till we reached a bungalow area with small houses with flat roofs. The bus stopped at one of these bungalows and we were told that this would be our new home.

The bungalow was sparkling clean and had four large bedrooms, a kitchen, and two bathrooms with a corridor in between. At the entrance there were two housemen waiting to take care of us. Each bedroom had two beds. We each selected our roommate and unloaded our luggage into our new home, which would be ours for the next two years. There was plenty of closet space, attractive furniture, two fans, and two lamps, one on each table. Our bedroom was painted white, and hanging over each bed was a mosquito net. We had a flourishing garden around the bungalow, and it all looked wonderful except for the heat and humidity.

Soon a waiter came and guided us to the mess hall, which was a few blocks away, next to a large kitchen. A long table was set for the eight of us with a white tablecloth, genuine silverware, glasses, water and a few bottles of wine. The food was excellent. The four waiters were running back and forth from the kitchen to our table and kept asking us if we wanted a second serving. They spoke very little English, but we understood them.

At the end of the meal, a handsome English man with a big mustache welcomed us. He told us how important our service was to the war effort. The refinery was very important for the supply of fuel to the armed forces.

Each of us received a note describing the department we were assigned to and the name of the head of the department. My department was construction machinery, and I was appointed to be the assistant to the superintendent of that department, whose name was Mr. Korless. I was only 22 years old, but I spoke English well and I had excellent references from the Brigadier General of the British mechanical engineers, whom I had worked for in Israel as a foreman.

Mr. Korless was an older English gentleman who had worked for the refinery for over 20 years. He was married to a lovely English lady, and they had two sons back in England. From the start, I liked him and it was mutual. He explained to me my responsibilities, which included 80 cranes and shovels, 120 tractors of all sizes, 300 welding machines, 100 dump trucks and a large workshop. Four foremen reported to me -- one Indian and three Persians – as well as 400 employees. It was overwhelming. However, I felt very secure. Although I had never supervised such a large group, I felt that I could do it.

The Indian foreman spoke fluent English, but the other three spoke very little English. The first week I learned the most essential words: yes or no, good or bad, slowly or faster, thank you, come, go, etc. I was amazed to find that, with only a few words, I was able to supervise my group.

At first, my foremen were skeptical about my knowledge. However, soon they found that I was an experienced mechanic and supervisor, and I had no problems managing the department.

Mr. Korless was very happy to see me taking over the department. He spent only four hours a day in the office and left it all to me to run things. He was relatively old, tired, and hot, especially in 120-degree Fahrenheit weather. But I had no problem with the heat; I just suffered in silence without complaint.

Every day we started work at 5:00AM. A small minibus picked us up and dropped each of us at our designated departments at 9:00AM. By then the heat had usually reached 110 degrees Fahrenheit. We were picked up and brought to the dining room for breakfast. Then, we went to our hot rooms to rest under the fans at 2:00PM. We had lunch, and when it cooled down at 3:00PM, we returned to work until 7:00PM. When we were done, we showered, had a light dinner, and went for a walk to the swimming pool.

We had Sundays off. Sometimes we went for a walk to the old city, but usually we spent most of the day in a large, beautiful swimming pool not far from our bungalows. We always went to the swimming pool in a group. Most of the people in the swimming pool were

Persians; we Israelis were the only foreigners in the pool. We were warned not to look at or speak to the girls in the pool. The Persian men were very jealous of their women and we had to be careful not to antagonize the local people. It was no fun having all these beautiful women around without even being allowed to admire them openly.

My work was getting more and more interesting. However, not knowing the language was a hindrance, so we approached the local school principal and requested his help. After negotiating a fee, we started taking lessons in Persian every day. Most of us were slow to learn. However, two of our group learned to speak the language fluently within three months. For me, it took over six months to speak well enough to be able to direct my supervisors and personnel in their own language.

After three months, our group of eight was evaluated, and the refinery management was satisfied with our performance and decided to recruit an additional 300 engineers and technicians from Israel to the refinery. Our private little dining room was enlarged to accommodate 300 additional men. The kitchen was likewise expanded to cook for them. Now there were more than 30 tables, each seating 10 men, and more than 60 waiters running from the kitchen to serve those 30 tables. Our table was closest to the kitchen. Our original waiters were still serving us, and to make things easier for us we bribed the waiters and the head of the kitchen, and so we received the best food and extras before anyone else was served. No one suspected our private deal. However, because of the jealousy we created, our small original group was not liked too much. In addition, by this time most of the original group had supervisory jobs, which meant that some of the newcomers had to work for us, the old group.

Included with the new group of 300 was a manager sent from the main office in Israel to manage the affairs of the groups -- personal affairs, the financing of the workers, and the payment for our services to the contractor, Solel-Boneh, who had brought us to Persia. The manager's name was Chay Yesacharov. Some years previously he had been the chief engineer who built the first turbine water driven power plant in Israel, which was built at the entrance of the water from Lake Kinert to the Jordan River. Chay lived in a separate bungalow and had two bookkeepers working for him. Chay was a personable man with tremendous engineering background and he managed the 300 engineers and technicians. But we of the first group who had signed up directly with the refinery did not feel that Chay had any authority over us and we shunned him, never meeting him or talking to him.

I was promoted to superintendent, working under Mr. Korless, who was promoted to a director's position. I was given a motorcycle with a sidecar and I was free to come and go as I pleased, and everyone was envious of me. I needed additional help for my department, so Mr. Korless approved two additional engineers to work for me. These men came from the new group from Israel. I gave them a test and made them supervisor of two of my many departments. I told them that friendship is one thing, but if they were ever late to work, they would be fired. As a result, they were never late.

One day Chay Yesacharov called me to his office with a request. He said that for reasons he could not explain, I must accept a young man to work for me. He told me that helping this young man, by the name of Yudka Rabinovitz, would have national importance for the Jews. I asked Chay if the young man was a mechanic. He told me that Rabinovitz knew only a little, but that I must keep him in my department nevertheless. Chay added that Rabinovitz might need some time off from time to time, and when he did, I would have to cover for him. Chay reiterated that this was a secret service and very important to the Jewish agency in Palestine.

So one morning, Yudka came to see me. I introduced him to Mr. Korless as one of my new assistants. He spoke a few words to Yudka and approved him.

I asked Yudka what he knew about being a mechanic. He admitted, "Not too much." At the time, I was setting up a new department repairing radiators, so I told Yudka that I would show him how to supervise a group of ten local mechanics who were repairing and building radiators. In no time, he mastered the job and I was happy with him. Yudka was a loner, so I did not talk to him much except when we had to talk about his job.

The radiator department became a very important department for the refinery. Because of the war, there were no spare parts coming from England. Since the weather was so hot, the cooling systems on most engines broke down. Once they started leaking after local repair, the radiator became unusable, and so was the engine, which left the heavy equipment idle. I had found that I was losing the use of most of my equipment because of the broken radiators. So I started looking for a junkyard for spare parts, and to my amazement, I came upon a mountain of all kinds of used, broken equipment parts and radiators by the thousands. Before the war, the junk had been shipped to Japan, but now it all piled up ten stories high. All the metal junk of the refinery was collected in one large pile. I realized that I had found a goldmine.

I brought in one of my large cranes and placed one of my assistants to supervise the separation of the junk piles, which contained all kinds of broken radiators, engines, gear axes, wheels, and all other equipment parts, many of them in good condition. We separated the radiator piles to various sizes. The pieces that were most suitable to our need we brought to the workshop, and I set up the radiator department.

A radiator is a cooling block of copper pipes with fins, which are soldered on both ends to small copper tanks. The bottom tank is connected to the engine, and on top, you fill the radiator with water, which runs into the engine. A pump circulates the water and a fan blows air through the finned pipes and cools the water. The pipes can be removed from one radiator and soldered to another, and the result is that you have a good functioning radiator.

Under the supervision of Yudka, the radiator department was a great success. Many of the refinery management personnel who had private cars brought their car to be repaired there. Mr. Korless was very proud of my department. The local Iranian workers were sitting on the floor holding the radiator parts with their feet and soldering the parts with their hands. All was going well, until one morning Yudka did not show up for work. I could not find him in his bungalow -- he had disappeared. I went to see Chay and told him about Yudka's disappearance. Chay told me that Yudka had a very important job to do for the Haganah, and that he would be missing for a while and I would have to cover for him.

I appointed a local foreman to supervise the radiator department and whenever Mr. Korless asked me, "Where is Yudka?" I told him that I had sent him to install the repaired radiators on the construction site. Every week I signed the weekly attendance for Yudka and Mr. Korless did not bother to check me further.

Through the years, Yudka came and disappeared often. I found out later, after he left to go back to Israel, that he was a high-ranking officer and head organizer of the Haganah, the Israeli underground army, and that he was moving Jewish refugees from the concentration camps in Europe to Israel.

The fifty thousand local employees in the refinery were mostly unskilled and very poor. Most wore rags. Some lived in mud huts next to the river with their families, but most were day workers and had no housing. At the end of the working day, after the shops were closed along the town's main street, the workers carried little bundles of their personal effects with them everywhere they went, whether it was to their place of work or to the street. They slept on the sidewalks along the street, thousands and thousands lying next to each other. The river was close by to the main street and canals were extended from the river into the shanty town. This was the only supply of water for the workers and their families. Washing, drinking and cleaning dishes were all done in the canal. It was an unbelievable sight. The pay to the workers was in pennies. The food they ate consisted of pita and a few dates a day. It was hard for us to get used to seeing this poverty.

Some of the machine operators and mechanics were very good and their living conditions were better. They had small homes and a living salary. Most of these had several wives and many children. I had no problem managing them.

My dump truck drivers were mostly Indian soldiers who had been prisoners in India, mostly for murders, and they had been given the choice to be released from prison if they joined the army and worked as drivers in the refinery. All were Indian of the Sikh tribe. They never cut their hair. They had long beards, which were tied over their heads, and a scarf around their head formed their hat. They were a very rough bunch, but they were very good drivers and mechanics. Their sergeant spoke English and reported to me.

I remember an incident with them, which nearly cost me my life. The dump trucks had to be cleaned, so I instructed the sergeant to fill buckets of kerosene and brush clean the dump truck bodies. Some of the drivers removed their hats and untied their beards, which were quite long. I had never seen the young Sikhs' beards unbound before. While they were cleaning, the beards were practically touching the surface of the trucks. It was quite funny. So I said jokingly to one of the soldiers that his beard looked like a cleaning brush in the breeze.

The soldier started screaming, pulled out his long knife and approached me threateningly. Several of the soldiers held him back and the sergeant took me in a hurry into the office. I could not understand what had happened. The sergeant explained to me that the Sikh's beard is a religious symbol and anyone insulting one's beard must be killed. To make sure that no harm came to me, the soldier was transferred from the refinery and I learned my lesson.

My welding machines, which were driven by gasoline engines, were working in various parts of the refinery. Each had a local Coolie who watched the engine to prevent it from overheating. As the heat reached 120 degrees the water in the radiator began boiling, and the water had to be supplemented continuously by the Coolie. On many occasions, they failed to fill the radiator on time and the engine burned down. After a while, I found that 40 percent of the welding machines were out of order.

I came up with an idea to develop several gadgets to overcome this loss of equipment. I had my own active workshop where I built several gadgets. One such gadget was a float with a switch for the water system. When the water got low, the switch would cut out the engine and stop it in time before the engine burned. To make sure the level of the oil in the engine was controlled, I built a float in the engine oil sump with a switch cutting off the engine once the oil level got too low.

Another problem I had was that the engine magnetos were being stolen. So I developed special protective bolts to attach the magneto to the engine – bolts that only a special wrench could remove -- and the theft of the magnetos stopped. My boss Mr. Korless was very happy with my achievements.

For such innovations as I had made, the refinery was giving out considerable monetary prizes. I had a great deal of debate with myself whether to register my innovation to my name or whether to give it to Mr. Korless, so that he would get the credit and the money. Since he was a great boss, letting me do whatever I wanted on my job, I decided to give the credit to him, and he entered the innovation in his name. This was a great sacrifice for me but a great pleasure for Mr. Korless and his wife. Mr. Korless was written up in the local papers and he received a 100-pound cash prize.

The day after the ceremony, Mr. Korless gave me the cash prize with a note of appreciation. I was happy that I had made the right decision. Our relationship was now better than ever and I was actually my own boss, which made me very proud of my position. I had reached the highest position of the Israeli group and many of the Israelis were very envious of me.

It was getting warmer by the day. The humidity was getting to 85 percent and there was an acid smell coming up from the refinery. There were many smoke stacks, which were burning the surplus gas, and the smell and smoke added to the heat made it very difficult to breathe. To cool off, we moved our beds into the yard. We covered the beds with mosquito nets to keep the mosquitoes off and tried to sleep outside. However, while the mosquito nets kept the bugs out, they also kept the breeze out, making us even hotter. So we had to move the beds back to our hot rooms again, and the fan in the room did not help much.

The refinery was surrounded by a high concrete wall and several iron gates. The local workers were searched each time they left the refinery; however, in spite of this, stealing was rampant. Tools, instruments, and products were disappearing from the work places. The police officers guarding the gates were on the take, and there was no way of stopping the thefts except to lock all the tools and materials in the work area every day after work. Any police officer or government official could be bought with a few dinars. This bribery was accepted and understood by all as the normal exchange of any services you wanted for money. They called it "baksheesh."

One of my friends, Berle Lubashevsky, was in charge of the instrument shop, repairing and maintaining the refinery's instruments. He was a genius machinist. In fact, it was his knowledge that kept most of the process equipment running. At the time, no spare parts could be imported from England, and so many parts of the instruments had to be made in the refinery. One of the most expensive materials used in the instrument department was quick mercury used in the measuring instrument. All instrument department workers were searched every evening before they left work. However, the mercury kept disappearing, and no one could figure out why. Most workers used bicycles to travel from their homes to the refinery.

It happened that one day, one of the workers working in the instrument department was passing through the exit door with his bicycle. As he was being bodily searched, his bicycle fell down. The guard wanted to help him lift the bicycle, but he could not lift it because it was so heavy. After inspecting it closely, they found how the mercury was being smuggled out: the liquid mercury was being pumped into the bicycle tires and frames. Thereafter the bicycles were weighed before they left the shop, and the mercury theft stopped.

There was not very much to do after working hours. We did not m ingle with the local population, and we were bored. Some of us attended classes in the Iranian school, some played cards, and some drank. However, drinking was not an Israeli habit and it was limited to only a few. We were all heavy smokers of cigarettes and pipes and played all kinds of betting games between us just to pass the time.

Berle, who lived next door, was always bragging that he could drink vodka all night and never get drunk. We gathered one evening in his room, betting with him that he could not drink a whole bottle of vodka in one evening. The bet was for 100 pounds. He drank the whole bottle of vodka in just five minutes. He got his 100 pounds, which at the time was a lot of money. While we were celebrating his success, he was getting sick, vomiting and fainting. We called the doctor, who rushed him to the hospital, and they pumped out his stomach. Berle was sick in bed for a week. No more vodka for Berle thereafter.

The next joke was on one of our young neighbors. We all usually talked about sex, and he was always listening with great interest. One night we told him that we had a sex pill, which he could take that would make him very sexy for a long time. He begged us for the pills. We did not give them to him, but we deliberately left the pills on the shelves. The pills were actually laxative pills. One day our friend proudly announced that he had swallowed some of the pills. A few days later, he told us that they were very effective…however; they had also caused him a heavy dose of diarrhea. In fact, it was so bad that he had to spend a few days in bed. We never told our young friend the pills were only laxative pills.

In the evening, we usually dressed up before dinner and then after dinner, walked over to the swimming pool, which was a cooler area, where we would just sit and talk, since there was not much else to do. The water in the pool was usually warmish. While talking we would dare each other and make bids on the dares: how much money one would get for swimming the length of the pool with all his clothes on, including his jacket, tie, shoes, etc., and who would be willing to do it and for how much. We started to pool the money and we got to 100 pounds. At first, no one took the challenge. We changed the condition: the only thing that could be removed before jumping into the pool would be the watch and the billfold. Before we knew it, one of our friends removed his watch and billfold, jumped fully dressed into the pool and swam the whole length. He got the 100 pounds prize and went home dripping wet.

My roommate Joseph was a great eater. He always had three or four servings at breakfast and dinner, and he could eat pistachio nuts by the pound. We started talking about how many pistachios he could eat, and he said as many as we could give him. We invented a plan naming a prize he could win if he could eat the quantity of pistachios we provided…but if he could not eat that much, he would pay us the amount of the prize, plus the cost of the pistachios. We prepared an evening for this occasion. To make sure that Joseph would lose, we went to the market, bought 10 large bags of pistachios, and hid them in the closet. We did not show Joseph how many pistachios we had. That evening, about twenty of us gathered in the room. Joseph sat at the table with a couple of bottles of beer in front of him. We negotiated the length of time he had to eat the nuts, and settled on four hours. He would win the prize if he could eat all the nuts we had bought in four hours.

We all sat around drinking beer and watched Joe eat the nuts. Joe never expected us to buy more than two or three bags of nuts, because they were very expensive. After two hours, he had finished two bags and he got suspicious. He wanted to know how many more bags of nuts we had. He said he had to know so that he could plan his speed of eating. We were opposed to the idea, but we finally agreed that after he ate the third bag of nuts we would show him our storage. It took him four hours to finish the three large bags. By that time, he was already in bad shape. Then when all of our twenty friends were ready to judge the winner, we opened the cabinet and provided another seven large bags of nuts. Joe nearly fainted. Not only had he lost the bet, he had to pay us for the other seven bags, which we had bought at a considerably high price.

From time to time, we met some Jewish families in Abadan. They were mostly merchants in rugs and jewelry. As Israelis, we did not think much about them.

In one family we met a gorgeous woman, a wife and mother with four small children. Her husband was a rich rug dealer. They kept a beautiful large home with several servants, and we noticed during our visit to them that there was a middle-aged man always hanging around, helping with the children and doing all kinds of chores. We thought at first that he must be a relative. We found out that he had a wife and three children of his own, but that he was under a "bad luck spell," in which the Iranian believed He had fallen in love with the rug man's wife -- not a sexual love, but a platonic "demon's love." He simply could not live without being near her, and had he been prevented, he would have committed suicide. He was, in fact, a slave to her. His family felt sorry for him but they could do nothing about it. The husband of this beautiful woman also was sorry for him and did not end this strange relationship. Most people in town knew and were also sorry for him and they all lived this way for years and years.

Our socializing with the local people was very limited. From time to time Mr. Korless and his wife invited me to spend an afternoon with them in the British Social Club, where only the British management personnel of the oil refinery spent their leisure time. Next to the club were the cricket field and a riding park. The British lived separately in their colony. Their homes were beautiful and each had three or four servants: a cook, maids, etc. They lived well: each floor of their homes was covered in Iranian carpets made to order, mostly Kashan or Isphan carpets. All of us Israelis bought these expensive beautiful carpets -- which were not expensive locally -- and brought them back to Israel upon our return home.

There were several Jewish families in town, but since we were not religious, we never attended the local synagogue where we could have met the local Jewish families. Likewise, we never befriended the local Iranians. We were treated like the British Foreign Management: we were respected, but kept at a distance.

The Iranians guarded their women, wives and daughters so that we could not speak or get close to them. It was a difficult life for us without having a chance to speak to women. For the local inhabitants, there were a lot of activities in town. There were also prostitutes in every section of the town, who mostly started at the age of 11 or so. We were advised that most were sick with syphilis. So for the two years we stayed in Iran there were no women in our lives.

The Indians also lived separately in another section of town. We were invited from time to time to an Indian musical concert. We had to sit outside fully dressed for such occasions in 100 degree heat, sweating all the time. Unfortunately, for us, the concerts sometimes lasted three to four hours. The music was monotonous and uninteresting and we had to sit and suffer for hours.

The hospital was divided into three sections: one for the British, the second for the management personnel and the third for the local workers. The standard health service was poor, so we tried our best not to visit the hospital, especially the dental department. There was no drilling or filling cavities in the department. Instead, if anyone came in with a toothache, that tooth would be pulled out. In fact, some of my friends who were unfortunately enough to go to the dentist found that all their teeth were pulled out. The local dentist's theory was that dentures were better than your own teeth. I kept far away from the dentist, although on occasion I had a terrible toothache.

Second Year

After a year of work in Abadan, I received two weeks vacation. Half of my vacation time was spent on traveling from Abadan to Israel and back. Most of the money I had earned, which was considerable, I left with my father. There was no opportunity in Abadan to spend my money. I spent some time at home in Jerusalem, met some of my girlfriends, and before long returned to Abadan for another year.

In my second year, I was the highest paid Israeli in the refinery. I was a full-fledged superintendent and very happy with the work, although the heat was getting to me. My younger brother Maza in Israel, who worked as a mechanic, also wanted to work in the refinery. I told Mr. Korless about my brother's request. In no time, he was accepted and he joined me in Abadan. Being that my brother was only a mechanic while I was a superintendent, his accommodations were somewhat less opulent than mine were and he roomed with other mechanics in another bungalow. I had different friends from his and unfortunately, we did not spend much time together.

Thinking back on my relationship with my brother when we grew up together in Jerusalem, this was actually the norm. He was five years younger than I was, and we never had spent much time together. We had never played together or been close like brothers should be. I have no memory of doing any activity together with him. By the time I was fourteen, I left for school in Haifa and lost all contact with him, except on some holidays when we spent an evening together at home. Through the years, I never took vacation and I was always out working.

Although I had spent only fourteen years at home, I loved my parents with a deep love, as well as my brother and sister. I felt very close to my father and mother. My father was a very gentle man who never raised his voice to us or to my mother. He was crazy in love with my mother, and she likewise loved him deeply. They never quarreled, because my mother was the aggressive one and my father respected her opinions and decisions.

For most of his life, my father worked for one company, Keren Kaimet Le Israel, first as an accountant and then as assistant controller. Keren Kaimet Le Israel was involved in acquiring land from the Arabs and lending it to kibbutzim and farmers for a term of 99 years. In addition, the company helped finance the kibbutzim's purchase of equipment. My father was responsible for the loans for the kibbutzim. Sometimes he extended himself beyond his responsibility and took chances with kibbutzim, which were in financial difficulties. I remember many nights on which he did not sleep because the loan he gave to a kibbutz was not covered sufficiently. If the kibbutz did not pay the loan in time, my father would be responsible for the debt. Fortunately, it never happened. Sometimes he just extended the loan date so that the kibbutz would be able to pay back the loan.

Until I got married at age 28, I never had a bank account. Most of the money I earned I sent to my father to keep, and he kept my records. Whenever I needed money beyond my salary, I could get it from my company; they kept my records and I never bothered to check how much money I owed them or they owed me. I simply did not need money. I just wanted to work for the cause of my company, Solel-Boneh, the largest construction company in Israel. It was thrilling to know that this company was building Israel and that I was a part of this great undertaking.

In 1942 my sister, whom I really hardly knew, joined the British Israel army, and worked as a driver of army trucks for several years. During the war, she drove supply trucks from Israel to Egypt. When she finished her stint with the army, she wanted to study gymnastics in Sweden. Since I had money saved with my father, I supported her in school for two years. When my brother wanted to go study in Haifa Technical School, which I had graduated from, I likewise supported him for three years. Somehow, I felt responsible for them. I was the older brother and they were my brother and sister, whom I loved but did not truly know.

After my short vacation, I returned to the Abadan refinery. Mr. Korless was very happy to have me back. In fact, he tried to convince me to sign up for another three years with a promise of a much higher salary, a separate bungalow, and the privilege of using the British Iranian club, which was reserved only for high ranking Iranian management and the British personnel. But by the end of the second year, I had had enough.

During that second year, Rommel was progressing in North Africa and the Germans were in the Balkans. The British were preparing for possible bombing by the German Air Force, and I was involved in setting up a smoke screen system around the periphery of the refinery. I set up barrels of oil drums connected by pipes, pumps which could be lighted up, and cause a large smokescreen to cover the refinery and hide it from view from the air. I had several hundred workers working for me on this project.

At the time, the United States had made Abadan a port at the center of shipping, unloading tanks and aircraft for the British Army and their air force. The ships from the U.S. were unloading this war material day and night, and tremendous quantities of goods were stored in port for shipping to Africa. Most of the aircrafts parts were in wood crates, and since wood was scarce in Iran, a flourishing black market business was going on. Some of the officers and local people as well as the Israeli storage manager were selling these wooden crates for large sums of money. By the time, our Israeli storage manager returned to Israel, he was a rich man. We all felt sick and embarrassed to see this happening, but there was nothing anyone could do because the locals and the officers were corrupt. Any Iranian official from a police officer to the director general could be bought, and this was the accepted way of doing business.

On several occasions, our original member group rented a sailboat and had a sail on the river, which was a mile or two wide in some sections. There was a great deal of shipping traffic on the river, primarily oil tankers and ships from the U.S. and India. Our sailboat would take us to a small island in the middle of the river, and there we would have a picnic. We always dressed properly for such an occasion: white shirt and shorts, white shoes and a heavy cork hat, which protected us from the sun. Although we always set a price for our sailing trip in advance, we often found after our picnic, when we returned to the boat, that the master of the boat requested additional money, because he claimed that we had stayed longer than he had expected on the island. Since we were stranded on the island, we had no choice but to pay him. This was a normal happening in Iran and we always were ready with cash for the unexpected.

By the time I left after two years, a whole colony of 300 Israeli engineers and technicians were working in the refinery, and the British refinery management was very happy with their services. We -- the original group of eight who started it all up -- felt very proud for being the pioneer of this project.

Chapter 3 - Abadan Iran, with the Anglo-Iranian Oil Company

View from the Air - Abadan Refinery

In front of our Bungalow

Boating on the River

Abadan Technical Institute

Chapter 3 – Abadan Iran,
with the Anglo-Iranian Oil Company

Fishermen's Boats
On the River

The Shanty Town
next to the River

Boating on the River

Picnic on the Island

Chapter 3 – Abadan Iran, with the Anglo-Iranian Oil Company

Going for a walk

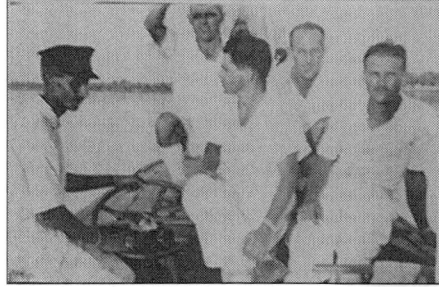

Boating on the River

Smoking Pipes in our Room

Inside the 30 million gallon fuel tank

Chapter 3 – Abadan Iran, with the Anglo-Iranian Oil Company

On my motorcycle

At the Dining Room

Yudka Rabinovitz sitting down on the right
Israeli Undercover Agent

At the swimming Pool

In the Swimming Pool

CHAPTER FOUR
BAHARIEN ISLAND

Airport Construction

In the spring of 1943, I was among twenty Israeli construction managers recruited by Solel-Boneh (the largest construction company in Israel) to build an airport for the British Air Force on Baharien Island. The general manager was named Yulish. His assistant was Avigdor, who had previously worked with Yulish on several large construction projects in Palestine, including Lida Airport and most of the main roads.

The flight from Palestine to Baharien took about three hours. Our group of twenty was sitting on benches on both sides of the DC propeller plane, and the noise inside the plane was unbelievable. There was no air conditioning and it was steaming hot. We could hardly speak to each other because of the noise. Finally, we began our descent. From the air, we saw two small islands that were connected. The land appeared to be mostly desert, with little mud houses near the water's edge.

We were happy to end this trip because we had no idea what was in store for us. After the landing, the plane doors were opened, and a sudden blast of boiling hot air with sand entered the plane. I was sure that it must have been from the D.C. propeller. It felt just like a furnace.

Avigdor was there to meet us. He was short, husky, and red-faced, and he wore short pants, no shirt, and a pleasant smile. He said, "Welcome to Baharien, boys." As we walked away from the plane, I realized that the heat we felt was the actual temperature outside. I said to Avigdor, "This is pretty hot weather." He said, "Wait, this is only spring here. Wait for the summer!" The temperature must have been over 100 degrees. It was very humid, and my shirt got completely soaked.

We drove to our camp in jeeps, which was a short drive from the landing strip. Our housing was nothing more than a long hut. The walls and roof were covered with palm tree leaves tied together with rope. You could partially see through them. The windows were just openings high near the ceiling. The doors were made of the same material as the walls. In each room, there were two metal beds with thin mattresses and mosquito nets hanging from the ceiling, a small table, one chair, a small ceiling fan rotating slowly, and a light bulb hanging next to the fan. All other necessities were outside the hut, about 100 feet away. The toilet facility was a hole in the ground covered by a wooden box with a cutout hole, surrounded by a structure made of the same palm tree leaves. Avigdor's remark was, "These toilets were specially made for you. Most of the locals do not have this luxury. Theirs are without a box on top of the hole."

For a shower, I fastened a 50-gallon container overhead with a hose and nailed an empty metal fruit can to it as a showerhead. The overhead valve was operated by pulling a string. For washing and shaving, there was a long metal basin on a wood stand. In the center, there was a long water pipe, with ten faucets on each side of the basin.

The dining room was made of the same material as our living quarters and contained a long table to seat thirty with long benches on each side. The kitchen was a short walk to the dining room. We jokingly called our living quarters "The Baharien Hotel" and our dining room "the restaurant."

Before unloading our luggage, we were assigned rooms and roommates. My roommate was an older accountant by the name of Meirson. He was the separated husband of the famous Golda Meirson, later known as Golda Meir, who became the prime minister of Israel. He was a small, quiet, very learned, middle-aged gentleman who always had a book in his hands. There was never much conversation between us. He ate very gingerly, rarely drank, and kept very much to himself.

There was only one time that we were able to get him drunk. It happened at one of the dinners we had with a group of high-ranking British Air Force generals who had just come from a visit to India. On their way back to England, they had stopped to inspect the progress that we, the contractors, were making in building the landing runway for the airport. We contractors had one of the best chefs from Palestine, and our restaurant was known to all the British high-ranking officers in our territory, who looked forward to eating dinners in the best restaurant to be found between India and Baghdad.

The general and several of his staff, all wearing red bands on their caps and lapels, sat down amongst our Israeli group. As a gift to us, they gave us several cases of whiskey, which they had flown from India. We all appreciated the gift. We told the general that Meirson never drank and asked him to help us get Meirson to drink for once in his life. So it was arranged that we would raise our glasses and drink to the Queen: of course, Meirson could not be rude and refuse such a toast. To help Meirson's intoxication along, we added some whiskey to the beer without his knowledge, and every time the general raised his glass and drank to the Queen of England, we filled Meirson's glass with whiskey and beer.

The dinner lasted several hours. In the middle of it, Meirson asked to be excused. He was drunk and felt sick. We practically carried him to his room.

When dinner was over and I returned to our room, I found Meirson in bad shape. He was vomiting and coughing, and then he appeared to faint. Frightened, we called our medical doctor, who placed cold compresses on Meirson's head and gave him some pills. I was left with him with instructions to watch over him. He continued vomiting all night. In the morning, he finally fell asleep. It was a hot night, at least 100 degrees, which did not help Meirson's recovery. He stayed in bed for the next three days, and we all felt very guilty for making him so sick. I do not think that he ever suspected that we had deliberately planned to make him drunk.

Baharien Kitchen

When we first arrived in Baharien, we brought with us a well-known chef named Moshe from Israel. He took his profession very seriously, and despite limited kitchen equipment and food supplies, he made our meals a great adventure. Every meal was different from the last. Unfortunately, the heat and humidity were so great that our appetites were limited. Some days the temperature got as high as 130 degrees Fahrenheit, and it never cooled much at night. The worst part was the humidity, which was 70 to 90 percent. You never stopped perspiring.

Each morning, our chef Moshe took his small truck and drove to the small village of Manhama. There he shopped for vegetables, eggs, chickens, and ducks with which he cooked great meals. But in time, there started to be a shortage of poultry. So Yulish, our general manager, sent me to find out where the ducks came from. It did not take me long to find the small farm where a small number of ducks were raised. However, most of them were sold to the market. After I reported this to Yulish, he met the farmer and bought out the farm. And after that, we were never short of ducks. Unfortunately, there was no other meat available. So every night, Moshe made a different duck meal with oranges, grapes, vegetables, ground duck, etc. Our favorite was always the roast duck with orange dressing.

When it came to desserts, Moshe's menu was limited. We searched for fresh fruits, but they were not available. However, we found out that the American Air Force kept a warehouse in town and that there were cases of canned American fruit there. So we arranged a barter deal: we supplied the American Air Force with our ducks in exchange for canned American fruit.

We began organizing our plans to start our construction operation. I was appointed as chief technical engineer, which meant I was in charge of all the maintenance equipment associated with the construction of the airport. I was also the liaison engineer between our construction company and the British Air Force engineers. I made a list of the equipment we needed: asphalt mixing plant, road spreaders, large and small rollers, stone crushing machines, 120 dump trucks, 4 cranes, 3 compressors, 3 generators, twelve caterpillar tractors, backhoes, and a lot of hand tools for our maintenance department. While waiting for the equipment to arrive, I directed the building of twelve maintenance garage bays and large storage areas for parts. A large fuel tank was erected. All the equipment arrived four weeks later from the British Air Force warehouses in India.

Each day seemed to be hotter than the last. The average temperature was between 110 degrees Fahrenheit and 130 degrees Fahrenheit, with 80 percent humidity. At night, it cooled off to 100 degrees to 110 degrees Fahrenheit. Our bodies were continuously wet. There was no point in wearing a shirt because it was always soaked with perspiration. Often we found our socks and shoes filled up with perspiration too. Our doctor gave us salt pills, as well as quinine pills to protect against malaria.

But the heat was not the only weather hazard we had to face. Sometimes sandstorms blew in from the Saudi Arabia Peninsula. When that happened, the desert looked like heavy fog, and we could not see ten feet in front of us. The sand was blistering hot, 110 to 120 degrees Fahrenheit. We had to cover our faces and wear shirts, and we could not touch any metal without a glove. In fact, it was hot enough to fry eggs on top of the tractor engine hood! Fortunately, most of the trucks and other equipment withstood this heat.

The only relief from the unrelenting heat came at the end of the day. We would take a much-needed shower, and afterwards the doctor would use a four-inch paintbrush to smear our bodies with a white mixture of calamine powder and water, in an effort to combat the prickly heat, which was spreading in patches all over our bodies, especially our arms. As the calamine dried, it cooled us, which felt wonderful. But sadly, this blissful feeling only lasted three to four hours. The fan in our rooms did not help much, especially since we had to use our mosquito nets over our beds. We would drink four or five bottles of warm beer, which was generally available in unlimited quantities, and finally fall asleep for four hours or so.

During our twelve-month stay in Abadan, all twenty of us Israelis got malaria. I was one of the last to get it. I got it just one month before returning home, just as I had been thinking that I would escape it. While I was in the hospital, despite the heat, (there was no air conditioner), I was shivering with cold. My teeth were chattering and I was hallucinating. I was extremely sick for fourteen days and weak for two months after that. Even after I recovered, the attack of malaria returned to me once or twice a year for the next several years.

Before starting our project, we recruited several local supervisors. Each had several wives and dozens of children. They spoke only a little English. Although they were relatively young, around 35-40 years old, they looked 50-60 years old. The unrelenting hot weather made people old early in life.

The locals had some customs that seemed rather unusual to us. For example, one supervisor (whom I soon promoted to head foreman) had five wives. He was looking forward to getting his first paycheck, because he planned to use it to buy another 14-year-old wife. Several months later, when we had gotten to know each other better, he offered to buy me a young wife for the duration of my stay and buy her back from me at half price upon my return home. I respectfully declined.

Since we did not have enough equipment and local labor was very inexpensive, we recruited over 2,000 laborers, including women. The women were chosen by our foreman; we never saw their faces, because they wore black loose dresses like sheets, which covered them from head to toe, and their faces were covered by a heavy veil with cutout holes for their eyes. Early each morning we sent our dump truck to town and loaded thirty or forty men, separately from women, into each truck. They all remained standing for their 30-minute trip from town to the airport. In the evening, they returned the same way, packed together on the truck.

Building an airport-landing runway is similar to building a road, except that a runway is a wider strip that is slightly curved on top, and on each side you must dig channels with drainage pipes so that rainwater will quickly run down to the side of the runway and keep it dry.

After clearing some of the soil and grading the surface, we covered it with eight inches of crushed stone and, on top of that, twelve inches of sand, flattened it with heavy motorized rollers. Then we used a special asphalt spreading machine to coat the surface with another four inches of asphalt mixed with sand, which was again compressed with the heavy motorized roller. When this was completed, we connected heavy steel plates with large holes to form a blanket metal over the runway. Each day we completed 40 to 50 feet of runway.

The most important factor in getting the project done on schedule was the continuous supply of material to the site, with no delays. A shortage of any one of the materials could cause complete stoppage of the operation. The delivery of sand, crushed stone, asphalt, steel plates all had to be delivered on time to the right place.

Of course, in the unbearable heat, machines did break down, and it was my responsibility to keep them running. I tried hard to keep spare parts around for my trucks and other equipment. All went fine at first. But after four months, most of the equipment and spare parts were directed to the war against the Germans in Africa, and I found myself without them.

I told my boss Yulish that I did not have enough spare parts and many of my trucks were sitting idle. The only way to acquire more parts was to dismantle some of the trucks for parts for the rest of the fleet. I got permission from Yulish to do this, and out of my fleet of 120 trucks, I dismantled 40 for spare parts. In this way, most of the remaining 80 trucks were kept in full operation, and after twelve months, we completed our contract on time.

Because of the unbearable heat, some of us developed boils on our bodies, which are very painful. One of our men got boils all over his body, hundreds of them, as well as a very high fever. After several days on medication, he had not improved, so the doctor decided to send him back home. We called our office in Palestine and arranged for him to be rushed to the hospital as soon as he arrived from his flight from Baharien. The flight took about six hours. Upon his arrival, the doctor inspected him. To his amazement, the boils on the man's body had disappeared. It seems that the change of weather had cleared up the painful boils and he was cured upon his arrival home. He never returned to Baharien.

Swimming

After we initially settled down in Baharien, we started to look for some recreation for our non-working hours. Baharien is a small island: you can easily get to the ocean by driving in any direction. So one day, we decided to go swimming. Eight of us got into the back of the dump truck and headed for the ocean. The sun was beating down on our heads and we were eager to get there... but strangely enough, the water's edge was not as close as we remembered. We drove over a flat sandy beach full of dried clams and finally, after another two miles, we found the water's edge. It was still shallow there, but cool. We started swimming and had a great time.

But before long, we suddenly noticed that the truck, which was behind us, was standing in water! We realized that the tide was starting to come in, and when it fully arrived, we would be two miles out to sea! We jumped into the truck and I started it, but by this time, the water was already halfway up the wheels. I had a difficult time turning the truck around, so I decided to drive it in reverse toward land. I drove the truck as fast as I could, but the water was catching up with us. We had just managed to arrive at our camp when the full tide came in. We were lucky: the tide in Baharien is about nine feet high, and if our truck had been stuck in the sand, we would have found ourselves two miles out to sea, struggling to swim to shore, with the truck under nine feet of water. All of us could have been drowned.

We never went swimming again because when the tide was in and the water's edge was close to us, the water was too hot -- the tide came in over the hot flat sand, which raised the temperature of the water to about 80 degrees. There were no swimming pools on the island that we could use, so for the rest of our stay we never had a swim in Baharien.

One of the most important requirements in building an airport landing strip is to always keep the surface dry. The water drains into both sides of the strip and through pipes underground, where it is collected into a pumping station from which it is pumped outside the area. Unfortunately, when we began our project, we did not know that the island was made of shells, rocks, and less than two feet of soil. There was also shell base rock, which is very hard and cannot be excavated with regular earth moving equipment like backhoes. The only way to dig through it was by hand, cutting through it with chisels and hammers. It was slow, grueling work: a laborer could get through only twelve inches a day and the chisels had to be replaced several times each day.

To accomplish this difficult task, our general manager, Julius, decided to recruit 1200 new workers, placing them all along the landing strip to chisel out the shell rock. As the heat was unbearable, it was essential to have a constant supply of water along the strip, so every 20 feet we placed empty asphalt drums, which were filled up with water by a passing water tank truck. As they chiseled the rock, the workers were able to drink and constantly pour water on their heads to keep themselves cool.

At the end of the runway, we were building a sunken pumping station, and there, too, we found that the only way to dig was to use chisels and hammers. As the rock was porous, no explosive could be used. Fortunately, we started digging early in our scheduled construction, because it took us five months to dig to the required depth.

When the digging was finally finished and we had placed all our pumps and pipes, we noticed that each morning there was a puddle of water on the floor of the station. We would remove the water, but the next morning we found water there again. As all the station surfaces including the floors were cemented and coated with protective asphalt, we could not understand where the water was coming from. Finally, one day we dried the floor and stayed all night to watch and discover the source of the water. We found that a small hole in the bottom of the floor station was spouting with water. However, upon tasting the water, we found that it was sweet water. In fact, in our digging we had hit a small underground spring, and whatever method we used to plug this stream, it always found another spot from which to emerge.

After several weeks of trying, we decided not to fight that stream. Instead, we placed a small pipe leading from the opening to the outside of the pumping station and let the water drip out of the station. When the inspectors came to inspect the pumping station they found the floor dry, and no one knew about the little pipe, dripping sweet water from the underground spring.

Pearl Diving

One morning during the summer, our trucks came back from the city half-empty of workers. We learned from the drivers that for the next three weeks, all the able-bodied workers were going to work for the Baharien sheik on his pearl fishing expeditions. It seems that generations ago, the sheik had begun the custom of lending his boats to the local pearl divers. They paid him back with pearls they harvested from the sea. However, if they did not have enough pearls to pay for the rental of the boats, they owed him this money. If they could not pay, eventually the debt was transferred from father to son, from one generation to the next. So most of our workers left us for three weeks to work for practically free for the sheik, paying him with whatever pearls they fished.

Since pearl diving was a big business in Baharien, we decided to try our luck in finding some pearls ourselves. On our day off from work, we rented a small fishing sailboat with a crew of divers. It was a very hot and humid day. We wore only shorts with large brimmed hats. The four divers wore just a string between their legs. On the boat were four divers, four crewmen, and six of our Israeli group. We raised sail and we sailed into the gulf for about two hours. There was just a small breeze and the boat sailed very slowly.

We noticed that three of the divers were blind in one of their eyes. We thought that probably they had some eye disease, but we learned later the reason was that by the law of the Baharien sheik, the divers were not allowed to wear goggles or any diving gear. While they were diving, the sea horses in the water attacked the divers' eyes and on many occasions blinded them. It seems the diving law of unprotected divers was made so as to control the production of oyster growth. With proper diving gear, the bottom of the sea would be harvested too fast and there would be no time for new oysters to grow. The divers were mostly middle-aged, very slim and dark-skinned, but they looked very old. We learned that the average lifespan of these divers is only 45, but the ones we met were so weather-beaten, they looked 75 years old.

When we arrived at the site, each diver tied a rope around his waist. A lead weight was also tied to his foot, and a small basket was tied to his left hand. They dove into the water holding the rope and quickly disappeared into the sea without goggles or diving gear. They dove to a depth of about thirty feet and stayed in the water for about four minutes.

Once they reached the bottom, they picked up the oysters and placed them in the basket. They signaled the man on the boat by pulling several times on the rope and they were quickly pulled up to the boat. The basket of oysters was dumped on deck, and the diver continued to dive for the next two hours, by the end of which the pile of oysters had grown to a sizeable heap of 300 to 400.

The divers were pulled out of the water and then, to make sure of their honesty, the crew asked us to sit around the pile of oysters and watch them open the oysters and remove the pearls. To our disappointment, most of the oysters did not have any pearls, and some, which did had only very small pearls. Altogether, we ended up with about ten small, unimpressive collections of pearls, which certainly did not pay for our expense of renting the boat.

Our expedition had been interesting, but nonproductive. It would have been much cheaper and easier to buy the pearls in the local jewelry shop in town.

Transferring Money

The construction of the airport was nearly complete. A large payment of two million British pounds was due. The question was how to transfer this money from a bank in Baharien to Solel-Boneh in Palestine. Yulish, our general manager, decided to carry it with him in one of the British Air Force planes, which was flying between the various British Air Force stations in the Middle East. Our relationship as a contractor with the British was excellent. The chief of the British Air Force for the Middle East was very friendly with Yulish and agreed to take him and me as his "luggage-carrying assistants" in his private plane to Palestine.

When the day came for the flight, Yulish and I carried the two million pounds in cash in two very heavy valises into the plane, which was a seaplane stationed in the sea just next to the island. Besides the two pieces of luggage, Julius carried several Iranian carpets, which he had bought on the island. One of them was a gift to the Air Force chief. We boarded the plane, which took off in the sea. It was quite bumpy until we got into the air. The flight took about four hours. Our landing was deliberately made in the Dead Sea so that there would be no problem with customs.

The Air Force chief was dressed in his full uniform with a red band around his hat and red lapels. Following the Air Force chief were his pilot, Yulish, and me carrying the two very heavy pieces of luggage. We got off the plane and into a small jetty. There was a single Palestinian custom policeman standing at the jetty, but when he saw the very impressively dressed general, he just saluted and never asked any of us for papers. In fact, he was asked to go into the plane and bring out Julius's carpets.

An Air Force car was waiting for us. The Air Force chief bid us goodbye and left in his seaplane. We loaded the luggage and carpets into the car and drove to Haifa. A week later, the plane came to pick us up and take us back to Baharien. The two million pounds, which Yulish brought with him to Solel-Boneh in Palestine, helped the company buy the large cement-manufacturing factory near Haifa.

Upon my return to Baharien, the only problem we had at the end of the contract was that we had to return 120 trucks to the Air Force, but we had only 80, since we had dismantled some for their spare parts. We planned to make a big party for the Air Force personnel with a lot of drinking, and return the trucks just before we left. We mounted the wheels on the truck chassis with only the outside of the body of the trucks mounted, without engines or any other mechanical parts below the hood, except for the steering wheel and the drivers' seat. Each of these "dummy" trucks was pulled by a regular truck.

Just a few hours before we left Baharien, we returned the trucks and received signed receipts for the 120 trucks. Most of us were drunk, including the Air Force personnel in the receiving parking lot. I believe that they knew what we were doing and that it was a mutual understanding.

109
Chapter 4- Baharien Islands

Aerial View of Our Airport
by our Israeli Artist

Asphalt
Spreading Machine

Standing in front
of my room

Our Baharien Hotel

110

Chapter 4- Baharien Islands

Moshe Yulish
General Manager of the
Airport Construction
with Minister Sapir

Pearl Diving
Sail Boat

A woman smoking a Nargila

Pearl Diver Ready to Dive

CHAPTER FIVE

AMERICA

Traveling To The United States To Study

During the time I had lived with Dr. Bardin and his wife in their luxurious apartment on Mount Carmel, facing the blue Mediterranean Sea, and met some of their friends (including teachers, musicians, professors, and singers), I found my views on life beginning to change. Mrs. Bardin helped me with my homework, and she always talked about higher education and the opportunities it could bring. My own background had been very limited. I had wanted only to be a mechanic and work and build the country, and all my efforts were directed toward becoming the best possible mechanic and working in a garage. Now all of this was changing: now, I wanted to live like the Bardins. It began as a vague thought, but over time, it grew. I wanted to have a beautiful home and beautiful carpets, furniture and all this luxury.

After working for two years in Abadan and one year in Baharien, I returned home and my company Solel-Boneh appointed me as a maintenance manager of equipment for the stone quarries around the country. I was not happy with this assignment. I was restless and wanted to further my education overseas.

I talked to my Solel-Boneh managers and asked if they would help me financially with my studies in the U.S. The plan was that first I would visit and study with various construction companies in the U.S. and then I would further my education at Columbia University. The money I had saved during my work in Abadan and Baharien was sufficient to pay for my studies at Columbia.

After the arrangements were made with the various equipment companies in the U.S. and Columbia University, I embarked on my adventure. It was 1946, the start of trouble with the Arabs. I made a reservation to fly with TWA from Israel, but flights at that time were discontinued and my reservation was changed to fly from Cairo, Egypt.

I traveled to Egypt by train and in Cairo, I stayed at the Sumeramis Hotel, which was very luxurious and beautiful and faced the Nile.

I was very excited, but also nervous. Everything was new to me. I had never before traveled out of Israel on my own. Previously, when I went to Abadan and Baharien, I was always with colleagues. Now I felt very uncomfortable being alone. I was very reserved and introverted, especially since my English was not very good.

My flight to the U.S. was initially scheduled to leave only a few days after my arrival in Cairo. However, there was an airline strike and the flight was delayed for two weeks. As a result, I ended up unexpectedly having to spend too much money, because the hotel was expensive. Since I was in Egypt, I could have visited the pyramids, but I did not. Later on, I never forgave myself for not spending a few days sightseeing while I had the chance. Instead, I spent most of the days just walking around the streets and sitting in coffee shops. It was the first time I had ever found myself alone in a strange town. I could have gone for a swim in the hotel's gorgeous swimming pool, but I did not have a bathing suit and I did not want to spend my money unnecessarily. I was bored and unhappy and I could not wait to fly to America.

At long last, the strike was over and we took off on TWA's four-engine propeller plane. It stopped to refuel several times during our 20-hour flight, and because of a storm in New York, we landed in Boston.

Luckily, on my flight was the wife of Ben Gurion, the future Prime Minister of Israel, and the man who met her suggested that I join her on the train to New York. I did not have a reservation for the hotel, but being with Mrs. Ben Gurion made it possible for me to get a room. It was the Empire Hotel and again the price was sky high, but I had no choice. For the next few days, until I made contact with my scheduler in Washington, I stayed at the Empire Hotel.

Across the street was a large cafeteria with endless varieties of food: hot and cold, meats, cheeses of all kinds, salads, etc. The serving line was moving fast and I could not make up my mind about what food to choose. When my turn came the only thought that came to me was a cheese sandwich. So I said, "cheese sandwich." But that was only the beginning of my trouble. The counterman asked me what kind of cheese I wanted. I pointed to yellow cheese. Then he asked me what kind of bread I wanted. I could not understand him and he was getting impatient. Eventually I pointed to the white bread. I got the sandwich and a cup of coffee. This was my first meal in America. The next few days I ate at the same cafeteria morning, lunch and dinner. I gradually extended my menu until I could order a hot meal.

After a week, I was contacted by a representative of the American Association of the Construction Equipment Association in Washington. The secretary informed me that they had made a schedule of visits for me around the country, visiting various construction equipment manufacturers such as Caterpillar Tractors, Alice Chambers, Barbar Green, and various other construction equipment manufacturers. For the next five months, I traveled around the country on a study mission. I stayed a week or two with each of the companies and I gained a great deal of experience in the field.

One of the companies was LeTourneau in Longview, Texas. The owner, Mr. LeTourneau, was a very religious evangelist, and each day the factory stopped working for half an hour for prayer. On Sunday, I was invited to participate in the prayer service at church. I told my supervisor that as a Jew, I could not pray with them. However, during the service I did stay in the back of the church, listening to the sermon and the beautiful singing of the choir.

One evening I was secretly invited to a Ku Klux Klan meeting. The men were preaching with masks on their faces, fiery speeches which I did not understand. At the time, I did not know what Ku Klux Klan meant. It was just an interesting experience, especially for an Israeli!

Another time, one of the managers took me out for dinner with his wife to a very luxurious restaurant specializing in Texas steaks. After the first serving of salad, they served a steak about 12 inches in size on a tremendous plate. I could not believe that anyone could eat such a steak! My friend saw my surprise and told me that I should eat only small parts of the various sections of the steak, which all taste different, and leave the rest, so I did. That sure was a waste of good food, but that is how they did eat in Texas.

My visit to the manufacturers was coming to an end. Next on my schedule was to attend the Industrial School of Engineering at Columbia University. I was very excited about it. I was admitted as a foreign student, taking into consideration my degree with the British

Institute of Engineering. I started my classes, got a lot of books and entered a new life of learning. At first, I had a great deal of difficulty in preparing my homework, but some of the other students were kind enough to help me, and gradually I developed into a regular student. There was so much to learn that I spent all my time in school and in the library or at home studying.

War In Israel, Recruited In The U.S., And Getting Married

It was February 1948 in New York City. I was twenty-seven years old, a hotshot young engineer, and had just started my second year in the advanced engineering program at Columbia University. I was doing well, and was learning a lot that would help me become a better engineer and would advance my career when I returned to Israel.

Like many American Jews and especially the handful of fellow Israelis I knew in New York, I closely followed the campaign for an independent Israel. We cheered, guardedly, at the United Nations resolution in the autumn of 1947 to partition Palestine and allow creation of a new state of Israel. But during the following three months, we anguished over Arab attacks on Jewish communities, especially after New Year's Day 1948, when the violence seemed to intensify. Jews were being wounded and killed almost daily, and their property was being destroyed or taken away by Arab gangs and militia. Drinking tea and coffee in little shops on the Upper West Side bars or sharing simple meals in cheap restaurants or in each other's homes, I anguished with my Jewish student friends, both the Americans and those like me from other countries, that the Jewish settlers seemed to be almost defenseless.

We talked about going home to fight – even the Americans called Israel "home" – and sometimes when people disappeared, it was whispered that they were on tramp steamers heading back to Israel to fight. We talked about sending money back to buy weapons and equipment, and to construct defenses against Arab attacks, if we could. But nobody I knew had any extra money.

Since the Arab attacks began, I had stopped receiving my regular monthly checks from my company. My bosses were sorry, but my education had become a luxury that they could not afford. The money that had been supporting me in New York was better spent on additional security for the company's employees and property. I did not mind. My tuition for the spring semester of 1948 had already been paid. I simply wrote to my parents, who dipped into my savings account and periodically wired me money to pay my meager living expenses.

In general, I was concentrating on my studies and minding my own business. But I wasn't all business, I must confess. Several months earlier, I had met Dalia, a friend from Israel who had been my family's neighbor in Jerusalem. She and her family had lived across the street from us. I had not known her personally, but meeting her in New York made us casual friends. She was working at the Jewish Theological Seminary as a Hebrew secretary. Her mother was in New York for medical care at the time. She had a broken hip, which had occurred while she was riding a horse in Jordan with her husband, who was the only Jewish officer in the Jordanian Army. Her uncle in New York was a very well-to-do diamond dealer, and Dalia and her mother lived with him in a very large 10-room apartment on Central Park West. From time to time, she threw a party for her Israeli and American friends.

For some reason, Dalia made me her personal advisor. She had many problems with her superiors at work, and I met her from time to time for lunch at the cafeteria at the seminar.

During lunch, she often talked to me about her friend Florence, who was also a secretary to her boss. It happened that during one of our lunches Florence joined us and sat down just across from me. She was a slim, pretty brunette about five foot four who happened to be wearing a light summer dress and dark sunglasses. All three of us began to talk casually about Israel and as she spoke, Florence removed her sunglasses. I looked into her eyes and was instantly mesmerized. She had large blue eyes the color of the sky. I was hypnotized. It was my first experience of falling in love. I truly believe that I fell in love with her right then and there. My heart was pounding and my ears were ringing. I knew that something incredible was happening to me. I found myself wondering if this was love at first sight. (Today I know the answer--it was!)

Unfortunately, I do not think that I impressed Florence. After lunch, Dalia asked me if I liked her friend. I said, "Very much!" She said that she was planning to have a party the following week and that she would invite Florence, so I would have the opportunity to meet her again.

Perhaps my falling in love with Florence was preordained, maybe it was because I already loved the color blue and she, somehow, became the embodiment of all it symbolized to me.

My love of blue had begun when I was six years old. My mother took me on vacation for the first time in my life to visit Tel Aviv. At that time, the ride from Jerusalem to Tel Aviv took many hours. When we arrived at the Tel Aviv shore, I looked at the horizon and asked my mother "What are these beautiful blue hills in front of us?"

My mother explained to me, "This is the sea, and the water of the sea is blue." I had never seen the sea before. From that moment on, blue was my most beloved color. Later I felt the same for blue flowers or dresses...and now Florence's eyes. I desired her more than any woman I had ever met. However, my expectations for success with her were very low. I was a poor Israeli student with no money, who hardly dressed properly. What could I offer her, besides my anxiety for her?

We met again at the party and I had the occasion to talk to her. She was attentive and interested in my stories about Israel. I think that Dalia, who knew of all my accomplishments and background in Israel, had told Florence about some of these and aroused her interest.

After the party, I accompanied Florence to her home, and that was the beginning of a great romance. I was crazy about her. A new feeling, which I had never felt before, came over me: "jealousy." I was terribly jealous of any other man who spoke to her. It seems that great love goes hand in hand with suffering, but such feelings only sharpen one's love.

We started to go steady. I was accepted warmly by her family and I was especially appreciated by her mother, who was a gentle, warm and giving person. I think she liked me too, and that encouraged Florence to allow herself to fall in love with me.

Coming home from classes one cold day in February 1948, I climbed the stairs to the top floor of the four-story tenement on 110th Street where I rented one of the three rooms in the apartment of an old Jewish doctor. He had emigrated from Germany ten years earlier, just before he would have been caught up in the Holocaust. He had tried repeatedly to pass the New York medical exam so he could practice medicine in America, but his English was so poor that he always failed. He was making ends meet by renting me one of the three rooms in his cold-water flat. He studied English for hours on end, every day, and pored over American medical books. I would have liked to help him, but my own English was worse than his.

When he met me at the door on that day, he spoke to me in Yiddish, as he always did. There had been a message for me, a phone call. He did not know who it was. Someone calling on behalf of a man named Davidka. I had never heard of Davidka, but I had been expecting a call and I knew what it was about. My father had told me some weeks earlier that his friends in the leadership of Haganah had talked to him about me, and had told him that I might be called on to serve. My father had said he had no idea what they might have in mind for me.

I put down my books, took off my heavy overcoat, and walked back down the four flights to the entryway and the pay phone that was shared by the entire building. I put a nickel in the phone, dialed the number, and asked the person who answered for Davidka.

The man's voice on the other end was brusque. Who was calling? I gave my name. The voice gave no hint of recognition and did not soften. The man gave me an address downtown, and told me to go there. When? Right now, the man said. And he hung up.

I trudged back up the stairs for my overcoat. The old doctor looked at me as I put my coat back on, but he did not say anything and neither did I. We both knew that the voice on the phone had been Israeli, and that the call would change my life.

A little over an hour later, after a subway ride during which I pretty much decided I was going to be conscripted into the Israeli army, probably the infantry, like so many of my boyhood friends, I found the address. It was a nondescript commercial building on Park Row, near Wall Street, with dozens of companies listed in the directory in the lobby. I went upstairs and found the office. The upper half of the door was frosted glass, and the stenciling read "International Commerce and Shipping." I knocked, and someone – it was the same voice on the phone – commanded, "Enter." The man who had been on the phone was sitting at a desk planted in the middle of a small office with a single window facing onto an alley. He told me to sit down in a chair just inside the door. Then he went through another door into an interior office.

A few minutes later, he reappeared and beckoned me to follow him into the adjacent office, which was just as small. There was no window. Four men were in the inner office, gathered at a desk beneath a single bare light bulb hanging from the ceiling. They obviously had been talking. Just as obviously, they had interrupted their conversation to look me over. Three of the men were standing. All wore cheap suits and needed shaves. The wooden desk in the middle of the room was old and battered, and the handful of chairs in the room did not match. Some of the tiles on the floor were cracked, and a couple was missing completely.

A slender, balding man seated at the desk seemed to be in charge. He was in his late thirties, I guessed. He had a long, serious face that was not only unkind, but that also indicated he had no time for small talk. His dark hair was starting to thin from the front. He beckoned me forward, and motioned with his hand toward the single wooden chair sitting in front of the desk. The men he had been talking with retreated to lean or sit in chairs against the walls. I sat down, still wearing my overcoat. No one had offered to take it. I was not frightened, but my heart was pounding. I knew that whatever these men asked – no, ordered – me to do, that I would do it.

"You are Efraim Margolin," the man at the desk began. "An engineer. A student at Columbia University. I am Davidka Nameri."

I looked at him more closely. He was wearing a khaki shirt and matching trousers. His sleeves were rolled up. His tanned, sinewy forearms, rough hands, and lean build spoke of thousands of hours of work -- hard work -- in the hot sun. His shoes had not been shined in a long time. His manner of speech, so direct as to be almost rude, was almost accusing in tone. He reminded me of my Uncle Moshe.

Then it dawned on me, and I nearly smiled in recognition. This man was a kibbutznik. I had never met him, never even heard of him before that day, but I immediately felt like I knew a great deal about him. People like Davidka who had grown up on kibbutzes in Israel in the 1920s and '30s created miniature social democracies in their farm communes on hillside and in the deserts, claiming land that would be part of the state of Israel and raising food that would give the rest of us the strength to make it happen. Like so many other men – both men and women, actually – who had grown up on kibbutzes, he would be short on the social graces. He would not care if he hurt my feelings. He would not care if I liked him. But whatever his job was – whatever he was doing for Israel – it would get done or he would die trying. Or, more likely, both.

If I thought I knew a lot about Davidka at that moment, it was clear that he knew much more about me. Occasionally glancing at some papers on the desk that seemed to be about me, he recounted some of the major particulars of my life – parents, schools, jobs, and the names of some of my friends, both in Israel and in New York. He even mentioned my girlfriend. I nodded in affirmation as he went through the papers.

Davidka then told me why I was there. He never asked me if I wanted to help, or tried to persuade me to volunteer. He never even said, "Israel needs you." Instead, he said that Israel needed vehicles from America, military surplus left over from World War II. Trucks. Tractors. Jeeps. All manner of vehicles that could be used in war, everything short of tanks. There was a man in Connecticut who had purchased many hundreds of such military vehicles from the U.S. government, and was willing to re-sell them to Israel. Speaking quietly but firmly, with authority in his voice, Davidka told me he would give me lists of what equipment to buy. My job was to inspect the vehicles in Connecticut, check them out, and select the best ones. If I was assigned to pick out an ambulance, I was to make sure that the ambulance was in perfect working order, and that it would not break down the first time, it carried an injured soldier to a hospital in Israel. Did I understand? I did. Could I do this job? In my own mind, I was not sure. What did I know about inspecting vehicles? But that wasn't the answer Davidka wanted. I told him I could do the job. Good, Davidka nodded. I was dismissed.

The entire meeting had taken barely ten minutes. As I left the small office, the three men in suits were returning to the center of the room and talking with Davidka, apparently about some other matter. No one nodded or waved goodbye. I took the subway back to 110th Street.

In my room, I opened my engineering books to study, but I could not concentrate. I somehow knew there would be no point. I closed my books with a sense of resignation and finality. I never went to another class at Columbia.

The next morning I was on a commuter train to Greenwich, Connecticut. I stared out the window as the train left the city behind. Then, as now, Greenwich was known as a rich suburb. The man who met me at the station in Greenwich was the owner of the company that was selling the military surplus vehicles. He was a wealthy American Jew who, he did not mind telling me, had made "a killing" buying and selling army and navy surplus. What the American military did not need, he had purchased for pennies on the dollar. He was confident that somebody, somewhere, would be needing this kind of equipment and would be willing to pay him nickels and dimes on the dollar. After all, there were always going to be wars, weren't they. When I nodded dumbly, he added that while he was not happy that it was the Jewish people in Israel who needed the equipment, he was grateful to be able to offer the cause such good bargains on such good equipment. I had no idea whether the vehicles were being sold for bargain prices or not. Fortunately, Davidka said he would take care of all the finances, including the negotiations. I would not be handling any money, or even talking about money.

In those early days, before there was a recognized nation of Israel, the United States was not as good a friend to the Jews in Palestine as it is today. The U.S. government was providing no aid to the Jewish settlers to defend themselves, and was doing very little diplomatically or in terms of financial aid to promote the cause of Israeli independence. In fact, there were tough restrictions barring Americans from selling weapons to Israelis.

As we drove, the military-surplus entrepreneur made a point of telling me that "everything was on the up and up," strictly legal, in his deal with Davidka. There were no restrictions on selling vehicles to Jews in Palestine, even if the vehicles might be used in battle. Davidka had not mentioned anything to me about legality one way or the other.

The owner guided his late-model Cadillac through Greenwich's quaint downtown village, past the small tidy houses near the center of town, and then past the tall hedges and vast lawns of the bigger houses, the estates and mansions on the edge of town and beyond. Some of the mansions were down winding lanes so long that I could only catch a glimpse of the houses. Some of the houses were bigger than almost any building I had ever seen growing up in Palestine.

Eventually the man pulled his car to a stop near a large fenced-in field, perhaps one mile square. The field was covered with former military vehicles large and small, nearly all of them painted olive drab, row after row. Another man came out of a small cinderblock building and the owner introduced him as Joe the supervisor, and we shook hands. My hand all but disappeared in Joe's serious handshake. "Nice ta meet ya," he growled in a rough voice. I would be working with Joe, the owner told me. He told Joe, who obviously had been expecting me, to give me everything I needed and to help me in any way I asked. Then the owner left.

Joe looked at me expectantly. I pulled a folded piece of paper from my pocket and looked at it. I did not really need to look at it. I knew that ambulances were at the top of the list. I asked Joe to show me ambulances, good ambulances, the best ambulances in the field. He directed me to a row of ambulances and pointed toward the first one.

"Is this the best one?" I asked. The supervisor shrugged. He did not know. It looked okay to him.

"I need to start it up and drive it," I said. "I need to get under the hood and check out the engine. We need to jack it up so I can look underneath. Can you bring me a jack?"

Joe was not happy. He sold lots of vehicles from that field, but apparently, no other customer had ever been so particular. Most customers limited their inspections to kicking the tires and maybe looking under the hood. Now here I was, this pushy young Jewish engineer who wanted to spend what sounded like hours checking out an ambulance. That ambulance was only the first vehicle on my list. I had a long list. And there were more lists to come.

The supervisor lent me a pair of overalls and reluctantly helped me check out that first ambulance, and the next one and the next one. When lunchtime came, Joe suggested we go to a nearby tavern. The food was hot and hearty and plentiful, blue-plate specials like meat loaf or baked chicken or some kind of roasted meat with potatoes and vegetables. Before we ordered, Joe suggested that we have a boilermaker. He said that is what most working men in Connecticut had with lunch: a boilermaker. I had no idea what a boilermaker was, but I was game for anything. I was a good drinker in those days. I could drink beer, wine, or whisky with just about anybody. But, as it turned out, I couldn't drink the way this supervisor drank. The boilermaker came – a beer with a shot of whisky. I watched as Joe took a long couple of swallows from his beer mug, set it down, and then threw back the shot of whisky. He looked at me, grinned, picked up the mug again, took another long swallow of beer, burped, and proclaimed, "Cheers!" I took a deep breath and then did the same: drank some beer, tossed back the shot, and drank again.

When we had drained our beers, Joe ordered another round. We eventually ate lunch, but I have no recollection of what I ordered. I do know that I was more than a little wobbly as we left the tavern. The supervisor said that when we got back to the field, he could show me several ambulances that he was sure I would approve without having to check them out so closely. They were in great shape, he said. I realized that he was hoping to get me drunk enough to rubber-stamp the vehicles. He did not want to crawl around, getting dirty. But by then I didn't feel like crawling around under vehicles, either. I knew I would not be able to do my job in such a muddled condition. I was woozy. I excused myself, telling him I had to call my office. I did not have an office to call, of course, but he did not know that. I did not want him to know I was too drunk to inspect any more vehicles that day, but I needed an excuse not to go back to work. I called Florence.

"I'm coming home," I slurred.

"What's the matter with you?" she asked, sounding worried.

"I'm drunk," I told her.

Back at the bar, Joe was up for another boilermaker, but the mere thought of it almost made me throw up. I declined, saying that my office needed me back in New York right away. He dropped me off at the train station and I told him I would see him the next morning.

I finally made it back to Manhattan and collapsed in bed in my new home, a tiny room at 86th and Broadway. The old doctor had asked me to move out the day after my first meeting with Davidka. He told me he had found another tenant who would pay him more money, but I suspect he was afraid that my involvement with Davidka – he never asked for details, and I never told him – might bring trouble to his door.

He was a timid old man with plenty of problems of his own, and I did not blame him. We shook hands and wished each other luck.

As I lay in my whirling bed that evening, Florence came by my little room to see if I was all right. I accepted the leftovers from her family's supper that her mother had sent along with her, and assured her that I simply needed to sleep it off. I had the leftovers the next morning for breakfast on the train on the way to Greenwich.

Joe was no doubt disappointed that second day in Greenwich when I again insisted on checking out every vehicle very carefully. We went to lunch at the tavern together again that day, as we did every day for the next several weeks. Joe and I gradually became friends. He continued to grumble about how picky I was, but I think he came to respect me for being so careful and meticulous. He grudgingly helped me check out all the vehicles on my various lists, not only ambulances but also Jeeps, vans, light trucks, heavy trucks, even armored personnel carriers. He did not believe there was anything wrong with any of the vehicles. It was true I did not reject many, but I did reject any vehicle that had even the slightest thing wrong, like a loose tailpipe. If an engine coughed or sputtered or if I just did not like the sound of it, I rejected the vehicle. If there was not a better ambulance, Jeep, or truck in the field, I went to work on the best one. Sometimes I rolled up my sleeves and tuned an engine that was running rough. I was driven by the thought that if I made a mistake, if I approved a vehicle that failed at a crucial moment, it could cost Israeli lives. I did not want to be haunted for the rest of my life by any doubts about whether I had done my best.

Some days I would spend my entire time in Greenwich on only one vehicle. If it got too dark to see, I took the train home and finished on that vehicle in the morning. Every time I rejected a vehicle or decided to take apart an engine that seemed to be running okay but not quite perfectly, Joe would shake his head and mutter, but over time, he came to respect me, and the way I approached the job.

A few evenings each week, whenever I would get close to the end of the latest list of vehicles required, I would go down to the office on Park Row and get a new list from Davidka. Over a period of almost three months, I selected several hundred vehicles that were shipped to Israel.

The routine was interrupted when I returned to Florence's one evening in April and her father told me that Davidka had called. Instead of going to Greenwich the next morning, I was supposed to go see him at the Park Row office.

I got there early, but Davidka was already in the office. He let me in himself. No one else was around. We sat at the same desk as before and he told me that I had done a good job in Greenwich. That surprised me. I knew I had done a good job, but I had not expected him to acknowledge it. He even smiled at me. He was a kibbutznik with charm, and that was new in my experience.

Davidka had a new job for me. "What do you know about boats?" he asked. I said I did not know anything about boats. He did not care.

"You'll learn," he said.

Then he asked if I had ever been to Florida. I said no. I asked if I was going to Florida. "This morning," he said. "You're taking a train to Florida with me." He smiled a little at what must have been an incredulous expression on my face. Then he continued. "We're going to buy some boats, and you're going to turn them into torpedo boats for Israel." No doubt, I looked even more incredulous, but he was no longer smiling. Again, he did not ask if I wanted the assignment. I never had a chance to volunteer.

I did not know anything about boats, and I really did not know anything about torpedoes. I didn't even have a toothbrush in my pocket, but I was getting on a train in two hours and going to Florida for who knew how long to help buy some boats and arm them with torpedoes. Once again, Davidka did not say anything one way or the other, but this time I was pretty sure that what we were about to do was illegal.

Smuggling Torpedo Boats

Looking back, I now know that Davidka – he was one of those people everyone called by his first name only – was not merely a high operative for Haganah. He was also one of the leaders of the underground military's intelligence wing, the future Mossad. While he had me inspecting trucks and ambulances legally in Connecticut, he was simultaneously in charge of many other people doing many other things, some of them illegal, such as buying and smuggling weapons to Israel. I was about to become an accidental, unintentional undercover agent. He was the real thing.

Before we left for Penn Station, Davidka let me use the phone and call Florence at the office where she worked as a secretary. I told her I was fine and that I was with Davidka and we were going out of town for a while. I could not tell her where we were going or what we were doing. I told her not to worry, which I know only made her worry more. If I made a point of saying do not worry, then there must have been something to worry about. She wanted to know when I would see her again. I did not know. I promised to get in touch as soon as I could.

The twenty-four hour train ride was a blur. It was just Davidka and me. He carried a small satchel, I noted with some chagrin. He was taking an overnight bag, probably at least a change of underwear and a fresh shirt, and no doubt a toothbrush. He could have given me a chance to go back to Florence's apartment and throw a few things in a bag of my own. But no. I did not say anything. It would not have mattered. He would have just looked at me, and then looked away without answering.

We did not talk much on the trip. He had a fat book, in Hebrew that he read when he was not dozing, balancing it on top of the satchel that he kept on his lap. I dozed, too, off and on, but mostly looked out the window, variously enjoying the scenery. I would have preferred the window seat so it would be easier to look out the window, but Davidka wanted me to sit on the aisle. He took the window seat even though he barely glanced at the passing countryside. Typical inconsiderate kibbutznik, I thought, though I had to admit I was beginning to like being around Davidka. He exuded a quiet competence, and it inspired my confidence in him.

The trip took all day and all night. We ate sandwiches from the dining car. We slept in our seats, sitting up, Davidka with his hands clasped around the satchel on his lap. I alternated between telling myself that I was involved in an exciting adventure and wondering what the hell I was getting myself into.

When the train finally arrived in Miami the next morning, I was stiff and cramped. We took a taxi from the train station to a small marina. I loved Miami at first sight. The weather and the vegetation reminded me of Tel Aviv or Haifa, though no city in Israel had anywhere near the number of tall buildings that Miami did. I was intrigued by the obvious Latin flavor on the streets, the Cuban influence in the shops and restaurants.

At the marina, Davidka spoke briefly with a man who told us to wait on the dock. A few minutes later, while I was admiring the small neat sailboats in the marina, the man pulled up alongside the dock in a small motorboat. We climbed in, and he took us across the bay to a small island – I think he said it was Virginia Key – where another man met us on another dock at another marina, this one with bigger, dirtier boats that seemed to be used for carrying freight. We walked through the marina to yet another dock. The man led Davidka and me to three grimy, rusting metal boats, moored side by side, each about thirty feet long. Each had a small wheelhouse or cabin. I guessed that maybe three or four people could sleep in the hold.

Davidka paid keen attention as the man showed us around the three boats, inside and out. He nodded, but asked very few questions. The man said the boats had been torpedo boats in World War II, but he had converted them to banana boats. They carried bananas from Cuba to the port of Miami.

I got only a brief look at the engines, but I tried to absorb as much as I could because I thought Davidka might ask me something later. I did not know what to expect from boat engines, but it turned out there was nothing extraordinary about these particular engines. They were standard General Motors diesels, configured to fit inside this style of boat. I could work with any diesel engine, and I could work with these. When the time came – "Can you work with these engines?" Davidka asked me – I said sure, no problem. "Do they need a lot of work?" he asked. I said I did not know, and I could not tell until I looked at them more closely, but I was sure that I could get them working as well as they could. He nodded, satisfied.

That brief conversation took place as we walked down the dock away from the three boats to a corrugated-metal shack where the man sat behind a terribly messy desk. Davidka took the only other chair, in front of the desk, and I stood by the door. The only window in the shack was in the wooden door, and the man moved me aside to pull down the shade so that no one could see in.

"Do we have a deal?" he asked.

"We do," Davidka said. "On one condition." He told the man he wanted the three boats delivered to Tampa. He handed the man a piece of paper with the name of the boatyard in Tampa on it.

The man frowned. "This wasn't part of the deal, this transport to Tampa," he said. "That'll add some expenses for me."

"If you can include transportation, we will meet your original asking price, and we will do the deal right now," Davidka said.

The man's eyebrows shot up. "Payment right now?" he asked.

Davidka took the satchel from his lap and set it on the desk. It was the first time since we had left Penn Station the day before that I had seen him take his hands off it. He nodded to the man, who opened the satchel, reached in, and began pulling out packets of twenty-dollar and fifty-dollar bills.

"Jesus!" the man exclaimed.

"Oy," I heard myself whisper. No wonder Davidka had kept the satchel so close! No wonder he had wanted the window seat, to make it more difficult for someone to snatch the satchel and run. I realized that I had come along to Miami not for my engineering expertise, but to ride shotgun. Davidka did not want to travel alone with that kind of money.

I wondered why he chose me. I thought of myself as a pretty tough little guy, but at five-foot-five, 140 pounds, I wasn't the most imposing fellow Davidka could have called upon.

He chose me because he trusts me, I thought with a certain amount of satisfaction.

Then I thought, no, maybe he chose me simply because all the big guys working for him were doing something more important.

"We will need the boats delivered in Tampa two weeks from today," Davidka said. The man nodded, counting the money. It took him a while, but when he got to $100,000 he said, "Done," and stood up and stuck out his hand. Davidka shook with him, and we left.

We went straight back to the station in Miami and got on the next train for New York. As we were boarding, I asked Davidka, "What if that guy doesn't deliver the boats? You did not make a contract or sign any papers or anything. What if he doesn't keep his part of the bargain, and skips with the money?"

Davidka stopped briefly, just for a second, and looked at me. A smile almost flickered across his face. He shook his head no, almost imperceptibly. It dawned on me that if the man cheated Davidka, it would be the worst mistake of his life – and quite possibly the last.

We found our seats and Davidka stepped aside to let me in first, holding out his palm to usher me into the window seat, where I sat for the entire trip back to New York.

Back in New York, Davidka told me to be ready to go to Florida again in three weeks. I was to use that time to wind up my affairs in New York; I would not be coming back. I would spend as long as it took in Tampa to get the three boats in shape, and then be part of a crew that would smuggle the boats out of U.S. waters onto the open sea and across the Atlantic, into the Mediterranean and on to Israel.

I felt obliged to tell Davidka that I knew nothing about boats, and that our motorboat ride to the island off Miami was the first time I had ever been in any boat of any kind. He shrugged and said all I had to do was get the engines to run. When I told him I could not even swim, he cracked a little smile and said that was all the more reason I should make sure the engines ran well.

I had no idea what would happen to me when I got to Israel. I asked Davidka, but he said only that there would be an assignment for me there. I mulled the possibilities. I always had assumed that I would become an engineer for the Israeli army, helping to build things and keep things running. That is what I wanted to do. I hoped Davidka would not want me to become a regular part of Davidka's network, a real spy instead of an accidental one. Davidka offered no clues. The one thing that seemed certain was that once I got to Israel – assuming that the little torpedo boats made it – I would not be returning to America for quite some time.

All I had to pack was my engineering books into one suitcase and my clothes into another. So I spent as much of the next three weeks as possible with Florence. She worked in the office at the Jewish Theological Seminary on West 120th Street, and every afternoon at five o'clock when she got off work, I was waiting for her. We would stroll down Broadway, stop for coffee or ice cream or a piece of pie, and then stroll some more. We often walked along Riverside Park, with the Hudson River on one side and the grand old apartment buildings of

Upper Manhattan on the other side. We talked about what it would be like to raise a family in one of those big old apartments, but we were not bold enough to talk about the two of us raising a family together.

I began eating dinner with her and her parents in their apartment every evening. Her parents were strong supporters of Israel, and vaguely knew that I was involved and becoming more deeply involved. We talked over dinner and sometimes through the evening about the news from Israel, which was mixed in April 1948. On the one hand, it looked like Britain really was going to pull out of Palestine soon and that Israel would be able to declare itself a free and independent nation.

On the other hand, the Arab violence against Jews and Jewish communities was escalating, and many shortages were hampering the efforts of Jews to defend themselves or fight back. The newspapers said that Czechoslovakia was the only nation in the world willing to sell weapons to the fledgling Israeli army, but I suspected that Davidka was smuggling weapons from the United States, too. Knowing that I was a small part of his organization, and helping in a small way, helped me overcome my misgivings about abandoning my studies. When I thought about Columbia, I reminded myself that some of the vehicles I had inspected were probably in Palestine by then, helping my countrymen.

On the day of my departure in late April, it was difficult to face the prospect of actually saying goodbye to Florence. She wanted to take the morning off from work and see me off at the station, but I discouraged her. I did not want her to be seen with me at the train station, in case anyone was watching. And I didn't want her to meet Davidka or any of his associates. I wanted to keep Florence separate – and safe – from my work with Davidka. So I walked her to her office, hugged and kissed her goodbye on the sidewalk, and told her I'd call as soon as I could. In truth, I was afraid I would never see her again.

At the station, I looked for Davidka. Instead, the man who had been in the outer office on Park Row showed up, handed me a ticket, and told me I would be traveling alone to Florida this time. In my seat on the train, I noted that the valise I carried was about the same size as the one Davidka had held on his lap all the way to Miami; but mine held only a couple of changes of clothes and maybe twenty dollars, not $100,000.

Davidka was waiting for me at the station in Tampa. He took me to an undistinguished, cheap but cheerful residential hotel where I was already checked into a small room under a fake name: Ed Black. Davidka told me not to give my real name to anyone in Tampa except the four men I was about to meet. In the hotel lounge, he introduced me to three other Israeli guys and an American Jew. Together we would refit the banana boats and transform them back into torpedo boats. We would live at the hotel. All of us were about the same age, mid to late twenties, except one of the Israelis who might have been in his early thirties. Davidka called him the Captain. Davidka said he was a real sea captain, and would be in charge of both refitting and sailing the boats across the Atlantic and the Mediterranean to Israel. My job was to overhaul the engines on all three boats, and the Captain would oversee the other three guys in working on everything else on the boats. Davidka told me the Captain would have money for the parts I needed, and at some point, I might get some helpers, some assistant mechanics. And then Davidka said goodbye, presumably headed back to New York.

The next day we walked to the boatyard. The boats were there, moored alongside long repair docks under a metal shed that opened onto the boatyard's small inner harbor. To see what we were doing, someone would have had to walk through the entire boatyard and peer directly into the shed. No one ever did, as far as I knew.

The nearly two months we spent in Tampa working on the boats turned out to be very enjoyable. The weather was good, and I enjoyed the sunshine and the sea air. The men I was working with were salt-of-the-earth guys; it was good to be back among Hebrew-speaking working men, though we sometimes had to explain our jokes and banter in English to the American. And the work was satisfying. Piece by piece, I took apart the engines on the three boats, and cleaned and oiled or replaced parts: pistons, cylinders, pumps, prop shafts, bearings, everything that needed to be done, I did. I loved doing this kind of work, and I knew how to do it well.

After several weeks, the Captain brought in a couple of local mechanics, Jewish men who wanted to help, and it turned out that they made the work go much more quickly. Whenever I needed money for parts, the Captain handed it over – several thousand dollars in all – and I got what I needed at one of the local marine equipment suppliers. I tested the engines periodically at the docks, revving them up with the boats still in their berths. They ran superbly, if I do say so myself, probably as well as when they were new. Maybe better. Meanwhile, the Captain and the other guys did everything else: cleaning, scraping, painting, and so on. It was gritty, grimy, backbreaking and, to me, boring work. I was happy to be up to my elbows in engine grease.

The Captain brought in a few more helpers, too, and eventually there were a dozen of us working on the three little boats. Gradually they began to look sleek, sharp, and dangerous, more like naval weapons of destruction and less like decrepit banana boats. I still did not know anything about torpedoes, but I helped the Captain clean out the torpedo tubes, two on each boat, and rewire them so that they would actually fire torpedoes again.

The Captain told me how the boats worked. Armed with a torpedo on either side of the bow, they would try to get as close as they could to unsuspecting enemy ships, usually at night when visibility was poor. The preferred targets were tankers, freighters or troop carriers. More maneuverable and better-armed vessels such as patrol boats or destroyer escorts would blow our little torpedo boats out of the water before we got close enough to do any damage. The idea was that once we got within a certain range of a target ship, the torpedo boat would come to full speed ahead. When it got close to the target ship, preferably amidships, it would fire one torpedo and then the other. "Fish," the Captain called the torpedoes. The boat's top speed was not that great, maybe twenty-five knots, but every little bit of additional boat speed increased the velocity of the torpedoes in the water. Once the torpedoes were away, then our boat was supposed to turn as sharply as possible and run in the opposite direction as quickly as possible.

It all sounded dangerous to me, and the Captain said it was. The target ships always had lookouts, and if they saw a torpedo boat approaching they would begin firing machine guns and cannons. Even if the torpedo boat got its fishes in the water and they hit the mark, there was no guarantee that the torpedo boat would not get hit. The target ship would also radio for help and sister ships – or worse, airplanes – would immediately begin chasing the torpedo boat as it ran away. Finally, even if everything went well – no enemy fire, no escorts giving chase, and a direct hit that would sink the target ship – the torpedo boat could be fatally damaged by repercussions as the target ship blew up. If we ever made a direct hit on a freighter with a full magazine of explosives, the Captain said, smiling nonchalantly, we would not have time to get away. We would be too close. We would be blown to kingdom come.

He saw me shudder, and laughed. He told me not to let my imagination run wild. Our job was merely to deliver the boats to Israel, not to fight our way across the Atlantic. He did not even think we would be carrying any torpedoes, but he did not know for sure. If so, they would be put on board literally at the last minute. I did not find this particularly reassuring.

I called Florence several times during the first couple of weeks in Tampa. I described the beautiful springtime weather, which was much warmer and sunnier than New York in May, and told her about some of the tourist sights in the area. I assured her that I was getting off work on the boats every night at six or seven o'clock, that I had a clean room in a nice little hotel, and that I had time in the evening to go to dinner and walk around town. I described some of the nicer restaurants, and a couple of nightclubs where there were floorshows and couples could dance. "Why don't you come down here for a visit?" I urged her. "Take a vacation from work and come and see me." To my surprise, she said yes immediately, without even seeming to think about it. Maybe she had been thinking about it already.

Ten days later, I met Florence at the station. She was so beautiful. She had the prettiest smile I had ever seen, and the bluest eyes. The desk clerk at the hotel did not raise an eyebrow when I checked her in as Mrs. Florence Black. We had a wonderful week. I would go off to the boats early in the morning, while she would sleep late and then spend the day as a leisurely tourist: she would take in the zoo, the botanical gardens, a harbor cruise, or just look around at the sights. We would meet back at the room shortly after six o'clock, and then go out to dinner either by ourselves or with the Captain and some of the other guys. They were friendly to Florence and respectful, but I could also tell that they were envious. How did a little schmuck like me get such a gorgeous, intelligent and personable girlfriend?

Florence was in Tampa on May 14, 1948, the day that Israel declared itself a new and independent nation. While I was working on the boats, Florence spent much of the day listening to the radio in the hotel lobby, absorbing the news reports of the British withdrawal the previous day and the expectations of increased Arab violence in the coming weeks. That night we went out to dinner, just the two of us. We rarely drank, but that night we each ordered a glass of champagne and drank a toast to Israel.

By the time, I put her back on the train to return to New York, I was more in love with Florence than ever, and the parting was more difficult. We talked about her perhaps joining me in Israel. Someday. Maybe. I would call her from Tampa before we left. There was just as much uncertainty as when we had said goodbye in New York, but this time I felt much more confident, somehow, that we would find a way to end up together.

By early June, we had almost finished the boats, and the Captain said our orders would be coming soon. He paid off the local Jews who had been working with us, including my two assistant mechanics, and they stopped coming to work. There were five of us left -- the original five who had been gathered by Davidka at the start of the refitting. We spent several days polishing and testing our work and provisioning the boats with canned goods and dry food for the long sea voyage. The Captain had us bring only a few food items on board the boats at a time, and we never carried more than one grocery bag. He said he did not want to call attention to our impending departure. The Captain told us to quietly sneak our belongings out of the hotel where we had been living, a few items at a time over the next couple of days. He planned for us to leave without paying the money we owed for the rooms. He told us not to worry about the food or our belongings on the boats. He had arranged for some trusted local Jewish men, including some of the workers who had helped us, to take turns serving as night watchmen on the dock and guarding the boats.

I began looking around the boats in the mornings to see if any torpedoes had appeared somehow overnight, but none ever did. One morning, however, I saw two new men on the dock, poking their heads in and out of the boats. The Captain said that they were captains, too. He would be in charge of the lead boat, and they would take command of the two boats that followed. That made seven of us for the voyage: a captain and a crewman in each of the three boats, and me as the third person in the lead boat. We would sail the following night, the Captain said. We were to get the last of our belongings out of our rooms and into the boats the next day. We were to leave the hotel separately at different times during the evening to avoid arousing suspicion among the hotel staff. We would meet the following evening at nine o'clock at one of the nicer restaurants just off the Tampa waterfront. We would have one last big dinner to celebrate and say goodbye to America. We would sail at midnight, on the tide.

That final evening in Tampa was soft and warm. I made one last, wrenching long-distance call to Florence. I did not give her any of the particulars, but she knew that I thought this probably would be my last call for a long time. I arrived at the restaurant shortly after nine o'clock. The other six seafarers were already seated around a large round table toward the back. We were all in a jovial mood, or at least putting up a jovial front. We ordered seafood specialties and good wine – though I noticed that all three captains barely touched their wine. The Captain happened to mention that the watchman at the docks that evening had been one of my assistant mechanics during the refitting.

By about 10:30 p.m., we had finished our main courses and were looking at the dessert menu when there was a minor commotion at the entrance to the dining room. It was the night watchman, my former assistant mechanic. He was gesturing toward our table, talking to the maitre d'. The Captain was up from our table in an instant, taking the night watchman by the elbow and guiding him outside. We stopped talking and tried to study our menus as if nothing was amiss.

The Captain was back in two minutes. He leaned over the center of the table, and motioned for us to lean in, too. He spoke quietly.

"There is a problem. The FBI has boarded the boats. They are waiting there to arrest us. I suspect they are waiting at the hotel, too. I do not think they followed the night watchman to this restaurant, though. They don't know where we are right now."

He pulled a thick wallet out, counted out some bills, and put them on the table. "I will take our engineer," he said, nodding toward me. "The rest of you know what to do." No one else spoke, but they all stood and shook hands with the Captain, and with me. On the way out, the Captain paused to explain to the maitre d' that something had come up and we wouldn't be having dessert, but yes, thanks, the meal had been lovely and the service, too. Yes, we would be sure to come back again.

Outside, the Captain hailed a cab and took me to the train station. Inside, I waited while he folded the wooden door closed on a phone booth and spoke to someone for several minutes. When he emerged he said, "Davidka wants you to call him when you are back in New York. He has another assignment for you -- a big one this time." At that, the Captain grinned and motioned for me to follow him to the ticket windows. He bought me a ticket on the first train out in the morning for New York, and then shook hands and said goodbye.

Once again, I was getting on a train for a long journey without a toothbrush, not knowing what would await me when I arrived. I spent a sleepless night on the hard wooden benches in the train station, and could not sleep on the train, either. If I was not looking over my shoulder, literally, for anyone who might look like an FBI agent, I was wondering what Davidka – and Israel – would have in store for me next.

Buying A Steam Boat

Back in New York, Davidka had been waiting for us for a few days. During that time, before we returned to New York, he bought a large steamboat, which he planned to convert into a transport boat for the transport of the Jewish Holocaust survivors in Europe to Israel. The ship was anchored at a Brooklyn pier. It looked huge to me as I had never seen or been on one before. Davidka told me that I was supposed to be the chief mechanical engineer on the boat and that I would have a month to learn about the boat's engine and its mechanical equipment and get an engineering license with the Panamanian Consulate. I told Florence about the plan and she went with me to a technical bookstore, where I spent over $30 for a steamship engine handbook.

When I boarded the boat, I could not believe what I saw. I was used to working on diesel engines, which are relatively small. But when I entered the steamship engine room I found a two-story high engine with colossal cylinders and connecting rods, twenty-four bearings, and various large pumps and accessory equipment.

The books I bought were very good. I studied feverishly for a month and then went to the Panamanian Consulate. To my surprise, the exam was very easy for me. I finished it in two hours, and three days later, I received my chief engineer's certificate.

Now the work on the boat started. Besides the engine and the accessories overhaul, we had to remove most of the inside hall structures and build five high platforms that people could sleep on. These planks were built all around the boat. Air blowers were installed to keep fresh air inside the hall down below. A bathroom was installed at the rear of the boat and water pipes for drinking were placed in several locations.

In the hall, light bulbs were placed along the ceiling. Florence came to visit the boat and she could not believe that this old boat could ever cross the ocean. She remembered this boat, Dewitt Clinton, which had been converted from a pleasure boat on the Hudson River to a troop carrier during World War I, and was now being converted again, this time to carry Holocaust survivors from Europe to Israel.

The time was coming for me to leave for Israel. Florence and I finally discussed our marriage plans. I suggested that she follow me to Israel and see if she would like to settle there with me. She told me I must be crazy. "I'm sorry, but I am not going to Israel on approval. If you love me, let's get married before you leave. Otherwise I cannot promise you whether I will follow you to Israel."

I was too much in love to risk losing her. I said, "All right. Let's get married." A week later, we were married in the Jewish Theological Seminary. In attendance were the boat crew, and also Mrs. Bardin, who was living in New York at the time.

A few days later, I left on the boat, which had been renamed Hagalila. Florence brought a load of food and especially cartons of cigarettes to the boat, because at that time was I smoking three packs a day. The boat's crew consisted primarily of Israelis: the captain, the first and second officers, myself as a chief engineer (with an assistant who was a Pan American engineer who had worked on the boat before), a navigator, and several young Israeli crew members. Since it was a steamship fueled by coal, there were also four Indian firemen whose job was to shovel coal into the boiler furnace.

We took off in the late afternoon. I moved down to the engine room, worrying about the engine and all the equipment, which was new to me. Before we got out of port, I was already feeling sick. The noise of the engines was deafening and they had to be constantly attended to. I had to keep the huge bearings oiled all the time by squirting oil and water into them while they were in motion. I moved a small folding bed next to the engine room and set it up next to a porthole window, which was just at the water level. The seawater splashed incessantly against the window.

For the next 10 days, I never left the engine room. I could not sleep because of the heat and the noise, and I was seasick all the time. Luckily, I did not throw up. The fireman and the oilman were working around the clock and I kept the engine room running continuously without major breakdown.

We arrived in the Canary Islands to load the boat with coal. I enjoyed every minute of our stay up on deck, sunning myself and catching up on my sleep. The oilman left the boat for two days leave. When the time came to continue on our trip, we realized that our fireman had not returned. Our captain informed us that by nightfall, we would set sail, with or without the oil man.

I asked the captain how he expected to sail without four oil men. He said, "You have to solve this problem between your Israeli crew."

I said, "You mean we should attend to the boiler and the furnace ourselves?"

He said, "Yes, it's only for the next five days. So go arrange the shift." So I did. All the Israeli crewmen came down and were divided into twelve-hour shifts and so they all took turns working the shift. I escaped because of my duties supervising the operation.

During our stay in the Canary Islands, known for their canaries, a salesman came on board with a cage full of canaries. They were all singing beautifully and their reddish-yellow color was amazing. Each of us bought a few canaries with a cage. We let them stay on the deck.

The next morning, when we came to feed them, we found that the canaries had lost their color and they did not sing. It turned out that the canary salesman had painted the canaries, and he was the one who whistled like a canary. He had duped us into buying simple little gray birds. We kept these birds until we reached Treast port in Italy, and then let them fly free.

We reached Treast four days later. First, we recruited four new firemen and relieved the Israeli crew from their engine room duties.

The next morning we boarded 1,200 refugees of all ages: mothers with their young children, young and old men poorly dressed. However, they had happy faces because they were excited about their voyage to Israel. They all marched down the ship's hall, mothers and children on the lower levels and men on the upper levels.

As soon as they all were on the boat, we sailed. The temperature down the hall was getting hot and most of the passengers went up onto the deck. The two lavatories, which I had installed down the hall of course, were not sufficient, and I had to build six others out of wood on the deck. I also built temporary showers and washing stands, which were used continuously.

The voyage to Israel took six long days. There was continuous commotion on the boat. Many of the passengers were terribly sick, and so was I.

139

Chapter 5 – America

3 Torpedo Boats in Repair
Tampa, Fl

Boris, Paul and Me in
Tampa, Fl

Boris Yavitz
New York Times Notice

Davidka Nameri

Our Ship, Galilah

Chapter 5 – America

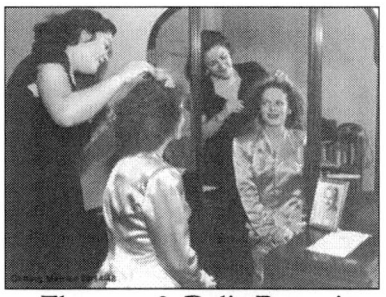

Florence & Dalia Preparing for the ceremony

Florence

Signing the Marriage Contract

Signing the Contract by the Rabbi

Getting Married Under the Chopa
Attending Mrs. Bardin and Boris Yavitz

Chapter 5 – America

Cutting the Cake

Florence and Me

Family Pictures

CHAPTER SIX

BEER SHEVA

Back To Israel

I was sure happy to see the shores of Israel and the end of my naval experience. As soon as we landed in Haifa, I reported to my company, received some money, and left to visit my parents in Jerusalem. By that time, I had not seen them in over two years. I spoke to Florence on the phone. After a few days of vacation, I returned to Haifa and received my first job assignment: to be the chief engineer supervising equipment maintenance in the port of Haifa.

Meanwhile, Florence was preparing to follow me to Israel, which was a tricky undertaking. The U.S. State Department did not permit American citizens to travel to Israel because of the war there. I suggested that Florence get in touch with Davidka, with whom I had worked before, to arrange a way for her to travel to Israel illegally without using her passport. After meeting Davidka in a small one-room office in downtown New York, my wife was told to travel to Europe and wait for instructions on how to continue her trip to Israel. She arrived in Trieste, Italy, and settled down in a small hotel to await further instructions.

After a week of anxious waiting, she finally received a call from an anonymous party telling her to travel to Marcel and wait there. After waiting in Marcel for another week, she called to tell me that no one had contacted her to tell her how to proceed.

I called my father, who had many contacts with the Haganah's underground forces, and he called the party in Marcel. Soon thereafter, Florence was contacted and arrangements were made for her to board a Romanian ship, which had been carrying Jewish survivors from the camps in Europe back to Israel. Florence spent five days traveling in that very crowded boat before finally arriving at the port of Haifa. Because I had control of the equipment in the port, I went on a small boat to meet her on the ship. I then drove to the pier where she was processed by immigration authorities.

Her first encounter in Israel was with a nurse who wanted to inoculate her with injections, as she had been doing to all the other newcomers. Florence strongly objected; however, before she knew it, she was being injected against her will. She was quite upset by the whole experience.

Our first living quarters together were in a small hotel near the port at which I worked. Later on, my company arranged a small apartment for us to move into in Mount Carmel. We brought in two army cots and a few wooden boxes to start furnishing our new apartment. I was busy working while Florence started to become accustomed to the unfamiliar environment. She did housekeeping and managed to keep the kitchen going.

Meanwhile, I was starting to become unhappy with my job at the port. The union was getting involved in every decision I made, and as a result, I did not have the freedom to do what needed to be done in the port. It was a difficult time in Israel. Food was strictly rationed to one egg per month, one quarter of a chicken per month, and so on. In fact, the port of Haifa was the only place in Israel where food was plentiful. But the port management, of which I was a part, was provided with breakfast every morning, which included eggs, ham, butter, fresh bread, and good coffee. I felt guilty, and wished that Florence could have breakfast with me.

The general manager of the port, Amos Landsman, was an extremely fat man who weighed at least 400 pounds. Every morning, his breakfast included twelve eggs, a pound of ham, and two loaves of bread. I had never seen a human being eat so much food in one sitting.

My daily routine involved inspecting the cranes, tractors, and other equipment; setting a work schedule; and attending meetings where I would outline the schedule to the representatives from the union. In the end, it was they who had the last word and decided what should or should not be done. The whole ordeal was unacceptable to me and eventually became so humiliating that I complained to my general manager, who worked in the main office of Solel-Boneh in downtown Haifa.

Hiller Dan was one of the general managers whom I had met several times before. He was short, slim and has a vibrant personality. He ran most of the company operations, which employed over 20,000 men. Setting an appointment with him was a tremendously difficult undertaking. He was in continuous meetings most days and nights and was often traveling in his car. While traveling, he would make appointments in each town to have interviews. One person would get into his car for a meeting that would last for the duration of time it took to travel to the next town or village, and then get out, so that another appointee could get in for the next meeting. I waited in his office for hours for my meeting with him. Eventually, he came out, apologized, and said, "I am sorry, but if you don't mind, I am going to the men's bathroom. If you sit in the next bathroom stall, we can spend some time talking together." I was embarrassed by his request, but I knew that I needed to tell him my problem. I desperately needed to ask him to change my job. So I spent fifteen minutes in the stall next to his, talking to him with just a thin partition between us as he did his business. In the end, he promised to change my job and gave me an opportunity to transfer.

Hiller Dan was one of the founders of Solel-Boneh and an active member of the Histadrut, which was the labor party in Israel. He himself had started as a laborer. In time, he had become one of the leaders of Solel-Boneh, the country's largest contractor building roads and houses. Previously there had been no organizations in Israel that could undertake building such large projects. The projects it led needed a large budget for funds and experienced workers. Histadrut, the labor party, was able to provide this. The British mandate, which had been governing Palestine, needed Solel-Boneh for various construction projects. Thus, Solel-Boneh was able to provide them with all the construction assistance they needed. In time, Solel-Boneh grew to become an incredibly powerful organization and was known for being financially capable of performing large undertakings. Hiller Dan had the brain, the vision, and the energy to head the company. He took me under his wing and had a plan to create a management position for me.

Meanwhile, Florence was settling down and running our home. The environment and the language were both so new to her. Buying food, cooking new recipes, and preparing meals were quite an undertaking, especially because our kitchen did not operate on gas or electricity. All she had was a small kerosene stove.

However, despite the odds, she managed well. Shopping at the market was very different from buying groceries in New York City. I remember one time when she went to buy a chicken. First, she had to choose a live chicken. Then they slaughtered it for her and placed it in her string basket to carry home. As she walked home holding the basket, the chicken still had its feathers and she could feel it moving. When I saw her, she was walking up the hill from the market crying, with the basket in her hands. She did not want to let it go, since it was the only chicken she could get for a month because of the food rationing.

Another time when she went to buy fish, they sold her a living carp. She had it in her string basket, and it kept snapping while she was carrying it home. After the long walk back to the house from the market, it was still alive. Our neighbor saw her crying because she did not know what to do with the live fish, so she took the fish from Florence, took it into her kitchen, and hit the fish on the head several times with a wooden mallet until it stopped moving. Ordinarily, Florence would have decided to forget about the fish, but again, since she knew it was the only fish she would get for the month, she kept it. It was not easy for an American girl to get used to this new environment, but she coped well and tried her best to adjust.

Since I was busy all day, Florence was getting bored. Besides taking care of the small, unfurnished apartment and cooking, she did not have much to do and was getting impatient.

Because Hiller Dan knew I wanted to change my job, he told me about an opportunity to start building a new town in the south of Israel. I went to the Solel-Boneh office to meet David Tuviyahu. A very imposing man, Tuviyahu was one of the famous construction general managers of Solel-Boneh who had built most of the main roads and the only airport in Palestine. Now, after the end of the War of 1948, the south of Israel was finally opened for settlements. Beer Sheva was to become the new central city in the south. David Ben-Gurion, who was the prime minister at the time, appointed Tuviyahu as the first mayor of Beer Sheva. Tuviyahu explained to me that this was the most important pioneering undertaking in Israel's history. With that, he then told me that he wished that I would serve as his mechanical engineer superintendent on this great endeavor.

I had heard of Beer Sheva before from reading the Bible: Abraham had lived in Beer Sheva. I knew it was in the southern deserts of Israel, but after having been in both Abadan and Baharien, that did not faze me. Nevertheless, now that I was married, I told Tuviyahu that I would have to check with Florence before accepting this wonderful opportunity. When I told her about it, I suggested that she go to see Beer Sheva first to see what she thought about us moving there.

My father, who was now working in Jerusalem as a controller with the Jewish National Fund, arranged for Florence to meet with one of the managers of J.N.F. who could show her Beer Sheva. At the time, Florence had met a friend of hers from New York whose husband was a rabbi studying in Jerusalem. She asked her friend whether she would like to join her in her trip, and she accepted. So both women traveled there by bus.

In 1948, Beer Sheva had just been conquered by the Israeli Army. The Arab population had left town, and only the Israeli army garrison was in town. Beyond that, there were just a few construction personnel and civilian government representatives who had moved into town. Florence and her friend arrived by bus looking for the J.N.F. office to meet the man who was supposed to show them around. After searching for him, they finally found him. Although he knew they were coming, he was completely surprised to see these two young American girls coming to visit Beer Sheva, this empty, unoccupied Arab desert town.

However, it was an exciting adventure for Florence and her friend after having been cooped up in the apartment in Haifa. My father's friend took both girls with him for a trip in his jeep all around the area. Because there were no roads, the ride was quite bumpy, very dusty, and incredibly hot. After a few hours of exploring, they returned. Since it was quite late, they had to remain in town for the night. The only place for them to stay was in the back of the J.N.F. office, which had small army beds with uncovered mattresses and a blanket. They had certainly never experienced that type of night's sleep before; however, it was exciting.

The next day when Florence returned to Haifa and I asked her how Beer Sheva was, she told me it was hot. She informed me that it was not a town at all, but instead just an empty, small Arab village in the desert. She said it reminded her of a town in the Wild West in America, but instead of having wooden structures there were small Arabian thick-walled stone houses. It was a village, but it was definitely in the middle of the desert. There was one small restaurant, an Arab mosque, a police station, and some army personnel. I told her that maybe if she wanted to, she should move in with my uncle at the kibbutz while I worked in Beer Sheva. That way, I could work during the week and then spend the weekend with her, as some of the other managers were doing. Florence told me that there was no way she would agree to that type of arrangement. She had come to Israel to live with me, and if my work brought me to Beer Sheva, she too would settle in Beer Sheva, no matter what the conditions.

In order to speed up the construction in Beer Sheva, Solel-Boneh bought special equipment made by LeTourneau in Longview, Texas. Since I was familiar with the people there, I arranged for them to deliver specialized equipment that would allow us to cast three to four houses per day.

Beer Sheva

The equipment we had ordered was among the largest pieces of equipment being used in all of Israel. I had been appointed by Hiller Dan to lead the building project with LeTourneau equipment in Beer Sheva. I was very excited to have been chosen for this project. My direct manager was David Tuviyahu, the general manager of Solel-Boneh's southern division. In fact, Tuviyahu was available to work in Beer Sheva because after his dispute with Solel-Boneh headquarters, they wanted to get rid of him. As they said in Israel, they were "sending him to Siberia" because southern Israel was the desert. At that time, no one thought much of southern Israel except for David Ben-Gurion, the prime minister who envisioned that the south and Beer Sheva would become the flourishing center of Israel's future. Tuviyahu did not have much choice but to move to Beer Sheva. Also, to my pleasant surprise,

Tuviyahu's assistant, Avigdor, one of my old friends from Baharien whom I loved and respected, was appointed to work with me.

I was very happy about the opportunity to move and build the new town from scratch. I felt I was fulfilling the Zionist dream of building Israel. To my surprise, Florence was also very enthusiastic about the move to the desert town. When we got there, I saw that the town only consisted of several hundred old adobe Arab houses, a mosque, a police station, a few trees, an old unused railway station, and a stone tower with two large metal tanks. Desert surrounded us as far as the eye could see. There was no electricity, no paved road, and the water supply was limited to one small well. At that time, the total population was about 200.

Before moving to Beer Sheva, Florence and I came down to see what our new dwelling would look like. Tuviyahu and four of his assistants, including Avigdor, brought us to an old adobe house that was surrounded by a high stone fence. It had two rooms, a small terrace, a tiny kitchen, a bathroom, and a small unkempt garden space. One room would be allocated to us, and the other would be given to a carpenter who would share our home. The walls were five feet thick and none of the rooms had windows. There was just a small opening high up near the ceiling. The floor was made of stone and the terrace was between the two rooms. Florence examined the new dwelling and, to my astonishment, she did not object.

After inspecting the house, she looked at the tiny bathroom. There was a small sink and a shower that stuck out of a water heater. With Tuviyahu and all of his assistants standing around, Florence turned to me and said, "I am sorry, but I am not moving to this house without a bathtub." I tried to tell her that there was no water system in Beer Sheva, but she insisted. Tuviyahu turned to Avigdor and said in Hebrew, "Don't argue with her. Give her a bathtub today." Avigdor told Tuviyahu that there were not any available in town, so Tuviyahu told him to send someone to Tel Aviv to get her a bathtub today. So, Florence got her bathtub that day.

Unfortunately, during our entire stay, Florence never had a chance to take a bath because there was never enough water in Beer Sheva. Looking back on the bathtub episode, I think that Tuviyahu was surprised that this young American girl from New York was not objecting to having to live in the old Arabian house and was relieved that her only objection was not having a bathtub.

A few days later, we moved from Haifa to our new home in Beer Sheva with our two army beds, table, chairs, and a few boxes with all of our other belongings. We brought along our kerosene stove, several pots, and some utensils. Florence operated the kitchen with the limited facilities we had and, on top of that, the rationed portions of food. However, she managed to cook very good meals and always served them properly on a clean white tablecloth with forks, knives, and napkins in place. The only restaurant in town had a very limited menu, but once a week we went there for a dinner out.

I was getting very busy. First, I had to move the heavy construction equipment from Haifa to Beer Sheva. The heavy cranes and large machinery had to be driven on narrow and sometimes unpaved roads. Some of the roads had to be closed for traffic while we were driving the equipment. It took us three days before we eventually arrived at our destination in the middle of the desert, about half a mile from the old town of Beer Sheva. There was not a tree or a bush to be found. However, I believed strongly that the new town would be built. In fact, several weeks earlier, David Ben-Gurion had arrived in this desert area with some of his ministers and Solel-Boneh management personnel (including myself). He had spread a large map on the ground. The chief government planner had used the map to show us the layout for the new town and point out where the main road would be laid out. He showed us where we would put the hospital, university, municipality, schools, recreation, and industrial center. While standing there looking at the map, I simultaneously looked around at the view of flat desert land around me. I thought to myself, "What a wonderful dream." I believed in Ben-Gurion and felt very proud to be one of the people that would have the opportunity to fulfill this historic dream.

While we were erecting the machinery, I started to recruit some local workers to work alongside my core experienced operators and my foreman who had come with me from Haifa. I arranged some living quarters for them in the old Arab houses.

The new immigrants, who had been transported at night directly from the boats at Haifa, had expected to arrive in Tel Aviv; instead, in the morning, they found themselves at the desert camp in Beer Sheva.

They settled in the tents, which I had erected, but it was a very unhappy scene. The women were crying, while the men were very aggravated and milling around. We tried to calm them down, assuring them that their stay in the tent-camp was only temporary and that very shortly there would be new buildings for them to settle into.

I selected some of the immigrants to work for me in building the new town. The new workers had no experience working in construction, digging trenches, handling concrete, or bending steel rods, so they had to learn these skills on the job. Training them was extremely difficult, especially when the temperature reached close to 100 degrees. (Fortunately, there was always a breeze and the air was dry.) Furthermore, most of them did not speak Hebrew. But somehow, we all managed. By the end of the day, work got done and all the men returned to their families, who were all still living in the small, crowded tents. When the rain came, all of the earth around the area became muddy and slushy. However, the anticipation of moving into newly-built homes gave them hope.

Florence was getting impatient doing nothing besides housekeeping, so she used the experience she had gained as a wartime nurse in a New York hospital to find a job working in the small hospital, which had just opened in town. The headquarters of the Hadassah Hospital were in Jerusalem, so she decided to make an appointment with one of the head nurses there. Early one morning, she took a bus to Jerusalem and met with the head nurses, but the interview did not go as well as she had hoped. The nurses could not understand why a young American woman would want to work in a hospital in Beer Sheva when even Israeli women refused to live in the desert town. Rather than being happy with her interest and qualifications, they were suspicious of her and asked for her references. Florence was disappointed by their cool reception, to say the least. However, she wrote to the head of the hospital where she had worked in New York and received a wonderful recommendation letter. When she went back to Jerusalem with the letter, they accepted her. She always wondered why they had given her such a hard time when there was such a shortage of nurses in Beer Sheva and no other nurses had wanted to move there. But I think that the women in Israel just could not understand why a young American woman would leave a luxurious life in New York for one of hardships in

Beer Sheva. They did not realize that she had been so motivated to stay because of her commitment to her husband and her love for Israel.

As soon as Florence returned from her visit to Jerusalem, she went to the hospital. She was given a nurse's uniform, which was a size too small for her, and placed on a 12-hour shift from midnight to 12:00 noon. Once she started, we barely ever saw each other. Besides being short of personnel, the hospital was also short of doctors, equipment, and medicine. To make things worse, there was always an overflow of patients. Many of them had been seriously hurt by landmines, which had been left in the desert during the war. Surprisingly, despite all these problems, there were very few deaths during the two years Florence worked in the hospital.

My construction sites were located about half a mile from the hospital. It took me about a month to install the heavy concrete casting machinery and prepare all of it for operation so that we could start digging the foundation for the new town. Since it was hard for me to believe that such a big town was going to be built in the desert, from Day One I started taking pictures of the building project with my box camera. In fact, I took the first and only picture of the first house that was built in the town of Beer Sheva.

The method we used to build the houses with our large equipment was unique at that time. First, we did the casting of the houses, which contained inside and outside steel forms. Then, between those forms, we placed windows and door frames, as well as electrical wiring and water pipes. Finally, we cast a layer of concrete on top and in the space between the forms. By the next morning, the inside of the structure could be detached. Using a very large crane, the outside form was lifted over the inside form to create the whole structure of the house. Once built, each house, which weighed over 75 tons, was transported to the site where the foundation had already been laid. Utilizing this method of casting, we were able to construct two to three houses per day. While some men dug and created the foundation for the houses, the others worked with the casting machines.

As we worked, the temperature often approached 110 degrees. Many of the workers had an extremely difficult time adjusting to working in this kind of weather. However, most of them had families to support and had no choice but to work for me.

There was a great shortage of water, cement, and electricity. Among other things, I was also responsible for the town's water supply. Any water coming into Beer Sheva came from a single, small well. Since we needed water to cast the new houses, I usually had to stop the supply of water into town during the day. Only in the evening was I able to redirect the water back into town. Each house in the old town had a small water tank on the roof, but the incoming water could hardly fill up the entire tank. Everyone had to make sure not to use too much water. Taking a shower was a luxury.

Florence did not want the hospital at which she worked to know that I was the chief engineer of the town. However, on one occasion, the hospital ran out of water during an emergency operation. Florence told the chief nurse that she could find a way to get more water to the hospital. As I was headed to the work site, she ran over and stopped my truck. She asked me if I could open the water supply so that it would go back into the town so that the hospital could get water. I had never done this before because it meant that I would have to stop pouring concrete at the site. However, for Florence's sake I directed the water supply to the hospital. Some of the nurses saw Florence talking to me and asked her how she knew the chief engineer of the city. Finally, she revealed the truth and replied, "He is my husband." No one could understand why Florence wanted to work in a small desert hospital when all the other Israeli nurses would rather stay in Tel Aviv, but after this incident, Florence's stock at the hospital was raised considerably.

Meanwhile, we were having our own troubles at the construction site, because cement was in short supply and the main cement factory was in Haifa and at times the cement trucks were diverted to other locations and we had to stop our casting. I decided to send one of my foremen to investigate what was happening to our trucks, which were supposed to be coming back to Beer Sheva. Upon investigation, we found out that the long trip was difficult for the drivers, so instead of coming to Beer Sheva, they were delivering cement to closer locations. So when the next driver arrived with a shipment of cement, I told him I would pay him for four additional hours, so he would get additional pay every time he came to Beer Sheva. After that, there was no shortage of cement for construction. The drivers were happy and so were we.

Cement was very expensive, so I had two watchmen guarding it at night. However, I noticed that, despite their presence, the cement bags somehow seemed to be disappearing. One night, I decided to take Florence with me in my blue semi truck for a ride to the site at midnight. I turned off the headlights and quietly drove around the construction site. Suddenly, I heard a sound. After listening a little longer, I realized the sound was that of a wheelbarrow. I switched on my headlights and saw a man carrying three cement bags away in a wheelbarrow. I pulled out my gun and pointed it at him. He stopped in his tracks and I asked him what he was doing. He looked at me and said, "I need cement to extend my porch. You have so much cement that I decided to take some for myself." I told him what he was doing was stealing but he still did not seem to understand why he could not take the cement. The watchmen were either asleep or knew about the theft. In the end, I loaded the thief on the tender and brought him to the police station.

Florence was very upset with me. She thought that I should have let him go. Two months later, I had to take a day off to travel to the courthouse at Richon Letzion, which was 50 miles north of Beer Sheva, to plead my case. The courthouse, which was located in an apartment house, was terribly disorganized. People were milling around from room to room, and I had to wait outside the house for hours before I was called in for my case. Eventually I got to stand before the judge. After asking the thief a few questions, the judge asked me to forgive him, because he had just come to the country and did not understand the rules. At the end of the day, the judge let him go with just a warning and I was very upset that I had just lost a whole day's work. Florence was right; I should have let him go.

Other than that, the construction on my site was moving very smoothly. It was becoming one of the highlights of Israeli construction. For the time, I had many visitors from around the country coming to see our project. Amongst the visitors were Israeli ministers, including David Ben-Gurion and Mrs. Golda Meirson (later known as Golda Meir). Mrs. Meirson was the Israeli Minister of the Interior and visited Beer Sheva very often. At that time, she was divorced from her husband, whom, coincidentally, I had shared a room with when I was in Abadan several years earlier. In fact, he was the man my friends and I had tricked into getting drunk when we were in Abadan. It was the first time he had ever gotten drunk in his life.

Florence was getting very busy at the hospital. The hospital was small and crowded, but she was able to manage the night shift practically by herself. The supervising nurse, who came from Egypt and lived at the hospital compound, had a new boyfriend, and most nights, she spent time with him and left Florence alone to tend the patients in the hospital. However, Florence did not complain. She was a very dedicated nurse, very personally involved with the care of her patients and committed to staying with her patients.

One patient was a small Bedouin boy who was four years old and had a muscular disease. Florence became very attached to him and gave him special attention, because he was alone. The young child's name was Ahmad, so Florence called him little Ahmad. His parents lived alone in their camp in the desert. His father was the sheik, which was the head of the clan. He was a very imposing, tall, handsome man who had many wives and children. Ahmad was the child of his youngest wife, and once every two weeks they came to visit Ahmad. Ahmad's mother came dressed in a black caftan, which covered her from head to foot. Only Florence saw her face. She was very young. Although Ahmad was very sick and in pain, he never cried. It seemed to be part of the Bedouin mentality; even if they were in pain, they did not cry. When Ahmad was finally getting well, his mother and the sheik came to the hospital to take him home. His mother fell to her knees and kissed Florence's feet. Through her tears of joy, she thanked Florence for taking such good care of Ahmad and presented her with a basket full of eggs. At the time, this was a great fortune because the food allocation was only one egg per month. Florence thanked her and also cried to see Ahmad go.

In the hospital, there was always a shortage of medicine and painkillers. Many of the patients suffered great pain, especially after undergoing operations. There were many serious operations performed in the hospital. Many patients had to undergo amputations because of land mines, auto accidents, or Arab ambushes. The only surgeon in the hospital was a man named Dr. Yedidia, who had come from a very lucrative hospital in London. With him was his small four-year-old son, Dov. Dov always hung around the hospital and was the pet of all the nurses. No one knew why the boy was always with his father in the hospital in Beer Sheva, of all places, and without his mother. In time, the information leaked out. It seemed that the surgeon, Dr. Yedidia, was divorcing his wife in London. Rather than lose custody of his son, he had decided to kidnap him and disappear. He chose to move to Israel, where he knew surgeons were urgently needed, and settled in Beer Sheva with the hope that no one would find them. When the people in the hospital became aware of this, they hid little Dov every time a policeman came to visit the hospital. Since Dov was born with an additional small thumb on each hand, the police always asked if anybody had seen a small boy with six fingers on each of his hands. In the meantime, little Dov was taken care of by the hospital nurses and was always playing around the hospital floor. He was never short of attention while his father was busy in the operating room.

Once a week, Florence was given a day off from working in the hospital. On that day, we often decided to make a trip to Tel Aviv. While I spent some of my time in the Solel-Boneh office, Florence shopped for food. At the time, each person received a ration coupon book. When you paid, you also had to give the proper number of coupons for the item you were buying. For sugar, salt, and meat, each family was only allowed one pound per month. You were also only allowed one egg per month. So Florence shopped for vegetables, which were in short supply in Beer Sheva. Usually, by the time we got back to Beer Sheva it was late at night. Driving back, the roads were bad and my tires got worn out. Many times, the car would get a flat tire on the way back, and I would have to take care of it at midnight. Sometime, we would arrive back home early in the morning and, after only two hours sleep, Florence and I had to get back to work.

Even with such strict food rationing, Florence was a good cook. She always managed to prepare a full course meal with the limited ingredients she had. Luckily, bread was always available and we were able to fill our stomachs with bread. One day, it happened that our next door neighbor brought Florence a chunk of meat as a gift. With this large chunk of meat, we set about preparing a feast. Florence placed it in her pressure cooker on top of her small kerosene stove until it whistled. However, when she opened the pot she found that the meat still was not cooked. She added some more water and boiled it again, but found the meat still was not cooking. This happened several more times. The meat was getting smaller and smaller, and a strange odor was coming from the pot. When our neighbor came over for dinner and the meal still was not ready, he came to see what had happened to the gift he had given her. When he found out that it still hadn't cooked, he apologized and told Florence that he had forgotten to tell her that the meat was camel's meat; unfortunately, it was also old camel's meat. In horror, Florence dumped the meat out of the pot and we decided to go out and eat dinner at the restaurant. Florence had to clean and boil the pot for a long time to get rid of the bad smell, and it was not until a month later, when we got our one-pound meat ration, that we had meat for dinner again.

To help alleviate the meat shortage, we decided to raise a few chickens of our own, so that once in a while, we could have chicken for dinner. I built a chicken coop a few feet above the ground in the backyard and used chicken wire as a floor mat. One of our neighbors was a kibbutznik who took care of sick cows in town. He brought Florence two small chickens as a gift. When she got them, she called the hen Saloma and the rooster Rusty, which was her brother's name. Florence fed the chickens well, because every night she brought home leftover food from the hospital kitchen. In time, several other chickens were added to our coop. We called one of the new ones Egen, after a beautiful Hungarian woman who lived next door to us.

The chickens were growing and becoming large, fat, and healthy…but our plan to supplement our meat ration with chicken backfired. The longer we had the chickens, the more we saw them as adored pets instead of a roasted chicken dinner. Each time a holiday approached, we could not think of killing our beloved chickens.

Once, I was woken up at four o'clock in the morning by the clucking chickens. Over the next few days, it continued to happen, and I could not sleep. I told a friend of mine and asked for his advice. He told me that usually, when chickens are clucking it means that they are laying eggs. Somehow, I had never thought of my chickens as egg producers; I had only seen them as sources of meat. So I started cleaning the chicken coop, and to my amazement and surprise, I found eleven large white eggs in the corner of the coop. It was such a fortune. We had eggs for breakfast and knew that we could not think of eating these wonderful egg-laying creatures. To our good fortune, the chickens continued to lay eggs every day for some time.

Every few months, Florence's mother sent us a package from the U.S. containing coffee, soap, and canned fruits. All of these were considered luxuries because they were very hard to come by in Israel. Our meals were getting better. We ate most of our meals outside in the small courtyard, which had to be swept each morning and night because of the sand that was continuously blowing in the air. During dinner, night flyers and black large bugs swarmed around our kerosene lamps, dove towards our heads, and got into our food, but we got used to them.

The white electric stove, washing machine, and dryer, which had been shipped to Florence from the U.S., were standing in the corner of the yard. They had not been used because of the shortage of water and electricity. As a matter of fact, the electricity was cut off every night by eleven o'clock. By the time the water was redirected to the tank on our roof, it was already night.

There were new people arriving in Beer Sheva every day. One of them was a young woman who had come from England with three small children and no husband. Her name was Miriam. She had worked in the Solel-Boneh office, and decided to settle in Beer Sheva. One of our construction superintendents, a middle-aged man called Vagman, was a tall, handsome, charismatic man who took her under his wing. He was constantly hanging around her and developed an intimate relationship with her, even though he was much older than she and had children her age. The young woman was beautiful, but she was dirty and a slob. Her skirts were all very short, and her blouses were always wet at her nipples because she was still nursing her small baby and never bothered to wash her blouse. But her older lover, Vagman, did not mind. After all, she was one of the few single women in town.

A year later, Miriam and her three kids found a new handsome young army captain. He was stationed in Beer Sheva and fell in love with her. After seeing each other for a little while, they got married. They moved to a nice home in town. Unfortunately, not long after they settled in their new home, the army captain died in an automobile accident. Miriam returned to England with her three children and one more baby on the way.

Life in Beer Sheva was difficult. Many young couples who had moved from large towns around the country could not cope with the harsh conditions and either left town or separated. There were no good schools or playgrounds, so families with children could not move there. Most married men who worked in town left Friday afternoon to stay with their families and did not return to town until Sunday morning.

Most members of Solel-Boneh management belonged to the Mapay party, which was the middle-of-the-road ideological party. When it came time for the election of the municipality, Tuviyahu was at the head of the list to be mayor, and I was chosen to be number 11 on the list as a member of the City Council as well as a member of the advisory board of the local bank. In this way, I was able to get involved in the political life of the new town.

In addition, the Israeli Flying Club approached me and asked if I wanted to be the head of the club. It had no members in the organization yet, but I took the position seriously, because I wanted to learn to fly a plane. We needed a local airport, and I felt that I could help by establishing the first flying club in Negev.

Before starting any of the activities, the question arose about how we could raise money to start the club. I asked Tuviyahu for some support, but he turned me down. There were more urgent needs in Beer Sheva than the club, and I did not have any money to spare. After a while, I got an idea to organize a concert or dancing event. If patrons paid an entrance fee, we could raise some money for the club. Since there was no large hall to accommodate such an event, I requested that Tuviyahu let me use the old Turkish Town Hall next to the police station and the old mosque. Before we could start, it had to be cleaned first. I recruited some of my construction workers, and in no time, we had a clean beautiful space for our event.

I went to Tel Aviv and arranged for a well-known jazz band to come for a night. Because it was the first time Beer Sheva had had such an event, I was worried that if the new immigrants might not have enough money and I would not be able to sell all the tickets, and the whole project would collapse. I wanted to make it a dressy event and stated "evening attire only" in the invitation. I estimated that if I got at least 100 couples attending, I would be able to pay the expenses for the jazz band and have some money left over for the flying club.

To my surprise, I sold more than 200 tickets for couples. In fact, I had sold so many tickets that I was getting worried we might not be able to accommodate all the ticket holders in the dancehall. It was a hot night when the jazz band arrived. We planned to open the doors at 8:00 p.m. I placed three of my foremen at the hall entrance to make sure no one entered the building without a ticket. To my surprise and astonishment, a large, beautifully dressed crowd entered the hall. The beautiful Hungarian and Romanian women wore long gowns and the men accompanying them were all well-dressed in suits. I could not believe my eyes. Most of these people lived in tents or in old Arab houses. I did not know where they had been keeping all these beautiful dresses and suits. It was just an unbelievable sight. I was thrilled; the bar in the dancehall was very crowded, the band was playing, and everyone was having a great time. I was standing at the door helping to control the crowd as they entered, so I hardly had time to spend inside the hall and enjoy the dancing. The jazz band was scheduled to stop playing at midnight, because they had to return to Tel Aviv; however, I gave them some additional money and they remained at the hall until two in the morning.

The whole thing was a huge success, and I had some cash left to start my Flying Club operation. When the club headquarters in Tel Aviv heard of my success, they demanded that the money I made should be sent to them and they would allocate some of the money to my Beer Sheva club. I was very upset, but to keep our relationship going, we settled on 50 percent of the money going to the headquarters. During next six months, I never received any support from Tel Aviv and lost interest in the flying club. I had too many things on my mind to fight with the flying club management for funding.

The construction of the housing project was moving along. The water pipes had been laid in the ground and the sewage systems were being constructed. Doors and windows were installed in all the houses and all of them were painted with shiny white paint. It was a wonderful sight, and I was very proud of my accomplishments. Although not all of the houses had been completed yet, we decided to start moving people from the tent camps into the new homes. My crew of workers, which had reached nearly 100 men, was grumbling about their pay. They wanted a raise. Tuviyahu, who was the final decision maker, was holding back, so I had difficulty in keeping the production up.

However, the day finally came for the official opening of the new town. Golda Meir, who was the Minister of the Interior, came, as well as the Foreign Minister, David Ben-Gurion, Tuviyahu, and many other dignitaries. But about ten minutes before the beginning of the opening ceremony, my foreman came to me and said he and the workers were not going to participate. They were going to walk out and go on strike. I was in shock. Tuviyahu was not available for discussion, so I had no choice but to promise them a considerable raise on the spot. It was the only way I could avoid a very embarrassing situation at the opening ceremony. Luckily, no one realized what was going on, the opening went on, and it was a great success. That day, the first families from the tent camps moved into shining white new dwellings.

I was elated. Each day, more houses were constructed and more immigrants moved into the completed houses. As the new houses were inhabited, the small gardens around them began to blossom. Each day as I passed them on my way to the site, I was proud of my accomplishments.

One morning as I was inspecting the properties, I noticed smoke coming from one of the apartments. As I approached, I could see that the door in the front entrance was blackened. Anxiously, I rushed in, thinking that the house was on fire. To my shock, I saw that there was a pot atop a fire in the middle of the floor in the apartment, which was billowing out thick clouds of smoke throughout the apartment. The freshly painted white walls were covered in dark black soot, chickens were running around, a small goat was stationed in the bathroom, and the bathtub was filled with straw. Apparently, the new tenants who had come from Yemen had never lived in a home like this before. The whole apartment was blackened by smoke, the floor was dirty as though it had never been cleaned, and overall the apartment was a real mess. We called the city's social workers, who came to teach the Yemenite family how to maintain and care for this type of dwelling. Keeping a house in Israel was certainly different from the customs they were used to practicing in Yemen. A few weeks later, I sent some of my painters to the apartment and, with a fresh coat of paint; they restored it back to new condition.

Half a century later, when I visited Beer Sheva in 2001, there were nearly 180,000 inhabitants. Among all the new buildings, I had a hard time finding any of the houses I had built in 1949. I could hardly recognize the site. At first, I could not find my housing project, because by then it had already been designated as the "old town" section. However, I was delighted to find that each one of the houses had beautiful little fences surrounding it, newly attached extension rooms, trees and flowers planted in the gardens, and impressive paved roads. It was such a beautiful sight, and I was very proud to have been one of the pioneers who made it all possible.

As the years had passed, more and more homes had been built, and new housing projects were developed around the area. Each project had its own style. Some houses were constructed with red tiled roofs, while others had simple flat roofs. Our construction style had been more minimal and, in a way, it was unattractive in comparison to the newer developments. However, it had fulfilled the urgent need to house the tent dwellers; the focus had been to relocate the families of new immigrants from tents into places they could call home. It had laid the groundwork for all that was to follow. Now the immigrants had all settled in and created a new town of their own. After we had built that section of town, David Ben-Gurion had arrived for a visit and decided to diversify the architecture in the new town. Right after his review, we stopped building houses with our method of construction, using the LeTourneau equipment. Unfortunately, I had to let my men go, and the project, which I had loved, came to an end.

Luckily, my new assignment was already set: I was being assigned to build a new ceramic factory in town. When it was finished, I would be the manager of the factory. I brought some of the men who had assisted me with construction at the Beer Sheva site to the ceramic factory. The plan for the factory was a very large plant that would supply bathtubs, toilet bowls, tiles, and sinks for the new buildings in the south territory. I was very excited about this opportunity.

Meanwhile, Florence was getting busy in the hospital. One of her patients was a Droze from the northern Galilee town. He had been working for the Israeli army searching for land mines and, during one search; a land mine had exploded and hit him. In order to save his life, they had had to amputate one of his legs. He stayed in the hospital for about three months. Although he could walk, he always wanted to be served by a nurse. Florence felt sorry for him and always helped him, although they never could communicate because he spoke only Arabic. When the time came for him to leave the hospital, a group of handsome Droze men from his family came to take him home. One of the men brought a basket full of grapes and other fruits from Galilee to give to Florence for helping the young Droze. They told her, "It's only for you, so don't share it with anyone." This was a treasured gift, because no fruits could be found at that time in Beer Sheva.

On another occasion, a young girl was brought to the hospital with a hand that was already discolored and swollen from gangrene. She was in great pain and crying. Yedidia, the surgeon, wanted to amputate her arm immediately, but Florence and the other nurses pleaded for him to wait. They felt that they could nurse the hand back to health so the girl would not have to have it amputated. He insisted on starting the operation, but the nurses told Yedidia that they would not enter the operating room to help him if he did. He had no choice, so the girl was left alone to be cared for by the nurses. They cared for her day and night for a whole week trying everything they could to restore her health. By the end of the week, the swelling had finally subsided and her hand had gone back to normal. They had been able to save her hand and arm from being amputated.

It also happened that the daughter of Golda Meir was rushed to the hospital from her kibbutz south of Beer Sheva, suffering from acute pain. By the time she was brought to the hospital, she had already fallen into a coma. Golda Meir stayed with her several days. Florence continuously attended her daughter, and Florence and Golda got to know each other. Golda had also come from the U.S. to Israel, and she was happy to find a young American girl like Florence working as a nurse in a place like Beer Sheva. Golda's daughter's condition was getting worse, so they had to fly her by helicopter to the Hadassah Hospital in Jerusalem. Fortunately, she recovered and was able to return to the kibbutz in the Negev. Some time later, when Florence and I were celebrating the official opening of the new town, Golda tapped Florence on her shoulder and asked, "Hello, Florence. Do you remember me? We met in the hospital." Of course, Florence remembered Golda -- she was an important minister -- but Golda was very unpretentious and lovely to speak to.

The winter in Beer Sheva was very mild. Seldom did it rain and during the days, it was usually warm. However, at night it would get pretty cold, so we heated our one room with a small kerosene heater. We lived near a wadi, which is a dry creek, and awakened one morning to what sounded like a train passing by. We rushed outside and saw a tremendous wave of water rushing over the creek. It was several feet high and close to our house. The skies were clear, and we could not understand where the water was coming from. Later on we were told that, miles away in the mountains of Jordan, a heavy rain had started the flood and, without warning, it had flowed down, drowning animals and men. Luckily, for us, the rush of water stopped as quickly as it had started and the creek was dry again.

During the winter, the main water line from the north of Israel from the Sea of Galilee was being installed all the way to Beer Sheva and the south. A deep trench was dug for a six-foot water pipe, which passed next to our house. The heap of dug–up earth was all around and practically covered the entrance to our house, making it immensely difficult to walk in or out of the door. It was especially difficult for Florence, because she had to walk next to the trench when she returned at midnight from her hospital shift. She had to put on boots and carry a small flashlight just to navigate her way in or out. There were no streetlights at the time, so I usually went to meet her at the hospital to accompany her home. One night, she had to leave the hospital early. As she was walking in the dark through the slippery mud, she lost her balance and fell into the deep trench. Finally, after struggling to grab onto the slick walls of the trench, she managed to pull herself out. When she arrived at the apartment, I could not recognize her. She was covered from head to foot in a thick coat of mud. I could hardly see her white uniform. It took her some time to clean up, because our water tank was practically empty, but it did not stop her from going to the hospital the next day. During her time working at the hospital, she never missed a day's work even if she was sick.

Several new small restaurants had opened in town. There were also a few food stores, a barbershop, and an outdoor movie theater with long benches. The ground in the theater was unpaved and never swept, so you always had to trek through several inches of sesame nutshells that had been spit out by people who were watching movies.

Tuviyahu was constantly on the lookout for promising industries so he could attract new settlers to his town. I traveled with him several times to the surrounding desert mountains, looking for minerals that could be exploited. When we explored, we were always digging for samples. On one venture, he found some areas, which had kaolin rock, which was a basic ingredient for the ceramic industry Tuviyahu realized that he could help provide this raw material to the ceramic factory, which we were in the process of building. We brought in a bulldozer to start clearing the topsoil and uncovered a large deposit of kaolin. In time, it became the main source of that material for all the ceramic factories in Israel. Further, down south near Eilat, Tuviyahu started searching for copper. It was known that five thousand years back the Egyptians had mined copper in that area and developed a large primitive copper industry, which had supplied them with the copper they used to make tools for building and cooking. Not long after Tuviyahu's visit, a mining shaft was opened there and the copper ore was mined and shipped overseas. For years, the mine produced large quantities of ore and employed many workers. When the price of copper fell, however, the mine was closed, because it could not compete in the world market.

Aside from short visits to Tel Aviv or Jerusalem, Florence and I had not taken a real vacation. As a matter of fact, I had never gone on a real vacation. I was too busy working and too caught up in doing what needed to be done. But now that I was married to Florence, she told me that taking vacations was a part of life and she convinced me to take one. It was very difficult for me to leave the piles of work I had to do in Beer Sheva, but I made arrangements for someone to cover my absence. I had a jeep, so we decided to travel north to the Sea of Galilee and stay in a hotel in Tiberius.

We found a small hotel near the shore where we went to swim each day and traveled throughout the beautiful hilly country. The Kinert, which is the Sea of Galilee, is a small beautiful lake between mountains with sky blue water. We visited the Jordan River and the water source above the Kinert, which starts in the mountains of Lebanon and is covered with snow for most of the year. Then we visited Nazareth with its beautiful churches, ate in several Arab restaurants, and bought some gifts in the bazaar. The weather was beautiful -- a big change from the hot, desert weather we were used to having in Beer Sheva. Each day, I walked to the post office and called home to see how my project in Beer Sheva was progressing. To my relief all was going well. The post office was a small one-room office with two employees. One day when I was trying to send an urgent message by telegram to some associates in Tel Aviv, the middle aged clerk could not understand what I wrote. He got upset with me and tore my message up into pieces in front of me. I was standing there with Florence, and I could not believe what he had done. I was outraged. I called for the supervisor to write a complaint that would be forwarded by the next day to the general post office in Haifa.

At about 6:00pm, the clerk came to the hotel holding my letter of complaint in his hands. He fell on his knees in front of Florence and me, crying and pleading for me to forgive him and take the complaint back. If it reached his supervisors in Haifa, he would definitely be fired and he had six children at home to support. He asked for my forgiveness and told me that he had made a terrible mistake. I did not want to listen, but Florence asked me to forgive him for the sake of his family, so I did. I took the complaint and tore it up in front of him. He kissed my hand and thanked me profusely. The sight of a grown man weeping on his knees before me left an indelible impression.

One morning we decided to go fishing. We went down to the lake and saw a young man using an unusual technique. He had a string at one end and a fishing hook with a worm on the other. I watched curiously, as he tied a loose stone near the end of the hook and threw it into the lake. As the stone dropped out in the water, the hook sunk further down into the water as well. A few minutes later, he pulled the string back up and, to our amazement, caught a fish. In the next hour, we watched as he caught several other fish. I did not have a fishing rod, so I decided to do the same. I went to the hardware store, bought some string and fishing hooks, and drove over to the mountain next to the lake to dig for worms. Florence was with me, but she declined my invitation to participate in the worm search. After I found nearly two dozen worms, we rushed down to the lake. The fisherman was just finishing up. He had a dozen fish and was ready to leave. Before he did, I asked him to show me his technique. He showed me how and left.

While Florence sat on the beach, I took off my shoes and tested it out. Somehow, I could not get the stone to stay on the string. The hook was not sinking into the water. I tried using this strange method of fishing and gave up after two hours with no success.

The time was coming close for our return to Beer Sheva. The next day was Christmas Eve. Florence wanted to visit Nazareth and be there at that evening to watch the Christmas Mass. Unfortunately, I got an urgent call from Beer Sheva because a integral piece of equipment had completely broken down, and so we had to return and missed out on the Christmas Mass. It could have been a once in a lifetime experience, especially for Florence, who loved visiting churches wherever she went. But all in all, it was a wonderful vacation. It was my first vacation, and I had enjoyed every moment of it.

Florence and I returned to work and got back into our busy schedules. The new ceramic factory, Harsa, was being built and needed a water tower. After deliberation with Tuviyahu, we decided to transfer the large metal tanks above the old Turkish railroad tower near the old railroad station to the ceramic factory. The cranes, which I had on site, were much too short for the job, so I had to build extensions so that we could reach and lift the water towers from the high stone tower to Harsa. It took several days to build this extension.

In order to separate the tank from the tower, we placed the two cranes on each side of it, wrapped steel ropes around them, and lifted the tank, which weighed over two tons. We were eventually able to lower the tank onto the ground. The second tank was corroded and collapsed in midair, sliding off the steel rope and crashing to the ground. Luckily, we all escaped and none of us was hurt. Even the cranes managed to escape without getting damaged. The undamaged tank was moved and brought over to the new tower. Each time I have visited Beer Sheva, I have driven back to the ceramic factory site and seen that my tank is still perched high above the tower. Every time I see it, I am reminded of that day we escaped death when the water tank collapsed.

For a while, Florence had been complaining that she was feeling ill. Every morning, it started all over again until she decided she would have to see a doctor. After her visit, she told me that she was not sick, but just was pregnant. Although we had been married for three years, somehow I had not thought of starting a family. I had been so preoccupied with my work and career, and not given it much thought. However, I loved the idea of having a child and becoming a father.

Before having the baby, Florence planned to visit her parents in New York. She would return to Beer Sheva before the birth and have the baby in Israel. It took some time for her to get an exit visa because of the strict regulations set for people leaving Israel. She wanted to buy an airline ticket using her own Israeli money, rather than asking her mother to pay for her ticket. It took months for her to convince the authorities that she had the right to buy her own airline ticket using her own Israeli money, but eventually she got it. I accompanied her to the airport, and she took off to New York.

While she was gone, I started to renovate our one-room apartment by extending the veranda, cleaning up the yard, and improving the plumbing and water systems. Florence expected to stay with her parents in New York for several months, so I had plenty of time. While in New York, she had a wonderful reunion with her large family and many of her friends. However, she still found that she was not feeling well. She went to her doctor and gynecologist, who told her that she had a bad case of pregnancy toxemia due to her poor diet in Israel. They advised her to remain in the United States for the remainder of her pregnancy. It was a surprise for the both of us. I did not want her to be without me when she had the baby, especially since she was sick, so I made arrangements to join her in New York. I made temporary arrangements with Tuviyahu to have someone fill in for me at the new ceramic factory, which was progressing nicely, and with a few personal effects, I left for New York.

168

Chapter 6 - Beer Sheva

Young immigrants waiting for their Home

Temporary Tent Camp

Digging the First Foundation in the New City of Beer Sheva

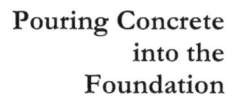

Pouring Concrete into the Foundation

169

Chapter 6 – Beer Sheva

Assembling the Inside Forms

Placing the Outside Form on
Top of the Inside Form

Pouring Concrete
On top of the House

First Cast House

Chapter 6 – Beer Sheva

Placing on the Second Floor

Beer Sheva Construction Group

Golda Meir's visit

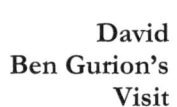

David Ben Gurion's Visit

Chapter 6 – Beer Sheva

Minister Moshe Sharet's Visit, Tuviyahu and Me

David Ben Gurion with Solel-Boneh Management Personnel

David Tuviyahu, First Mayor of Beer Sheva

Mr. Rubik Danilovich, Current Mayor of Beer Sheva

Chapter 6 – Beer Sheva

The First Housing Project

Beer Sheva Visit 1994 - Updated Photo

Aerial View of Beer Sheva 1994

CHAPTER SEVEN
SETTLING IN AMERICA

Returning To America, Adjusting To a New Life

When I arrived in New York, I found Florence different in size. She was in her eighth month of pregnancy and living in her parents' home in upper Manhattan. Florence's mother, Hanna, received me with open arms and made me feel at home. The apartment was on the sixth floor and had three bedrooms, a living room/dining room, a small kitchen, and a bathroom.

Both of Florence's parents worked. Her father, Max, was a glazer and had a glass and shades store across the street from the apartment. While Max worked outside installing glass windows in the neighborhood, Hanna cut and sewed shades and tended the store.

Max was an introvert, so I hardly had an occasion to speak to him. Hanna, on the other hand, was the opposite. She was a jolly, warm, and giving person, a great cook, and full of energy. All in one day, she would work in the store, shop for food, and cook great meals. She loved to entertain all her relatives and made big meals on the weekends and holidays. Whatever she cooked always turned out to be a feast.

Max was a hard-working man who worked without an assistant. Even when installing window glass on a high floor with half of his body sticking out of the window, or when actually working from the outside of the window, he managed to do the work alone. This was dangerous and hard work; however, he did this for years without complaining.

He had few pleasures in life, which included smoking cigars at home against the objection of everyone in the family. He liked to read the Yiddish paper every day, and took a coffee break at the diner next door to his store every morning. In the evening, he would watch television or read the paper. He and Hanna seldom went on vacations or holidays. The house was always full on the weekends with relatives coming over to eat meals, which Hanna had prepared between her working days.

Florence and I had a small room next to a long corridor, which housed three bedrooms. We prepared one bedroom for our future child. We went to buy a crib and bassinet for washing along with a few pieces of furniture for the baby.

Florence did not feel well, and the doctor warned her that she might have a difficult birth. When I left Israel, I had not taken much money with me, and we were running out of cash. Florence's parents were unable to support us, and Florence had to go to the hospital emergency room for medical attention.

When the time came for her to have the baby, she went into the hospital's general wardroom. She had a very difficult time and was in the hospital for two weeks before she finally gave birth to our son, David, on December 11, 1951.

Because it had taken so long, Florence was very sick and David was born with pneumonia. To make sure that they were okay, Florence and David had to stay in the hospital for another week.

When they finally got better and were ready to come back home, we put David in the spare room next to ours. My plans to return to Israel had to be postponed because I had to stay with Florence and David. The little money I had brought with me was running out, and there was no source of income to support us except for our free rent and food from Hanna. We had barely any money. It was shocking for me, and I was beside myself. I had never been in such a predicament, especially since I had been such a big shot in Israel. I found myself lost in this new environment with no friends or relatives besides Florence's family.

To make matters worse, I had no idea how I could find a source of income. At first, I thought that I would be able to work in the construction industry, but my English was not good enough for me to supervise people. I started looking in the newspaper every morning in the "Help Wanted" pages, but I could not find any openings suitable for me. There were, however, many job openings for engineers and draftsman, so I decided to search for a job as a draftsman. I had good knowledge of supervising draftsman and engineers, but had not worked on a board myself for many years, so I decided to polish my drafting knowledge first. I went downtown to the bookstore for technical information and bought a drafting instruction book, a cheap drafting board, and some drafting instruments. Every day, I sat for hours polishing my handwriting and proper numbering skills. Technically, I knew the subject, and after two weeks of practicing exercises for ten hours each day, I decided to apply for a job as a mechanical draftsman.

The whole situation depressed me. Just a few months before, I had been a big chief managing many engineers and large projects in Israel, and now I was starting all over again as a draftsman in a foreign country.

I dressed up in my best suit, polished my shoes, bought a new tie, and went in for an appointment with an engineering company that was advertising for a mechanical draftsman at $75 per week. In my resume, I did not mention that I was an engineer or manager. I just wrote that I had been a mechanical draftsman working in Israel in an engineering office. To my surprise, after a short test and just one interview, I was accepted by a large engineering company in midtown called Knappen Tibbetts Abbett McKarthy Engineers.

There must have been several hundred engineers and draftsman working at the company, and I was assigned to a group that designed material handling equipment for coal transporting conveyors, which were loaded from a railroad station onto a large ship docked at a pier on the waterfront in South Louisiana. There were nine engineers and draftsman in my group. I had a very nice drafting board, but I had to buy my own drawing instruments, and I was given the responsibility of developing the details for part of the project. My boss was a young Jewish chief engineer who helped me settle down.

My early experience of being a draftsman was coming back to me. I enjoyed working on the board solving technical details for the project. At night, after bathing David and having dinner, I worked on my drawing board at home for hours to solve some of the problems I had encountered in the office during the day. When I started the next morning in the office, I progressed very quickly with my drawings, and my supervisor was very surprised to see my progress, not realizing that I had solved the problems at home the night before.

All the draftsmen and engineers were very well dressed, so I also bought a new suit, several ties, and a new pair of shoes. I changed my image from being that of a construction worker to that of an office man.

To my surprise, I enjoyed the work and my new friends in the office. Each day, a group of five of us draftsmen and a few of the engineers walked to a small French restaurant a few blocks away from the office for a light inexpensive lunch during our lunch hour. It was a very noisy and busy restaurant, but eating lunch there together added to the pleasure of working. Each day, I looked forward to working to gain experience and make some money to keep us going.

Florence was recuperating slowly from David's difficult birth and he was also recuperating from his pneumonia, but things were settling down. Unfortunately, David did not sleep well during the night. He kept Florence and me running in and out of his room most nights, and we were worn down.

My company in Israel was calling me often to find out when I was coming back to Beer Sheva. However, I did not have an answer for them, because Florence and David needed me and I could not return to Israel at that time. The salary I had was small and hardly kept us going. We did not have health insurance and our medical expenses were high. I was looking for additional work at night to supplement my salary.

My work at the office ended at 5:00 p.m., so I searched for work I could do in the evening. I came across an ad for driving school instructors at a school, which was close to my office. On my lunch hour, I applied to work there in the evenings from 5:30 to 7:30pm. I was accepted, and the pay was $5 an hour plus tips.

Right after finishing my drafting job, I would rush to the driving school where my student would be waiting. It was easy work for me, and the $5 an hour plus the tip of $2 to $3 added another $60 to $75 per week to the $75 I received from my drafting job. It was considerable, and Florence and I kept our expenses down. She kept records of all her expenses, and I kept just enough money in my pocket for daily expenses. Medical and hospital expenses for Florence and David were high, but since the rent with my in-laws was free, we were doing fine with the extra money I made as a driving instructor.

My company in Israel continued to inquire about my return, but I still could not leave Florence and David at this stage in the condition they were in. In six months, I received a raise from my engineering job from $75 to $90 a week. I stopped my evening job working as a driving instructor, but I desperately wanted to improve our financial conditions.

The thought occurred to me that if I could invent an item that answered some specific need, I might be able to sell it to a marketing company. Feeding David with a spoon was always a difficult project for me, and if I could invent a swiveling spoon, that stayed upright no matter how it was moved, it would be easier to carry the food on the spoon directly into the child's mouth. By then we had saved a few hundred dollars, so I suggested to Florence that I could spend some of the money to make a sample spoon, patent it, and sell it to a baby food manufacturer.

I rented a space on the fourth floor of a small workshop on Canal Street, and after working hours and on Saturdays, I would rush to the shop to build my baby spoon samples. It took me three months to accomplish this task. I made a working sample, which I fed David with, and made a nice package to market it with. I registered the name Margolin Products for my invention, and with my meager savings, I applied for a patent and then I mailed several hundred promotional letters to baby food manufacturers and advertising agencies. I also mailed additional samples that I had made, but unfortunately, no one showed interest in my invention. All along, Florence had supported my effort, even though I was spending money, which we could not spare. With all the work and money I had spent, it was difficult for me to accept the fact that I had failed.

Two years had passed and my company in Israel decided to open an office in New York to buy machinery and equipment for the growing industry in Israel. Hiller Dan, who was my boss at Solel-Boneh in Israel, came to New York and offered me a job running an office with another Israeli financial manager. I would be the technical buying manager and Mr. Weissberg from Israel would be responsible for the financials. The salary was much better than that of my present job with the engineering office, offering in the range of $100 to $150 per week. I was elated. I was going to work with my old Israeli company in New York again and buy machinery and equipment for the various manufacturing companies in Israel. This job was just the job I had been dreaming of. For the time being, the question of my returning to Israel was postponed.

All this time, our house in Beer Sheva was closed. All the equipment that Florence had brought, including the refrigerator, washing machine, and stove, had been placed in storage with our personal effects. This was a great loss to us and a painful reminder for Florence. I requested that my father sell all these items and get all of our other personal effects into a warehouse, and he did. It was very difficult for him because, besides bookkeeping, he never was involved in any other activities that required packing, moving, or selling. I did not follow the matter, because I did not want to embarrass my father. It was painful for Florence to lose all her worldly goods, which had been so difficult for her to acquire and ship to Israel in the first place.

Since our income had finally improved and stabilized, we decided to move out of Florence's parents' home and into a small rental apartment on 100th Street and West End Avenue. It was a two-bedroom apartment on the sixteenth floor with a dining room and a small kitchen. We took out a loan to buy new furniture and were very happy to be on our own. David was growing up to be a charming little boy. He was very active and kept Florence occupied.

Meanwhile, my new job kept me very busy. At times, I had to travel, inspect new products, and negotiate with the machinery suppliers or the equipment manufacturers from various Solel-Boneh companies in Israel. From time to time, I had visitors from managers in Israel such as Hiller Dan, the innovator who had helped expand Solel-Boneh from building construction company to a giant industrial enterprise. During the last five years under Hiller Dan, Solel-Boneh had become the leading force in Israel's industrial development and had more than 25 manufacturing plants in various parts of the country.

During Hiller Dan's visit to New York, I spent some time reviewing our relationships with suppliers with him. I also spent time shopping for his and his wife's personal needs. Whenever he needed money for his expenses, we gave it to him from our bank account. Through the years, all Solel-Boneh management claimed that their salary was the same as ours (the lower ranking management). However, somehow they managed to build beautiful, well-furnished homes for themselves, while the rest of us workers did not. I never found out how the high-ranking management had the money to build their expensive homes on a salary, which they claimed was equal to ours.

Besides Hiller Dan, I had one of my previous managers who ran all the stone quarries of Solel-Boneh. The company was called Even-

Vesid Stone, which meant "lime" in English. I had worked for this company in Israel for a year as their technical manager. The director's name was Kav-Venaki. He was very a likeable man. I had heard that some years earlier, he had had a stomach operation and most of his intestines had been removed. However, he had survived and was able to lead a normal life except that he had to eat very sparingly. When he visited our home, Florence had to cook special meals for him. During his visits, he shopped mostly at Macy's for appliances and personal goods. Sometimes Florence accompanied him, and like the other high-level managers, he too had no shortage of funds to buy all these goods on the "meager" salary, which he was supposed to have been living on.

Our third visitor was old Margolin. Although his name was like mine, he was not a relative. He claimed that he was, but he really was not. An old bachelor, he was one of the founders of Solel-Boneh and only lived for the company. He never had any interest in anything besides Solel-Boneh. He lived in a single room in Haifa, had no car, wore old clothes, and was always looking for ways to save money for the company.

I remember one of his visits to a large stone quarry near Jerusalem, where I was responsible for managing the machinery. We were having an inspection tour, and while walking along, he picked up an old bent rusted nail, showed it to me, and said, "Efraim, you should take care of these old nails. You know they came all the way from overseas, traveling in boats to ports, then in boxes to warehouses, and then to your storage facility, taking part in building your factory. Then they get bent and rusted lying on the ground waiting for you to pick them up and use them again. So please, whenever you see an old nail, pick it up and use it again." Of course, I said yes to Margolin, but I did not bother to follow his unreasonable talk. That was the nature of old Margolin.

Nevertheless, he had a great influence on the company. In time, Solel-Boneh management recommended that Margolin, the old bachelor, get married and settle down. They found him a nice younger woman, and against his will, he got married and settled down in a small apartment in Haifa. He had a son, became a normal homebody, and was less active in the management of Solel-Boneh.

During his visits to the United States, he always came to our home in New York. He loved Florence's cooking, and he loved watching television. After dinner, he would stay with us until two or three in the morning before going back to his hotel. Every visit he made wore us down. Nevertheless, he was a wonderful human being who deeply cared for people as well as his company, Solel-Boneh. He always told me that he expected me to be a part of the next generation of management once I returned back to Israel.

Our office in New York was called Solcoor. I was buying equipment and traveling around the country visiting various manufacturers who had been bought out, transferred to Israel, and established a new industry in Israel. Time was passing, and I had already been working with Solcoor for four years. However, my salary was practically the same as when I had started. Whenever I asked for a raise, I was always told that I would be returning to Israel soon and, therefore, did not need a raise.

The longer I stayed in the States, the more I felt I wanted to remain in the States. The opportunities with Solcoor were unlimited, and I wanted to progress, but it was not clear in my mind how I would augment our income. Luckily, Florence found a secretarial job with a small Jewish organization and worked three full days a week while David went to kindergarten, so our financial condition was improving.

American Technion Society, New Job

A friend of mine who worked for the American Technion Society, which supports the Technion Israel Institute of Technology in Haifa Israel where I was a student at the Technion High School at the age of 14, approached me and told me that he was planning to leave his position. He had been the technical director of the society, but was leaving because he had gotten a better job as the director of a large hospital in the city. He suggested that I apply for his job at the Technion Society. In fact, he even recommended me to the Technion Board, so I was invited for an appointment. The offices of Technion were just across from the Metropolitan Museum on 80th Street and 5th Avenue in an old five-floor mansion.

I felt like a traitor to Solel-Boneh and Israel by going for the job, but I was beginning to realize that if I was going to stay in America permanently, I would have to give up my future in Israel. It was a very difficult decision to make. I loved working in the U.S. and was finally feeling comfortable after years of hardship adjusting to my new environment. It had taken years to become part of this new society and feel as comfortable in the U.S. as I had felt in Israel.

Becoming an American was a very slow and painful process. My thinking had to change, my relationships with people had to change, and it was a new life that was completely different than what I had had before. It was painful to think of losing my Israeli identity and becoming an American citizen. But no matter how long I was away, part of me would always be Israeli. Over time, I had lost some of my identity, but I knew I would never lose it completely.

I had several interviews with members of the executive board. They were outstanding industrialists and were important members within the Jewish community who were committed to Israel and to building the Technion Engineering School on Mount Carmel in Haifa. Most of the members of the board were large donors and active fundraisers for the institution. They felt that Technion had a great future and role in the development of science and technology in Israel and believed that it could help Israel become one of the most critical industrial centers in the Middle East.

Most members of the Technion Society were engineers, scientists, attorneys, and heads of various industries around the country. I was very impressed by these great people and thrilled by the opportunity to associate with them. I felt extremely lucky when the board accepted me for the position of technical director for the society. The best part about being accepted for the job was the salary they offered me, which was nearly double my salary with the Israeli Solcoor Company.

I was shown my office on the fifth floor of the old mansion facing the Metropolitan Museum. As a matter of fact, I had a great view of the museum and its American flag from my window. I had a large old mahogany desk that was situated right in front of my window, and the walls of my room had impressive wood paneling. The executive director introduced me to the five employees in my department. Bill Schwartz, my boss, took a liking to me from the first day we met. It made me happy to have a boss who liked me when I was starting out in my new job. Florence was very excited about my new position, especially since my salary had greatly improved our standard of living.

My job entailed several duties. First, I was responsible for purchasing instruments and laboratory equipment for the new facilities, which Technion was building on Mount Carmel. The new engineering and science building was growing very fast, so I had to purchase and ship equipment to Haifa. There were three women who worked with me in the purchasing department who helped me accomplish these tasks.

Besides purchasing vital equipment, I also assisted the board by recruiting professors for the institution, which gave me the opportunity to meet with many outstanding academic professors and researchers in various scientific fields. I managed a lot of the correspondence between the United States and Israel.

My secretary was a very accomplished writer and a fast typist. Because my English was still lacking, she handled all of my correspondence and made sure that all of it was perfect. Because there was a continuous flow of visitors arriving, primarily Technion scientists and engineering professors who had come to study or participate in meetings or conferences in the U.S., I was extremely busy arranging their visits to various universities.

While working for Technion, I also initiated several programs to help develop our relationship with our members who were industrialists and Israelis. One of my programs focused on bringing young graduates from Technion to the United States to get experience working in America. I received authorization from the state department for the program and, during the next five years, I succeeded in bringing more than 100 young Technion graduates to America to work in a wide range of factories, which were generally owned by our society members. The program was incredibly successful. The young engineers were able to acquire the latest methods and skills in American manufacturing and apply them to Israel's growing industry.

Unfortunately, after living in the United States for two years, many of the engineers who participated in the program decided to remain in the States. Consequently, I had a lot of difficulty with the state department, which was insisting that these young engineers be sent back to Israel. We experienced several unpleasant encounters with the Immigration Department; however, some of the engineers were eventually permitted to remain in the United States. Ultimately, the program was discontinued.

In getting to know many of the society members, I recognized the potential they had to help Israel beyond just raising money for Technion. I suggested that the board allow me to organize a consulting service. The program I developed would help Israeli manufacturers by providing free consultations to help improve Israel's developing industries. I formed several groups that were led by members that specialized in particular industries, so that Israeli visitors would have free technical assistance.

One case in particular which stands out was with an Israeli visitor called Seth Wertheimer who owned a small manufacturing company for carbide tools. When he came to my office, he wanted assistance selling his products in the United States and was seeking a contact in that industry. While looking through our list of members, I came across one in New Jersey that owned the Adamas Carbide Company. I scheduled a meeting for Wertheimer and learned that it went very well. They started working together and continued to work together through the years. The Wertheimer Company prospered, becoming one of the most outstanding companies in Israel, and eventually bought out the U.S. Adamas Carbide Company.

Another case, which I was very proud of, was a relationship I fostered between one of our members that owned a large air conditioning company and a company in Israel. I knew that Israel wanted to develop its manufacturing industry, so I suggested that the small appliance manufacturers in Israel start manufacturing air conditioners under our member's licensing. Our member agreed to donate the licensing income to Technion in Israel, which amounted to 5 percent of sales. In time, the deal went through and Technion earned a licensing fee for securing the deal in Israel. This fee, in fact, was a donation from one of our members to Technion. Several years later, when the fees had become quite substantial, the Israeli company came to us with the request to buy out their future payment in one lump sum. Because Technion needed the money, we agreed and decided on an incredibly satisfactory settlement. I was very pleased to have been responsible for closing this deal. On one hand, I had been able to help establish a large air conditioning industry in Israel and, at the same time, I had provided Technion with more income.

Every two years, Technion gave me a raise, so by this time my salary exceeded $18,000 per year. Our lifestyle was changing dramatically and getting better. We took short vacations, and most summers we were able to spend a week or two renting a cabin at Lake George and spending time there with my in-laws.

David was growing up to become an intelligent boy who was active all the time. However, we found that the school he attended in our district was very poorly run, so we decided to change it. The school next to my office on Madison Avenue and 80th Street was one of the best in town. I knew that the Israeli consulate had the right to choose what schools its citizens could join in the city, and since I was an Israeli citizen and had a good relationship with the Israeli consulate, I filled out an application for David for the school on Madison Avenue, and David was accepted. Every morning thereafter, I took David on the bus with me across town to his school, and Florence picked him up in the afternoon. For lunch, I crossed the street from my office and met up with them at the museum restaurant. Often, we also made visits to the museum exhibitions.

Our society was growing; we were getting more members as well as more funding. One of the largest donations we were given at the time was over $3 million from Girard Swoop, the past president of General Electric. He was introduced to Technion by his attorney, Mr. Abraham Tulin, who was an active member of the board. As a matter of fact, Mr. Swoop was not a practicing Jew. However, in his old age, he wanted to be connected to Israel, so Tunin introduced him to Technion. This was a great accomplishment for Mr. Tulin, who was one of the most outstanding attorneys in New York and an active member of the board of directors.

I also had the opportunity to recruit several professors to Technion and get acquainted with some great engineering and science teachers from various universities around the country. I enjoyed being associated with them and being able to expand my knowledge in many areas.

One of my most memorable experiences was with Professor Ollendorf, the professor in charge of the electrical engineering department at Technion. I knew him from when I was a student at Technion High School in Haifa. He had taught several courses about electricity, and they were the most exciting classes I ever had. He was originally from Germany, where he had been one of the most outstanding professors at Berlin University. When Hitler came to power, he immigrated to Israel and settled down at Technion in Haifa.

At the time, he was working on developing electronic eyesight for blind people. It was one of the earliest experiments using electronics, which had not been developed much at that time. His work was known around the world, and he came to the United States to present his work to the U.S. Department of Health. I accompanied him during our visit to Washington, and it was very exciting to participate in meetings at which he introduced his new development for improving eyesight-using electronics that were connected to the brain. He was looking for a grant to support his further work, so we spent two days in various departments meeting with top scientists that were reviewing Prof. Ollendorf's research in detail. It was very interesting to follow all of this discussion and learn about Prof. Ollendorf's ideas. I do not recall whether Prof. Ollendorf eventually received a grant for his research or not.

While I enjoyed the work and the exposure to the Technion Society and its members, I was getting restless. I had a difficult time adjusting to being under the control of the board, which thought of me as just a clerk and servant. I was beginning to feel degraded, especially at the board meeting where I had to be a waiter and serve them coffee. This part of my job was driving me crazy. Although it happened only once a month, I could not stand it and always dreaded it. I was also starting to become very jealous of these great, successful people who were supporting me with their donations. Everything else with my job was perfect, but I always felt like I was a lower class employee. The negative feelings I had were out of proportion to the benefits I received from the position.

I was becoming very unhappy, and Florence could not understand why. We had a good life, associated with wonderful people, lived on a good salary, and everything seemed fine, but I was unhappy. I wanted to be on my own and run my own life. I knew that I had no future to grow with the position I had at Technion. I was already in the top position I could achieve there, being the technical director of the organization, and I could have spent the rest of my life working with this wonderful organization if I wanted to. However, I could not see myself settling for this life. I knew that I could do more on my own.

I started looking for opportunities to start a business on my own while I was still working full time at Technion. I came across an opportunity to export automotive parts. I could do this by corresponding with companies overseas. So I set up an exporting company and corresponded with the companies at night. During the day, I hopped into a cab at lunchtime with my sandwich and drove to an office in midtown to arrange shipments of orders. It was a small business, and I spend a lot of time and effort with very little results. However, I felt that I was building some business for myself. After a year of trying and eating my lunches in a cab, instead of at the restaurant in the museum with Florence, I gave it up. There was no way I could make enough money running this small exporting business to make it worthwhile.

The second opportunity came to me when I met a friend of mine. He was starting a business selling liquor to travelers going overseas. If the travelers bought their liquor in advance and it was shipped to them back home, they could avoid paying tax. In order to advertise, the business had to print hundreds of thousands of pamphlets and distribute them to travel agents who got commissions on any purchases made through them.

Since most of this work could be done at night through correspondence by mail, I decided to partner with my friend. I invested a small sum of money printing pamphlets and setting up distribution to travel agents. There were hundreds of small orders for liquor, which were mailed by visitors overseas. I had to process the orders, register them, and pay commissions to travel agents all around the country. My partner took care of shipping orders to the buyers in the United States. It was a tremendous amount of bookkeeping work, which kept me working nights, but I was optimistic that it could develop into a successful business alongside my regular job at Technion.

To Florence's and David's dismay, I took a week of my vacation to visit Europe and distribute thousands of pamphlets to hundreds of travel agents in Vienna, Venice, Madrid, and Athens. I was so busy visiting all these travel agents and airline offices that I did not have a chance to sightsee in any of the beautiful towns. I was lonely and missed Florence and David, but I hoped that my sacrifice would eventually pay off. When I returned to New York, I was exhausted. I was happy to be back at my regular job at Technion and happy to be back to my regular routine. I had been neglecting Florence and David working two jobs, but I was convinced that I would eventually be able to develop a business for myself and be independent.

Unfortunately, after two years of hard work, I still was not producing much income relative to the amount of work I was investing, and we had to discontinue our business because the government had changed its liquor import regulations. Ordering liquor by mail and shipping it to customers in the U.S. was no longer permitted. Two years of my efforts went to waste and all of the time and money I had invested was lost. However, I was not discouraged. Somehow, I believed that I would eventually be able to develop my own business rather than being an employee.

David was getting older, so we registered him with the Boy Scouts of America. We became active parents with his troop. During the summer, we drove him to camp in New Jersey on Friday and picked him up on Sunday. He did very well and added badges to his uniform every year until he passed his master scout test. He specialized in fingerprinting and said he was planning to be an F.B.I. agent. I brought him to police stations so he could see how fingerprinting was done, and Florence and I bought him all the equipment he needed for his project.

During this period of time, Israel was developing its industry and looking to export its products to the United States. I had many visitors coming to Technion for advice and guidance, and I was continuing to introduce them to our members who would help them introduce their products to American markets.

One of these visitors was David Levy. He had come from Haifa and received an allocation from the government of Israel to establish an exporting company that would sell Israeli products in the United States. David visited my office several times, and we spent many hours planning how he would launch the marketing operation. While discussing this matter, he asked me whether I would be interested in leading the company and opening an office in New York. From such an office, I would help to import various products from Israel, market them in the United States, and raise money from members of the society to expand the new enterprise. I was very excited about this opportunity. I believed that I would finally have a company of my own that I could run and manage and, at the same time, I would be able to help Israel expand its industry.

David Levy was a very smart and sophisticated Israeli man, and I was comfortable having him as a partner. He would run the operation in Israel, while I would take care of business in New York. I decided to take the plunge and left Technion after seven wonderful years of working there with wonderful people.

This was a difficult decision to make; however, I felt that I would still be doing something patriotic by helping Israel. At the same time, it would open a new avenue for me and allow me to finally run my own company and become my own boss. Looking back, it was a naive decision, but at that time, I felt it was the right one. Florence was unhappy with my choice to leave Technion, but she went along with it, because she understood that I wanted to help Israel. She saw that it was an important undertaking, and we both knew that it was essential for the future of Israel's economic growth.

Starting My Own Company and Going Bust

Although it was a risk, Florence went along with my plan to leave Technion and start the new company. We called it Amtis Corporation. David and I recruited a number of Technion members and some of David's acquaintances to form a board of directors. They would invest a small amount of money for the operation and my salary, which was half of what it had been at Technion. I felt that I could handle this reduction in my salary because I thought it would be temporary. I did not see it being more than a year or so until it got better. At home, we had to tighten our belt and watch our expenses. Florence was not too enthusiastic about it, but she went along with it, because she too believed that it would get better in time.

The money that David had raised from the Israeli government together with the money we had put together from our board of directors was sufficient to last two years. We figured that after two years, we would be making enough money to pay me a full salary and expand our operations. David was recruiting Israeli manufacturers who were interested in exporting their products to the United States, while I searched for customers in the U.S. to develop a market for those Israeli products.

The first customers I found were members of the Technion Society. One in particular, Norman Sieden, owned a large sprinkler manufacturing company. For Norman, we searched for sprinkler parts, which could be manufactured in Israel. One of the parts was a brass pin that controls the flow of water into the sprinkler. After sending a sample of the part to Israel and evaluating how much it would cost, we found that we could offer a competitive price and received an order of 250,000 pins. The quality of the brass was very important as well as the accuracy of the parts. The parts had to be slightly oiled before being shipped in boxes so they would not oxidize while they were on the ship. We were very excited and happy to start importing such a large order.

It took us about two months to deliver the parts. When the day came for the shipment to arrive from Israel, we gathered to celebrate. During the ceremony, the factory inspector came with his micrometer to check the parts and found them satisfactory. We were all happy with the results, and we were expecting to get paid within two weeks and make some money from the deal.

A week after we delivered the pins, I got a call from Norman Sieden asking me to come to the factory because there was a problem with the parts. I rushed to the factory the next day, and the inspector opened several of the cases to show me that the pins had green mildew covering them. The manufacturers in Israel had forgotten to coat the brass pins with oil. While the parts were being shipped, the salty air from the sea had caused the brass pins to oxidize, and now they were covered with mildew. With this minute amount of mildew, the brass had swollen, so the pin could not fit into the sprinkler and could not be used. There were hundreds of boxes with pins, and when we opened them, we saw that they were all covered with mildew.

It was heartbreaking. All of the 250,000 parts were useless to our customers and we would not get paid. By this time, the Israeli manufacturer had already been paid, so we were stuck with all of these brass pins.

The owner of the business, Norman Sieden, felt very sorry for me. He tried to help me and suggested that I could recuperate some of the loss by selling the brass parts. To brass commodity buyers, they could buy it by weight and not as parts. We had to load the whole shipment on a truck and deliver it to a foundry. We got paid but, rather than making a profit, we found ourselves with a large loss. This was a bad start and a painful experience. David Levy, our board of directors, and I decided that I should travel to Israel to meet with the Israeli manufacturers and review their qualifications for manufacturing products for the U.S. market.

I stayed in Israel for a week. During this time, I saw many factories and evaluated whether they could be potential suppliers. Most were consumer product manufacturers. The problem was that their cost for manufacturing the products was too high to compete with U.S. manufacturers. I concluded that only small number of selected manufacturers in Israel could become our suppliers. An additional avenue, which we thought could be developed, was to introduce Israeli artwork to the U.S. market. We thought that this could possibly succeed, so I brought back some samples of jewelry and art from several known Israeli artists and, upon my return, set up a small showroom in my office.

My one-room office, at that time, was not sufficient for all the samples we imported. Besides, we planned to keep some forthcoming products in stock in New York, so I started to look for a space for our new office. I found a warehouse space on the fourth floor of a building on 24th Street. It was an empty loft with a large elevator. I liked the space because it had a whole wall of windows and was airy. I brought in a carpenter, and he built a corner office inside the warehouse for me. It was quite a cozy setup. Florence approved of the space, especially since there were so many windows. Unfortunately, there was not much of a view, because the windows faced the building across the street.

I was elated. Now I had a place to work and expand my operation. I was spending most of my time traveling and promoting the sale of our products, but it was still a hard sell, for several reasons. First, we had a limited number of products. Second, most of the prices from Israel were too high. However, I did find several customers, mostly for plastic products, and we placed new orders in Israel through David Levy, who was our representative managing the operation in Israel.

Each day, Florence spent some of her time typing my letters, paying bills, and answering the phone and now, I needed additional help, so I recruited a young bookkeeper and an all-around helper to manage the incoming and outgoing goods from Israel. Our sales were expanding, and we developed new products, which required some manufacturing and assembly in-house. I set up several assembly tables with drilling equipment and had a few temporary workers working on the line.

We were making progress and some money, but it was not enough to cover our expenses. Fortunately, David Levy had sent us some subsidized money from the government in Israel to promote our sales, and that kept us going until we could make enough money to cover our expenses.

I had been working very diligently to get a large order of crystal-looking plastic plates for the Woolworth chain of stores. This order could have put us on the map. The requirements were very specific: we had to ship a selected number of cartons to each store around the country and make special labels with bar coding, which I had to acquire from a bar coding company at a considerable cost. We sent special packaging instructions for the plastic plates to our manufacturer in Israel, and we carefully advised them how to wrap each plate securely in paper and pack them in strong cardboard boxes. The shipment had to arrive in October so it could be sold in the stores before Christmas. We were eagerly awaiting the arrival of our first large order.

Eventually a large truck arrived, and my bookkeeper and I started unloading the cartons and carrying them into the elevators. While moving them, I noticed that the boxes felt flimsy, and I could hear the sound of broken plastic rattling around inside. I was getting worried. By the time the whole shipment was unloaded into the warehouse, I realized that I had a big problem on my hands.

It seems that the factory in Israel did not follow our instructions for packaging the plastic plates properly in strong cardboard boxes with paper in between them. We realized that nearly all of the boxes had broken plastic plates and, of course, could not be shipped to Woolworth. By now, half of the warehouse was full of broken boxes and shattered plates, and none of the shipments could be made on time, and the order would automatically be cancelled. It was such a terrible loss.

Nevertheless, I hoped that we could possibly salvage some of the plastic plates and sell them to another customer. We started with two part-time assistants who helped open the cartons, remove the broken plates into one big heap, and pack the unbroken plates in new cartons. It took us over two weeks of working 24 hours a day to get through the shipment. We found that over half the shipment was broken. The loss was horrendous. We sold the broken plastic plates to a junk dealer and received 10% of their original value. I sold the rest to a local house wares store at half of our original price. The members of our board of directors were very upset. We all realized that Israel was not ready to export its products to the U.S. market.

There were other products in the warehouse, which we had difficulty selling because they were of poor quality. I was running out of money for our operation. My partner, David Levy, suggested that I come to Israel and present our case to the Israeli government, which had initially supported our effort to sell Israeli products in the United States.

While I was planning my visit, a large shipment of window glass from Israel arrived for our customer in Brooklyn. We delivered the shipment and hoped that we could use the payment to continue our operation. A few days after delivering our shipment, our customer called for us to come and see a problem they were having with the glass plates. I went to Brooklyn with great trepidation. When I got there, I saw that the crates were well made according to our instructions, and there was no breakage. I was relieved; however, it turned out that there was another problem. Our manufacturer in Israel had placed newspaper between the glass rather than special wax paper as we had instructed. Everything looked good at first, but on closer inspection, we saw that the print from the newspaper had left its imprint on the glass, and removing the newsprint would cost a fortune.

I was standing in front of the glass crates and felt like crying. After all, of the work I had put in to get the glass for Mrs. Bininfeld, who really wanted to help Israel, we had failed miserably, and it was heartbreaking. All was lost. However, in hearing of this damaged shipment, Mrs. Bininfeld felt bad for me. She said that she would take the shipment, sell the damaged imprinted glass for industrial purposes, and pay me when it was sold.

At that time, I realized that I had a big problem on my hands. I had run out of money and could no longer afford to pay for my operation, rent, salary, or telephone. My last hope was that my trip to Israel to meet with the Israeli government would help me and save our importing company, which we had started so enthusiastically with the blessing of the Israeli government.

I left Florence to manage our office and flew to Israel. It was winter, and the weather was rainy and cold. David Levy made a hotel reservation for me on the outskirts of Tel Aviv. We met in the hotel and planned our meeting with the various Israeli government agencies in Jerusalem.

My hotel room had no heat except for a small electrical heater, and I could not sleep because it was freezing cold. When I requested another room, I was told that all the rooms were the same, with only one electrical heater available. They gave me two more blankets. I bundled myself in the blankets and slept a few hours that night.

I planned to stay in Israel for a week. I checked in with Florence every morning on the phone. Some small orders were processed and shipped, and Florence and our young bookkeeper were taking care of things

Every morning after breakfast, I left for Jerusalem to meet with the government officials who were very pleasant and helpful. However, I could not get any positive action or commitment from them. All they did was refer me from one department to the next. They were all very polite and helpful, but there were no results. Two weeks passed with no progress. I told some of the officials that I needed to return to New York. They asked me to stay, saying that a decision and money were forthcoming. I was running out of money, so I called Florence and asked her to send me some money from our personal savings.

Two more weeks passed with no results. Back in New York, Florence was trying to fend off our creditors. When I called the office, Florence was not there. Then I called home, and she told me that one of our creditors had put us into receivership. She could not enter our office because it had been locked by the sheriff. As soon as I heard this bad news, I packed my bags and took the first plane back to New York. All my negotiations with the Israeli government had been of no use.

Florence was shaken up. Some of her personal effects were still in the office. My considerable inventory, which still had some value, was under lock and key, and I could not enter the warehouse. My largest creditors were my carton box manufacturer and my landlord. They placed us in this situation because they did not hear from me while I was in Israel. They thought that I had skipped the country and left them high and dry. I visited each of them and explained that I could pay them off as soon as I got into the warehouse and sold some of my inventory. I got a reprieve, opened the warehouse, and immediately sold most of my inventory to several of my customers for prices that were way below the cost, and so paid off most of the creditors.

With all of the financial difficulties I had had, our creditors and my board of directors were very understanding. They were sorry to see me in this situation, and the American goodwill attitude of "live and let live" helped me to survive this hard time.

I was now very depressed. My experiment of having my own business had failed miserably. I found myself without a business or a job, and I had lost a considerable amount of my small personal savings. I had made a grave mistake leaving my job at Technion. I was back where I had started years ago.

Looking For a New Job, Personnel Agency

Now I urgently needed a job and a source of income to support my family and pay my rent. I was fortunate that with all the difficulties I was going through, Florence understood me and my efforts to be on my own. To help out, she went to work as a secretary in a small office on Park Avenue. She had four jobs: working in the office, taking care of the house, cooking for us, and taking care of David and his schooling. Every morning, I spent time looking in the New York Times for a job.

First, I decided to look for a job as an engineer, salesman, or customer service representative. I prepared several hundred resumes and started mailing them out. To my dismay, I did not receive any replies. Whatever inquires I did receive did not offer the minimum salary I needed to make a living. After a month of mailing, phoning, and inquiring, I decided to approach employment agencies, which were the last option on my list. Some of the ads, which the agencies placed in the paper, outlined jobs that I could potentially fill.

I put on my best suit and visited some of the agencies. I was surprised to see that most of the agencies were located in beautiful offices and most of the personnel were young men and women. They all dressed very well and they looked very prosperous. I called one of the agencies, which had advertised for an engineer that fit my experience, and made an appointment with a young lady who sounded very pleasant and anxious to see me. She interviewed me, but once she started questioning me, I realized that she did not know anything about engineering. All her questions were not real inquiries about my professional experience. However, she sent my resume to the company in Long Island.

The next morning, she called me and set up an appointment for me to meet with the president of a manufacturing company in Long Island. I was very excited. I needed a job badly. Although the job was far out in Long Island, I decided to go. I dressed up well, put on my best tie, and took off with my old car to Long Island. It took me about an hour and a half to reach the plant. I got there early and was anxious to be interviewed.

I was given a form to fill out and sat down in the waiting room with two other men who were possibly applying for the same job. I was the last one to be called in by the president. It had been over two hours since I came in for the interview, and I was getting very nervous.

At long last, I was called in. The president was very busy on the phone and, at the same time, looking over my resume. When he finished his phone call, he turned over to me and said, "I am sorry. There must be some misunderstanding by the personnel agency. You are much too overqualified for this job, and I don't understand why they sent you over to me." I was sick to my stomach. I did not even have a chance to be interviewed. Spending all this time waiting there for nothing was terribly degrading. I drove back home very depressed. Florence was waiting anxiously for good news, and she too was quite upset to hear that the interview had been a failure.

Next, I read another personnel agency ad in the New York Times, which fit my background. Again, I dressed up in my best suit and left for an interview. The agency was located in a beautiful building downtown. It had a large waiting room with beautiful mahogany furniture, and it looked luxurious and expensive. Again, I filled out an application and, in a short while, I was called in by a young, well-dressed personnel manager. He sat me down next to him. I realized immediately from his questions that, like the previous interviewer, he had no knowledge of my profession. However, he said he had a job for me in New Jersey. While I was in his office, he faxed my resume to the company. A few minutes later, he informed me that the company in New Jersey wanted to see me the next day. From the description, he gave me of the job, it sounded very promising. The job was quite far away in New Jersey, but I did not care as long as I could start to work and make some money.

The next morning, I started early because I wanted to be sure that I got there on time. It took me about 2 hours of traveling in traffic, and I got lost. I was getting very jittery. Fortunately, I got to the factory a few minutes before my scheduled interview. The factory building was an old, dilapidated structure. The entrance to the factory was untidy, and the waiting room had four old, worn-out chairs next to a glass window. Behind a pane of glass sat an untidy-looking receptionist. Through the glass window, she handed me a form to be filled out. She hardly spoke to me. What an ugly receptionist, I thought, but I kept saying to myself that it did not matter, as long as I could get a good job. My unemployment check could barely keep me going. It was difficult for me to understand how, with all my experience, I had, I could not get a simple job quickly.

While waiting, I tried to read an old sports magazine with a dirty cover and waited patiently for my interview. By this time, the receptionist had left the glass window and time was passing.

After about an hour, the receptionist returned and told me that she was sorry, but her boss was busy and could not see me today. She said that I should come back tomorrow at the same time. I was beside myself. After all the time I had spent, all the hopes I had were gone. It was most depressing, especially facing Florence. She was waiting to hear some good news at last, but that was a fact of life that I had to bear.

The one thing that stuck in my mind from this whole experience was that all the agencies I had visited were prosperous, but their personnel managers did not know much about the professions they were handling. And yet, without any knowledge, they were still making money. I thought that this must be a good business to be in. With my experience, I could probably do it a lot better than they did.

I had some experience placing the Israeli engineers in various industries at my job at the Technion Society, so I decided to try and get a job as a personnel manager. If I was not successful, at least I might find a good job for myself. The next day after my fiasco looking for a job in New Jersey, I looked in the New York Times for a personnel agency managerial position that specialized in placing engineers. The agency I found was located on 39th Street and Madison Avenue and was very convenient to travel to from home. I applied for a job, but I filled up my application form without mentioning any of the management positions I held. Instead, I told them that I had placed engineers with the Technion, which was true, and after five minutes of being interviewed by the manager, I was accepted. The salary was $75 per week, plus commission on my placements. The money, of course, was not enough, but I needed the experience.

I started the next day. There were five placement managers in this office. I was seated at a small desk with a telephone and was given a telephone book. After about an hour, I had my first draftsman applicant sent to me for an interview. I was very happy to have the opportunity to review his qualifications, and immediately I knew exactly what he could do. The next step was to find him a proper job. I had to get on the phone, call companies, and find out if they needed a draftsman. No one in the office had instructed me on how to make a placement, but that did not worry me. I knew how to use the phone, and this was the main tool in the employment business. But after making over fifty phone calls that first day, I had no results.

When I got home, I looked over the "Help Wanted" section in the New York Times for draftsmen. I noticed several ads from companies looking for draftsmen. I decided to call these companies the next day and find out whether they would like to interview my draftsman. The only problem I had was that if my draftsman was looking in the paper himself and saw the same ad, it would conflict with my call. But I decided to take a chance, call the company the next day, and introduce my draftsman for the job. To my pleasant surprise, the first company I called was interested. The next morning, I called my draftsman and made the appointment for him. I followed the interview up with a phone call. Unfortunately, the draftsman did not meet the company's requirement, and they turned him down.

The thought occurred to me that rather than calling companies out of the phone book, I could cut out all the draftsmen ads out from the paper and follow them up by asking the company whether they wanted to interview my draftsmen. I was very busy on the phone all week. On Friday, I was looking for my first $75 check, which I needed badly. When I asked the owner for my weekly check, he said that he was short of cash and would pay me on the next Friday. I was quite upset. However, I was progressing nicely with my experience. I decided to wait and gain more familiarity with the process. The next week, I cut more ads out of the paper, pasted them on cards, and had a small file of available jobs for draftsman. I had also interviewed two engineers who were looking for jobs, so I started cutting ads out of the paper for engineering jobs as well and created a small file for them too.

On the second Friday, I asked the owner for my two weekly checks, and again he put me off, telling me that I would get paid on Monday, because he was short of money. At that point, I realized that I was working for the wrong agency. I had gained some wonderful experience, and I felt that there was a great opportunity for making money in this business, but I was not going to find it with a cheating boss. When the boss left, I took most of my files off my desk and decided not to return to work next week.

On Sunday, I reviewed most of the ads in the New York Times for a position for placement managers. On Monday, I started visiting their offices to apply for a job. I covered about five agencies, but most were not interested, because they either thought I was too old or not exactly in their field of specialties.

One agency, on the second floor of a building on 43rd Street and Madison Avenue, was very appealing. It was a quiet office with a large carpeted waiting room. The furniture was nice and the receptionist was very pleasant. I filled out my application and, shortly thereafter, I was ushered in to see the manager. He was a nice-looking, tall, young Italian gentleman by the name of Gaspar Campanelo, and he had quite a pleasant voice.

Behind him, I saw about ten placement managers. Some were women. They were all young and beautifully dressed and were sitting at small desks with telephones. They were all busy, and jazz music was playing from the speakers on the ceiling. Gaspar Campanello spent about half an hour with me. He told me that his agency specialized in accounting and computers; however, he was interested in starting an engineering desk for me. The starting salary would be $75 per week, and I could start the next day. I was somewhat hesitant to accept a job so quickly, so I told him that I would let him know the next day.

However, I did not call him the next day, because I was not sure if I wanted to start to working with an agency that did not place engineers. In the evening, Gaspar called me and asked me why I had not called. He said that he was very interested in me. He thought that I could do well in his agency, and asked me to come to work for him. I was flattered that someone wanted me, especially since I needed a job so badly. Gaspar following up his offer with me on the phone was a lesson for me that I used for years to come. If I wanted someone, I should not wait; instead, I should follow up the call again. I found out that this was one way to be successful in the personnel business.

They next day when I came to work, Gaspar took me over to each of the managers and introduced me to them. All the managers were very young, in their twenties, a nice-looking group, and looked very prosperous. The receptionist was a young Greek woman who liked me, and we got along very well from the start. I was given a small desk next to a window facing Madison Avenue. Looking out from the window reminded me of the beautiful view I had had at Technion, facing the Metropolitan Museum and the American flag in front. Somehow, it felt like that was another lifetime. However, I felt comfortable and at ease.

The only problem I had was the music, which was playing over my head. It was mostly jazz, which I did not particularly like, and, at first, it disturbed me. However, once I started to make my phone calls, I did not notice the music. Gaspar checked with me to see if I was comfortable, and I appreciated his concern. I asked him what the hours in the office were, and he told me that I could work any hours I wished. As a matter of fact, I could get the key to the office, come in as early as I wanted or even on Saturday or Sunday, and leave at any time at night. He said, "The phone is your life blood in this business, and the more you call, the more money you will make."

However, I noticed that most of the managers came late in the morning and left at 4:00 in the afternoon. I told Florence that I was going to start working many hours, from 7:00 a.m. to 10:00 p.m. six to seven days a week, because I had a great opportunity with Gaspar to make money. I was the first person to get to the office every morning and the last person to leave. Gaspar placed ads for me every week on in the Sunday New York Times, so there was a continuous flow of engineers and draftsman coming for interviews with me.

During the weekend, I cut hundreds of ads from the New York Times for engineering and draftsman jobs. I pasted them on 4" x 6" cards, dividing them into their specialty groups. When I interviewed my applicants, I had all the jobs available in their specialties in front of me, and I called the companies to set up appointments for my engineers. Once the engineer was accepted, he was committed to pay the agency a fee of 5% of his yearly salary. Out of that portion, 35% of it would be my share. That meant that if the engineer's salary was $30,000 per year, the fee was $1,500. Out of that amount, I got 35%, which was $525. At that time, that was a real fortune for me.

I realized that my hunch of making money in the personnel business was correct. The best part of the business was that, at long last, I was becoming my own boss and controlling my own destiny. The job did not look glamorous like the jobs I had had through the years in Israel, Abadan, Iran, Baharien Island, or Technion. It was like a clerical job. However, it gave me great satisfaction to successfully find a job for someone who needed to support his family. I knew how happy it made the family when my applicant finally found a job. Whenever I successfully made a job placement, I always remembered the hard times I went through looking for a job. It was a traumatic experience, which I am sure it is for many who are looking for a job. I was glad to make the job search easier and more pleasant for my applicants, especially when this work paid me so well.

Most of the young managers, who were half my age, could not understand my working habits of working all hours and being happy doing so. They did not understand the hardship I had gone through, the disappointments I had had in my failing businesses, and my need to make money to support my family. At long last, I had found the business I liked. It had no glamour, but it paid well. To my astonishment, after only three months, I was already making $1,000 per week. I could not believe my luck. I just hoped that it would continue.

Florence and David did not see me much during that period. I was working at all hours and, during the weekend, I was busy looking over the New York Times ads. I had cut all the ads up and pasted them on my 4" x 6" cards. By now, I had several boxes with these cards broken down into specialties. It always amazed me to find that my job seekers had never bothered to make phone calls to the ads themselves, and instead preferred calling the agency and paying for our service instead.

Most placement managers in the office did not understand my type of business. Most of them handled computers or bookkeeping personnel. They complained about the type of personnel I brought to the waiting room. They dressed differently from the young women and men who worked in the plush offices around town. Most of my men were engineers, draftsmen, and mechanics, so they were dressed casually. However, Gaspar did not mind it, and he always defended me. My Greek receptionist always helped me and took good care of my applicants while they sat in the waiting room.

The owners of the agency were three young men. Gaspar was one of them, and each of them managed a separate agency around town. Each agency had 15 to 20 desks in a good location and each was beautifully furnished. They ran the agencies very efficiently and made a great deal of money. Each of them had a beautiful home in town, a summer home, a boat, and several expensive cars. They were all nice, young, successful businessmen who were very professional and ran their business very well. Sitting at my little desk in front of my window facing Madison Avenue, I was amazed to realize that with the right business, one could make money by just having a desk and phone.

Things at home were getting better. We could afford a better car, dress somewhat better, take vacations twice a year, and go to concerts and operas more often. Florence loved the opera. Unfortunately, she had not been able to afford to buy expensive tickets to the opera for years, and she was always glued to the radio listening to the opera. Now that we finally had some money, we started going to the opera more often, and that made Florence very happy. We also got David into a private school in town, which we could now afford. We were also able to start saving some money in the bank. Our life was finally beginning to stabilize.

After a year at the agency, I wanted to expand and enlarge my department. I wanted to have someone work for me so that I could make more money. Gaspar thought that was a good idea, and I recruited a young man to sit at a desk next to mine. I started training him. When he started making placements, I would receive 10% of the money he produced. There were several personnel managers in our office that had two or three personnel agents working for them, which increased their income by 10%.

My background as an industrial engineer came in handy. I set up a system of bookkeeping and a cardex system that helped me follow the available jobs from the New York Times as well as keep records of my applicants according to their professional specialties. The system worked well, particularly for each applicant whom I interviewed. I had several cards with matching jobs, which made it possible for me to send applicants to several interviews. In time, the break down of the cards was so accurate that I had several jobs to call for each applicant. That was the cornerstone of my success.

Most of the personnel managers in my office did not understand what I was doing and never bothered to copy my method. I was becoming one of the top producers of the agency. However, there continued to be a conflict regarding the type of personnel, which I brought to our office, and the other applicants who were very well dressed. This disparity continued to bother most of the other personnel managers in the office.

Although the agency was growing, my next request to increase my specialty department was turned down, because the growth of the agency was in the computer and bookkeeping field. The technical and engineering specialties did not really belong in the agency program. I was becoming unhappy, realizing that there was no more opportunity for growth in the agency, so I decided to look into the possibility of starting my own agency.

I had some money saved in the bank. However, I was worried and unsure that I could make it on my own, especially since my income at the agency was considerable. Florence was also worried, but she said that whatever I decided was okay with her. I started looking for another small agency to partner with and spent most of my lunch hours visiting potential agencies.

Eventually, I came across one that was interested in having me as a partner. We prepared an agreement, which I found satisfactory. I took it to our attorney, who was actually my father-in-law's attorney. His name was Sam Feldman, and he was a large, pleasant, and soft-spoken man. The first time I met him, he looked over my agreement and then asked me, "Why do you need a partner? You can do this on your own." I was surprised by his remark, because I had expected him just to review my agreement and not change my decision. He noticed that I was upset and explained that from his many years of experience, he had found that most partnerships do not work out through the years. He told me that I was experienced and successful, so I should take the chance and do it on my own without a partner.

I was quite upset, because I was practically ready to go into business and now I would have to start my search from scratch and look for a place on my own. I was worried that I might not be able to be successful by myself. But despite my fears, I took his advice and cancelled my meeting with my future partner. I think it was the first time in my life that I decided to listen and follow someone else's opinion.

204

Chapter 7 – Settling in America

My Son David at age 2

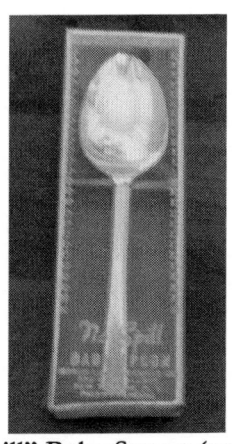

"No Spill" Baby Spoon (page 177)

David in the Boy Scouts

My Invented Plant Stand
Patented in 1975
(See Chapter 8, page 236)

CHAPTER EIGHT

DEVELOPING MY OWN BUSINESS

Starting My Own Personnel Agency

For the next three months, I spent my lunch hours looking for a new space. I wanted it to be close to the office where I was working, so I checked listings in the same area. The new office needed to have at least one room with large windows. This was a must for Florence and me. Nevertheless, the idea of signing a three-year lease worried me. I thought, "What if the business fails? How will I be able to pay rent for three years?"

After visiting several spaces, I found a room on the sixteenth floor of a very nice building on 42nd Street. Because my new landlord was worried about my ability to pay the rent, he made me sign the lease under the condition that I pay six months rent in advance. Financially, this was a huge undertaking for me. I was worried sick, because if I did not succeed, I knew I would be in great trouble.

As sick as I felt, I finally decided to take the risk and sign the lease. I told Gaspar that I was leaving and, to my surprise, he said that he was sorry but wished me success and the best of luck. He even offered to help me whenever I needed a hand. To this day, I have never forgotten all of his generosity. Years later, I heard that Gaspar had contracted the AIDS virus and died at a pretty young age.

I decided to name my agency after myself, because many of the companies I had been working with knew me personally and it would make it easier for me to start working with them on the phone. I bought some inexpensive furniture and a few filing cabinets. Then I installed a glass partition in the center of the room to create a waiting room for my clients on one side and a working space with my two desks on the other. Finally, I placed a telephone at each desk.

Florence agreed to work for me and be my secretary under the condition that she was paid a salary as soon as the business started making a profit. She wanted to have some money of her own. At first it worried me; however, over the years I found that it was a good idea; because having a salary insured that she would be eligible for Social Security in the future. And of course, I could not have asked for a better secretary. She was very supportive and helped make the agency a success.

I opened the agency with great trepidation. Because the office had very little furniture, I could hear an echo every time I was on the phone. Fortunately, it disappeared when visitors were sitting in the waiting room. I placed an ad in the New York Times listing several jobs I knew were available and, to my surprise, I had several applicants come for interviews the following Monday.

I had four chairs in the waiting room next to Florence, and it was beginning to get crowded in the office. In fact, the visitors that came in were so close to Florence that they could practically see what she was writing. However, we didn't mind. It made Florence and me happy to see the agency's potential.

The method I had for keeping my cardex systems up to date enabled me to start making telephone calls while applicants were sitting in the waiting room. After only a few hours on the first day, I had already succeeded in getting two of our applicants' job interviews. I was very excited and happy that I had my own business at last.

Every morning, I got to the office at 7:00 a.m. and Florence came in at 9:00 a.m. In the evening, she left at 5:00 p.m. and rushed home to prepare dinner and feed David, while I remained at work until 8:00 p.m. Because I got home later, I would usually have a late dinner. I also came into the office alone on Saturday, because there was so much to do.

In order to call the right companies for my applicants, I bought a 1,000-page directory which listed all of the industrial businesses in the area. When I found a good applicant, I would review my cardex system for any appropriate job listings I had cut out from the New York Times. Then I made a list of viable options for my applicant from the industrial directory. Following this process increased the number of companies I could call for a job opening.

After working with the directory for a while, I came to the conclusion that if I made a cardex system using the directory, I could have a card for every specialty that was available. So, I started to cut out all the pages in the directory. From each page, I cut out the company's name, address, and specialty and then pasted the information for each on a 4" x 6" index card. The whole process took me three months to complete, but when I finished, I had a complete breakdown of all of the companies in the New York City area on index cards. I could make hundreds of calls by just consulting the cards while my applicants were sitting in the waiting room. I could easily make fifty to seventy phone calls a day, and the more I called the better chance I had at making a placement.

Three months had passed since I had opened the doors of my agency, and I was pleasantly surprised. Numerous qualified engineers, mechanics, supervisors, and architects were coming to my agency looking for jobs. "Margolin" was becoming well-known in the personnel agency field. I was interviewing six to eight applicants a day and making at least three to four appointments for them with companies looking for their expertise. Out of every ten appointments I made, I generally got one placement and earned an average fee of $400 to $750. At that time, the person who got the job through the agency had to pay his own fee, which was 5% of his yearly salary. Six to ten weeks after starting his job, he would be responsible for paying us our weekly fee.

Most of our applicants were professionals with years of experience. My technical and engineering background made it easy for me to evaluate each applicant and determine whether his experience met the requirements of the job. I was always pretty close to the mark. The companies I sent the applicants to appreciated my understanding of their needs and maintained a good relationship with me. I always remember how bad I felt when I was looking for a job and how difficult it was to go through the whole process. No matter how busy I was, I always treated every applicant who came to see me with respect and made him feel wanted. I always made sure to make him feel like he was important to me. Even when I did not have a job for him, I made sure he left with a good feeling and had hope that he would find a job.

I could visualize how each man prepared himself for an interview with me. I imagined how his wife made sure that he dressed properly in the morning, gave him a kiss before he left, and greeted him when he returned home in the evening. I understood how his wife and kids anxiously awaited his arrival to hear how the interview had gone and to learn if there were any good prospects of him getting a job through my agency. This picture was always clear in my mind when I interviewed each applicant. I understood how important each and every interview was for each person I was interviewing. The respect and attention I gave each person would always remain in that person's mind. If I gave them that respect, I knew they would come back to the agency again and again over the years.

Since the average number of years a person is employed with a company is generally two, four, or six years, I could expect that many of the men who visited my agency would come back to me several times during their lifetime. I understood this fact and always kept the future in mind by treating each person with kindness and respect. This is what eventually made my agency very successful.

During the agency's first year, I could not afford to take a vacation, but during the summer, we drove to Jones Beach on Sundays and spent the day relaxing on the beach.

In the evenings, after I was done with work and had eaten dinner, I spent at least an hour or two reviewing the job listings in the "Classified Ads" section of the New York Times and pasting the ads on my 4" x 6" cards.

By this time, I had several boxes of cards. To my amazement, the jobs which were advertised often went unfilled for weeks. When I called the companies, they were usually willing to interview my applicants, because they had not gotten many job seekers calling them. I was becoming very busy, and my waiting room, which accommodated only four chairs, was not big enough to serve everybody who was coming in seeking a job. On many days, five, six, or seven applicants had to wait outside in the corridor for their turn to be interviewed.

Because I had two more small desks in my section of the room, I decided to recruit a personnel manager who would help me place the outstanding number of job seekers who were coming to the office. One of the engineers who came for an interview was an elderly man called Joe Steiglitz. He had many years of experience; however, I could not find a job for him. When I interviewed him, I asked whether he would be interested in training to be a placement manager for me. He would specialize in placing the tool and die makers who were coming to the office in droves. I offered him a small salary of $150 per week as a draw against his commission. The commission was 35% of the income we received for the toolmakers we placed. Fortunately, Joe agreed. The next week, I set up another desk with a telephone and started training him.

He was a slow learner, and unfortunately, I found out that he liked to smoke his pipe while he was working. Although I did not like it, I decided to keep him. Florence, who was on the other side of the partition, objected to his smoking, but I told her to be patient, because he had already started making some appointments and had good prospects of making some job placements and earning money for the agency. Over the next six months, Joe consistently made placements and was soon bringing in more than enough money to cover his draw of $150 per week.

Meanwhile, Florence was very busy answering the phone, registering applicants, and handling the books, but despite her best efforts, the paperwork was piling up and spinning out of control. Reviewing the fast growth of the agency, I realized that I would have to set up a system that could grow over time and accommodate thousands of applicants. My index card system would have to correspond to all the applicants' various specialties and professions. Since I had knowledge of industrial engineer systems, I envisioned that I would have approximately 50,000 registration forms in the next ten years. I knew that I had better set up a system that could operate efficiently years later.

When I finally broke down all of the professions into specialties, I had over 150 headings and subheadings. In a way, it was ridiculous to have a system like this at such an early stage in our operations; however, I knew that if the company started growing without a system in place, we would not be able to properly manage thousands of files. I was optimistic because I believed that eventually I would have a large agency. It was just a dream for the future, but I fervently hoped that one day I would be able to fulfill this dream.

Meanwhile, there was a lot of work that needed to be done. I decided that I would have to employ a part-time secretary to help Florence maintain a proper flow for all the paperwork. Florence suggested that we inquire whether any of the local secretarial schools had any students that we could recruit. We wanted a student with some experience who could work for us for two hours after school, from 3:00 to 5:00 p.m.

My Bookkeeper Sidney

Ever since I started the agency, Sidney Goodfriend had been my bookkeeper. For years, he had worked with my father-in-law. He was a quiet, pleasant, middle-aged gentleman, and he came to Margolin to work on the accounting books once a week. He also had several clients around the city.

Sidney had a wife, a daughter, and an old mother, whom he was very close with. Each morning before going to work, he traveled half an hour by train to check on his mother. Many times when his mother felt sick at night, he rushed to her house to take care of her. His wife was very close to their daughter, who lived in California, and spent a great deal of time with her, leaving Sidney alone in New York.

Aside from his work, Sidney did not have many other interests. Occasionally, he read the New York Times Business Section. He had an exceptional mind for figures and, in his unassuming manner; he was a genius in the stock market. From time to time, he spoke to me about the stock market, which was of no interest to me. I was too busy with my business and did not understand what the stock market was all about. Years passed before he was able to convince me to invest some of my money in stocks.

After a while, I gave him the authority to invest some of my savings in the stock market, yet I never paid attention to where he decided to invest the money. I trusted him; he was a very honest, knowledgeable man. He was always telling me that the economy in the United States would always grow and that the safest money was in the stock market. Years later, I found that he was right, and I always appreciated his guidance in my business affairs.

Most of the years, he lived alone while his wife spent her time with their daughter in California. Eventually, his mother died, and his wife got sick, so she returned to New York. She had a bad case of diabetes. It affected her eyes, and she was going blind. Sidney's wife was a very demanding woman, and he became her nurse. She did not want anyone else to take care of her.

A few years later, gangrene set into her toe and it had to be amputated. However, the gangrene spread further, and they had to amputate her leg. Sidney was very busy taking care of his wife and had to give up his bookkeeping practice.

His daughter became a professor at a university and wrote a few books about famous American women. Sidney moved with his sick wife to North Carolina, because his wife wanted to live in the country. At least once a week, Sidney called me, talked to me about the stock market, and inquired about my business.

Sidney's wife was now completely blind, and her remaining leg was amputated, but she still insisted that only he take care of her. By this time, Sidney was ninety-one years old, but he was still in relatively good health. Eventually his wife died, and Sidney went to live alone in North Carolina. He continued to call me once a week. I tried to convince him to move to a nursing home in New York, but his daughter objected. In time, his calls to me became very mixed up and unclear. Later on, I learned from his daughter that he had died and been buried in North Carolina. His interest in the stock market had paid off for her. He left his daughter with 5 million dollars in his will. I always remember Sidney fondly as one of the most gentle, quiet, and wonderful people I've ever met, and someone who helped my business prosper.

Stealing My Hard-Earned Money

As the agency progressed and grew larger, most of my new office personnel were first interviewed by Bob and then introduced to me for final approval. Usually, I did not doubt Bob's ability to make a good selection.

Maria was a young woman that was recruited for a clerical position. She was a nice and pleasant person, just out of high school, and a pretty good typist. When she introduced herself to me, I noticed that she came from a poor background, because her dresses and shoes were too big for her and she was very uncomfortable being in an office on Madison Avenue.

However, a month later, I noticed a drastic change in her. With the first paycheck she received, she had already bought a few nice, new dresses and shoes. She even started to get her fingernails painted like the other women who worked in the office.

In fact, Maria had come from a very poor background. She was the oldest of two brothers and three sisters. Her father worked as a janitor in a public school in the Bronx, and her mother, who had not married him, left her father. Three of Maria's siblings were actually children from her father's second wife. At first, they lived with their grandmother, who worked nights cleaning an office building downtown. We felt sorry for Maria and her hard upbringing. We felt that she should have the chance to have a better life, so we tried to make her part of the agency's family.

Despite her humble upbringing, Maria was very bright. She was a quick learner and excelled in any duty she was assigned to complete. Bob, her direct boss, always recommended her when a better position opened up in the agency. After several years, she was assigned to work for the controller as one of his bookkeeping clerks. She was doing very well in the office.

However, her personal life was very difficult. Her father was a drunk and beat his children frequently. At times, he disappeared with other women, leaving his children and his wife alone without any support beyond welfare. Now, Maria was helping her family with the small salary she was earning at Margolin.

Three years after she joined us, she met a young plumber who was a family friend, and they got married. They moved to their own small apartment, close to her mother, but she continued to help her younger brothers and sisters. Somehow, all of these hardships did not affect her excellent work in the office.

Before long, she had her first baby, a beautiful little girl, with dark hair and big dark eyes that she named Jana. We gave her two months of maternity leave, and everyone in the office loved the baby when Maria brought her in for the first time. We were all very happy for her.

But things were not going well for her at home. Two of her brothers were on drugs. They had been jailed several times for theft and selling drugs. Two of her sisters, one aged 15 and the other aged 16 were already single mothers. They were being supported by welfare. Their apartments were paid for by the city, and their boyfriends, who were much older men, lived with them on and off.

Maria's husband Joe was doing well as a plumber and, in his spare time, he raised bulldogs. He had a kennel in their apartment. I understand that he made good money selling the ten or eleven puppies that were born from each litter. However, it seems that this income was not enough for him, and he got involved in running an illegal dog fighting business in the Bronx. There, he made bets and lost money gambling during the dog fights, which took place in an underground arena. He also got involved in an illegal rooster fighting business and was getting entangled with gangs in the Bronx. During one of his fights, he was shot in the leg and was rushed to the hospital. Consequently, Maria had to take several days off in order to take care of him.

Even so, all of this family trouble did not visibly affect Maria's performance in the office. She was getting more and more responsibility and was now supervising two other girls in the accounting department. Her daughter, Jana, was growing fast. When things got difficult for Maria at home, she would bring little Jana into the office with her to spend the day. Jana painted and drew pictures at the desk next to her mother's. Maria got a great deal of sympathy, particularly from the women in the office. We all knew what a hard and unfortunate life Maria had. We all felt sorry for her, and we all wanted to make her part of our life and take her away from the horrible situation she had at home.

Time passed. Jana was now 11 years old. She came to the office often with her mother. She was very bright like her mother and proudly showed us her school report card.

With time, we had noticed that Maria was dressing in more expensive clothes and jewelry. There was clearly a great change happening in her life. Maria told us that her father, who had moved to Florida, was doing well in some business. As a result, he had become a lot more generous towards her and was sending her money from time to time. She was also moving to a new apartment in Brooklyn and bringing her mother with her. We were all very happy for the change in her situation. She deserved a better life. Now that she was an important part of our agency, Maria was carrying a great deal of responsibilities.

All was going well in the office. But it was only a matter of time before Maria's family situation turned and started getting worse. Now, her two sisters were in jail for possessing and selling drugs. Her brother had left the city, and neither Maria nor anyone else in the family knew where he had gone. Maria seemed to be the only point of stability in her entire family. We felt that she had escaped the life of crime, drugs, and jail. I was always annoyed when my bookkeeper Sidney Goodfriend was skeptical of her and said, "People don't change. They always return to their unstable roots."

While all this was happening, our business income was faltering. My comptroller, Sam, had a heart attack and was away from the office for two months. Sidney tried to cover for Sam, and Maria was a great help in keeping up the books. Nevertheless, I was having a very difficult time financially. We were short of money and, for the first time in my life, I had to take a loan from the bank, which upset me very much.

Sidney started working in the office every day, looking over the bills and checking the books. He looked very upset, and I thought it was because he could see the gravity of my financial condition; yet when I talked to him, I could feel that there was something beyond that. He was very tense and noticeably disconcerted. The whole time he was investigating where we had faltered, he did not speak to me much. He was very busy, and I was also busy trying to keep things going under pressure. From time to time, I would spend lunch with Sidney so as to have quiet time with him to review the issues at hand over lunch.

To my surprise, one day he unexpectedly asked me to go out for lunch, because he had important matters to discuss with me. I was worried, because I was afraid that he wanted to quit. Over the past few months, things in the office had been very hard to deal with and at this point, losing Sidney was the last thing I needed. I thought, "What would I do without him now, while Sam is sick and away from the office?"

We went to a beautiful Italian restaurant called the Trattoria in the Pan American building, which was one of our regulars, for lunch. As soon as we sat down at our table, Sidney said, "Efraim, we have a very serious problem." While working on the books, he realized that someone in the office was stealing my money. He said that it was an inside job and it had been done very cleverly. Finally, he professed that he suspected Maria was the thief.

I was shocked. I could not believe it. I could not believe that Maria, whom I had treated like a member of the family for the past fifteen years, was the main suspect. Sidney said that we were having such financial difficulties because Maria was forging checks. She had been siphoning money out of our checking account, and he estimated that by that point she had already stolen over $90,000.

It took me a while to believe him, but then I started putting the pieces together. I had noticed a visible change in Maria. I thought, "No wonder her finances had improved so much." The money she was getting was not from her father but from my bank account. I felt so betrayed, thinking, "How could she do this to me?" She had been working with me for over fifteen years, and I gave her a good salary. We all treated her like a member of our family, and yet while I was talking to her every day, she was stealing my money. She never showed a trace of anxiety in her behavior and had appeared to care about the company's financial situation. I could have never suspected that she would be capable of doing this. It was so awful and depressing. All of the money which we had all worked so hard for was gone.

Sidney calmed me down and said that we were lucky that we had caught her in time. When our lunch arrived, I could not touch it. I was terribly upset. I asked, "What should we do now?" Sidney suggested that we close our bank account, move our money to another bank, and say nothing about what we had found out to Maria. Then he said that I should go downtown and talk to the DA to get his advice about the case.

Sidney coaxed me to eat some of my meal. He said that in this time of crisis, I needed my strength. Facing Maria without showing a trace of my disgust was very difficult. A few days later, when we closed the bank account and transferred our money to another bank, I told Maria what we had done. She did not show any surprise or change in her attitude, but I knew she was very smart and suspected that I was aware she had done something. Maybe she thought that I was never going to find out how she had done it and that I would not be able to expose her. She told me that she was going to take a vacation and visit her father in Florida. I suggested that she should postpone her visit because of pressures in the office, but she insisted that she had to go because her father was ill – or so she said.

While she was away, we brought in two bookkeepers to go over the last two years of our checking and banking accounts and determine how she had been stealing the money. The method she had used to embezzle the money from us was simple and smart. As my bookkeeper, she first presented our bills to Sam, our comptroller. After he approved the bills, she wrote checks with erasable ink and presented them to me for my signature together with the approved bills. Once I saw Sam's approval, I signed the checks. Next, Maria chose the checks she wanted to embezzle, erased the name on it, and substituted her own name. Rather than mail the check, she cashed or deposited them to into her account. When the supplier demanded the money, she presented the bill to the comptroller again and erased his previous approval. Eventually, she was busy covering her theft from month to month and from one customer to another. She got away with it because Sam was ill and was not following up closely on what Maria was doing. We had all trusted her and never imagined that she would steal from us.

After she left for her "vacation", Maria never returned to the office. When we changed our bank, she must have realized that we had discovered that she was embezzling money from us. She knew that we had caught up with her scheme and she was no longer able to come back.

When I showed all the records which Sidney had prepared to the DA, he looked at them with amazement, remarking that Maria had been very clever. Shortly thereafter, Maria was arrested and convicted of fraud. She was found guilty; but unfortunately, the judge was very lenient towards her. She only got 45 days in jail, five years' probation, and an order to pay $10,000 to us over the next six years. This was barely more than 10 percent of the money she had stolen.

The whole event was very upsetting and discouraging. Even though Maria had committed a serious crime, it had indeed paid off for her. The penalty she received was minute in comparison to the loss and hardship she caused me by stealing nearly $100,000. Having to pay so little time and money would surely be an incentive for others to do the same thing. This had been an easy way for her to make money without working for it. Meanwhile, honest people that were working hard for their living every day, as I have done all my life, were sacrificed.

Romance In The Office
Jay and Mira

The first student we got was Jay Fishman. He was a small, quiet young man. He did not know how to type, but his handwriting was amazing. In fact, it was so small and clear that it looked like typed print. From the beginning, I liked him. He spent three hours a day with us, three days a week. Although he was tense and spoke very little, he kept himself busy all of the time.

From time to time, he would get on the phone and speak quietly to his young sister at home or to his father. We later discovered that his mother was critically ill with cancer. Jay was taking care of his young sister (who was still in high school), caring for his mother, cooking meals for the household, and doing all of the washing and cleaning to keep the family going, because his father worked late hours as a tailor in a store downtown. Even with all this going on, Jay was very efficient and always kept to himself. No one would suspect how much he had on his mind.

After a while, Jay unexpectedly left us without giving me a notice or making a phone call. Three weeks later, he came back to the office and asked if he could start working again. When I asked him what had happened, he finally confessed that his mother had been very ill and she had just passed away. His younger sister was always calling him on the phone with complaints, but he was always very patient and gentle with her. He spoke to her quietly and calmed her down. Now that their mother was gone, she was helping him keep the house going.

A year later, he asked me if I could use any additional help in the office. He had a friend from his college who was looking for a job. I was sure that anyone he recommended would be good, so I told him to bring her to the office. He introduced me to Mira, who was a nice young girl, and she started working for me. Jay saw her as a friend, but we could all tell that she was really crazy about him. Jay, on the other hand, never paid much attention to her. Later on, I found out that his mother had met Mira some time back and really had not liked her. Perhaps it was because Mira came from a lower-class Jewish family.

Two years passed, and Jay and Mira graduated from college. They left the office, but visited us from time to time and kept us informed about their progress. Jay's father, who was a concentration camp survivor, eventually retired, and Jay continued to take care of the house.

A few years later, Jay and Mira decided to get married. They invited Florence and me to their wedding, and we continued to keep in contact with them and their growing family. Now Mira and Jay work in Jersey City. They have three grown up children and own a beautiful house in New Jersey.

Sarah

Just three years after Jay and Mira left, Florence's friend Sarah was looking for a job. Sarah had worked with Florence many years before at the Jewish Seminary where Florence and I had gotten married in 1948. Florence asked me if we could employ Sarah because she had just lost her job. Our business was growing, and I had room to add another clerk in the office, so Sarah started working for us.

Sarah was married to a young electrical engineer called Edgar. He was a troubled boy who grew up in an orphanage school. He and Sarah had a young daughter. Sarah was young, small, and quite pretty. She was not very smart, but she was very friendly, and all the men around her thought that she was very sexy. Edgar, on the other hand, was a very serious individual. Most of the time, he was tense and reserved.

This was Sarah's second marriage. Previously she had been married to a man named Allen, but soon after they got divorced.

All her life, Sarah had a difficult time with men. She was always attracted to men with problems and always surrounded herself with the same type of men. Her father was a divorced recluse, and both of her husbands fit the same description. Her mother was illiterate, and unfortunately Sarah had a very difficult upbringing. Over and over again, she fell into the same trap by choosing to live with and marry two difficult men.

She was not very smart around the office, but I kept her because Florence liked her. Years later when her husband Edgar got lung cancer, he could no longer work as an engineer. He asked me if I could employ him, so I did, and he worked in our office for two years until he passed away.

By this time, Sarah had moved on from working at Margolin and was working in an office in the city. She was now a widow and was taking care of her daughter alone. Her new boss liked her very much. While she was working for him, they spent their lunch hours together in the office. But eventually, her boss moved to another location and she lost her job.

Sarah was getting old and having a difficult time paying her rent. Florence was very worried about her and kept trying to think of a way that we could help her out. The thought occurred to Florence that Edgar's father, who was also living alone, might be interested in meeting Sarah, and marriage and companionship could be beneficial for both of them.

The opportunity presented itself when we were invited to one of Edgar's family weddings. We brought Sarah along with us and introduced her to Edgar's father. He liked her, they started seeing each other, and shortly thereafter, they got married. They bought a house together in New Jersey and are still living there now.

Now that we had a larger team, it was getting too crowded on my side of the partition. My neighbors were complaining about the crowds of applicants that were always standing outside waiting for their interviews, and my landlord was getting upset. Luckily for me, my next-door neighbor was leaving and his office was available. It was a much bigger office, but it was quite expensive. I was worried about taking on such a great financial burden for the next three years, but after talking it over with Florence, I decided to take my chances and move to the larger space with the hope that the company would grow.

Financially, my small agency was doing well, and I had some money saved. We had to build a large partition to separate the office space from the waiting room, and we added a glass window for the receptionist. The new waiting room could accommodate about twelve chairs. I bought another three desks, chairs, and filing cabinets. The office was located in the corner of the building and had a lot of windows, which made Florence very happy.

We moved to the new office six and a half years after I started my agency, and now I had a commitment to pay rent for this new space for the next 3 years. Business was improving, and I looked for additional personnel managers to join the agency. From my experience, I learned that a good placement manager must come from the profession he was placing people in. His detailed knowledge of the profession would help him evaluate applicants thoroughly before sending them out for an interview. He would also understand the job requirements and send the right professionals to the right jobs. I always remembered the degrading experience I had when I was interviewed by a placement manager who had no knowledge of my profession. I vowed that no applicant to my agency would have that experience.

Bob Lerner

While interviewing my applicants, I always looked for candidates that could work for my agency, and when I came across a good one, I offered him a position with our agency. One of my prospects was a man called Bob Lerner. He had been working as a production manager. His technical background was very good, and he seemed to be a smart, quick, young man. To make sure that I was selecting the right person for the job, I sent him out to take a psychological test. However, I found that the results of the test were inconclusive in determining his ability to be a good placement manager. I debated whether I should employ him, and after another interview, I decided to overrule the test report and hire him anyway. That was a gut feeling, which I never regretted. Bob became one of my most successful placement managers and, eventually, became one of the head managers of the agency.

I trained Bob for six months, and he always said he would do better than me. He tried hard, but never caught up with me. He was making good money and was happy with his new profession. The agency was growing, and I was looking to expand to different specialties such as jewelry, tooling, architecture, mechanics, engineering, plastic, and so on. Bob and I were continually searching and interviewing for the right candidates. For the architectural department, we searched for someone who had been employed in the architectural field, and for the plastic department, we searched for someone with experience working in a plastic factory. My basic idea was correct, but ultimately success depended on the knowledge and background of the person being placed.

I made Bob my first manager, and he managed several placement managers. For incentive, I gave Bob 10% of the money his managers produced. He trained the new managers and they followed my original index card system.

In six years, we grew to five placement managers, one secretary, one receptionist, and three part-time, secretarial students. Our waiting room was always full. The office hours were from 8:00 a.m. to 6:00-7:00p.m, which gave us the opportunity to see many job seekers before their work started or after their work day ended. On Saturdays, we were open half a day. For incentive, I brought hot fresh bagels with cream cheese and coffee every Saturday morning. We all sat together enjoying our breakfast. This continued for many years to come.

David

A close friend of mine from France had a son named David who was a student at Washington University and wanted to come and work in New York. My friend asked me if I could find a job for his son. At the time, I was expanding the business and found that I could use another person in our recruiting department.

When David arrived in the office, I saw that he was a tall, handsome, and very personable young man. Although, I did not find him to be particularly smart, I thought that he could fill the position I had in mind. I introduced him to my office manager who would oversee his affairs and, for a while, I did not have much contact with him. I saw him busy on the phone at his desk, but I also noticed that many of the women in the office were giving him the eye. They were coming to the office better dressed, attractively made up with fashionable hairstyles and they were always passing David's desk to smile and talk to him. To stop this parade and chatter, I moved him to a desk that was closer to mine. That instantly stopped the show. Now, nobody was passing his desk as often as they had before.

I found that David did a good job, but he was always talking to someone on the phone in a quiet voice. It never occurred to me that he might be talking to some of the women in my office, but in time I found out that this was exactly what he was doing. By that point, he had already slept with a large majority of the young women in my office.

They loved him and he returned their love. So long as it did not reduce his efficiency at work, I did not mind. In fact, maybe I was somewhat jealous of how successful he was with women.

David was on a temporary visa in the United States, but he wanted to become a permanent resident. During a week of his vacation, he traveled to Washington to stay with his girlfriend. She was a professor of his from the university and was much older than he was. He hoped to marry her one day and become an American citizen; that way he could remain in the country. But their relationship did not work out, and he stopped traveling to Washington.

One girl in the office, Rebecca, who was not particularly pretty, was absolutely crazy about David. When he was looking for an apartment, she suggested that he move in with her. She knew that he was still active with other women, but she did not mind. Some time later, Florence and I were having lunch at a restaurant nearby the office when we noticed David and Rebecca sitting in one of the booths. They were very close together and were hugging each other. When they saw us passing, we just waved to them. When we walked out, after our lunch, David and Rebecca waited outside for us and joined us while we were walking back to the office. David turned to Florence and said, "I'm sorry that I didn't tell you before, but Rebecca and I got married yesterday." It was quite shocking news, but we knew that David had married her because he wanted to stay in the country. Rebecca did not mind that he had only married her so that he could stay in the country, and she probably hoped that he would fall in love with her one day, but this never happened. When the time came that David became a permanent resident, he left her and moved to California.

Sheila

While we were expanding, I felt that we could add another department to deal with point of purchase and marketing staff. One of the applicants was a young, beautiful woman called Sheila. She was very elegant and had a great personality. In talking to her, I felt that she could be a good recruiter. I suggested that she should try and see whether she might like working as a recruiter for the agency.

I introduced Sheila to George, the department manager, and he trained her for her new position. She sat at a desk next to George's. Meanwhile, most of the employees sat at their desks watching Sheila with admiration. Most of the female employees looked at her with envy, because she was very elegant and beautiful.

In the next few weeks, I noticed that some of the younger men were showing up to work better dressed. They were always trying to help Sheila, who was progressing very nicely in her new job. George, who had a very jealous wife and two grown children, also showed up better dressed; kept his hair nicely combed, and made sure his shoes were shined.

Sheila knew her effect on the men in the office; she was used to this kind of attention. Even though there was some tension with the other girls in the office, she was friendly to them, and at times they went for lunch together.

After a while, I found that George was spending more time with Sheila than was necessary. He always sat next to her desk and gave her instructions. He was very charming towards her. Even though I realized all this, I did not do anything about it because George was the manager of his department. As long as all the men and women in his department were producing placements and getting along, I was satisfied and did not get involved.

However, as time went on, I noticed that George was going out for lunch at the same time that Sheila was missing from her desk. I suspected that they were possibly going for lunch together. Once when I came back from lunch, I passed a hotel across the street and saw George walking out. Moments later, Sheila followed. Each arrived in the office separately. I was somewhat surprised; I had never expected George to cheat on his wife. But so long as Sheila did not mind, I did not mind. This romance went on for a while and, eventually, it was no longer a secret.

Now that Sheila was doing well at her job and making good money, I suggested that George move her closer to my desk, so that she could progress further in the company. I would be lying if I said that the thought did not occur to me that maybe I should try my luck with Sheila, but I always dismissed the idea. I never wanted to have any close association with any of my female employees even if I was tempted.

I noticed that the relationship between George and Sheila cooled down after George's wife visited the office. I think that she had been suspicious for a while and wanted to see the person in the office for herself. Before long, I noticed that Sheila was going out for lunch with John, who sat next to her. You could sense that there was a new romance between them in the air.

For the next five years, Sheila had the occasional romance with a number of my male employees. She was happy with her success, but the women in the office had become quite unhappy with her and seldom went to lunch with her anymore. After a while, I noticed that while Sheila was interviewing male applicants at her desk, she was very charming with them. But as long as she was spending most of her time on the phone, no one could tell whom she was speaking with. It did not matter to me as long as she was producing and making money for the company.

Time passed and the office had grown. Now I was sitting at the end of the office and did not see much of Sheila. She worked at the other end of the office. I was told that she had a steady boyfriend whom she had met while she was conducting an interview. Not too long afterwards, I was invited to her wedding. It was quite an elaborate affair, and I met most of her family. Her new husband was nice. He was also very handsome and tall, and he was a highly skilled professional.

Ten years had passed since Sheila first came to work for me. She was pregnant and asked if she could take a leave of absence. Of course I said she could – but afterwards, I never saw her again. I heard that she and her husband had relocated to Arizona and had two children. Later on, I got a New Year's card with a picture of her family.

The Mugging

Every Friday evening, I remained in the office alone later than the rest of the team, taking care of my books and records before closing up at 6:00 p.m. One evening, I was supposed to go to the opera and meet Florence at the entrance at 7:45 p.m. While cleaning up my desk, I noticed that a tall, well-dressed black man with a nice leather briefcase had entered the waiting room. Through the secretaries' window, he asked me if Mr. Adams was available. I could not hear him well, so I opened the door to see what he wanted. As soon as I reached him, he grabbed me by the neck. At that point, I realized that he wanted to hurt me. Perhaps he was unhappy with the agency. I pushed him back, rushed into my office, and locked the door. I ran to my desk to call 911, but while I was on the phone, he extended his hand through the secretary's window and pointed a large German Lodger handgun at me. He screamed and told me that he would shoot me if I moved.

Then I realized that this was a stick up. Before I knew what was happening, the man had pushed himself through the narrow window and crawled into the office over the reception desk while pointing the gun at me. I hung up the phone. By this time, he had reached me and was pointing the gun in my face. I still did not understand what he wanted, because we did not have any money in the office. We were always paid with checks.

The intruder was silent, saying nothing. He did not ask me for money or anything else. As the cold gun pressed against my head, I decided to fight him off and pushed the gun away from my face. Instantly he slammed his gun on the side of my head and I fell to the floor. I was so agitated that I had tried to stand up to him. The blood was streaming down my face.

He got close to me again and said, "Get on your knees and crawl, you son of a bitch." My white suit was soaked in blood. I decided that even if it meant my death, I was not going to crawl on my knees for anyone. I had lived long enough, and if I was going to die then I would die on my feet. I said, "I am not going to crawl." The mugger got so upset that he hit me again with his gun. I fell to the floor. He rushed over to me, turned me over so that my face was down on the floor, and used handcuffs to restrain my hands behind my back. Then he took my white jacket, which was behind my chair, stuffed the sleeve into my mouth, and tied it up over my head. He removed my wallet from my pants and left, locking the office door behind him.

I was lying on the floor with blood running over my face and my coat sleeve stuffed into my mouth. I told myself to calm down, not to move just yet, take it easy, and breathe slowly, because otherwise I knew that I would choke and die. I was lucky that he had not shot me or kicked me in the head. After about five minutes, I had calmed down, so I tried to get on my feet. It was difficult, because my hands were handcuffed behind my back. Eventually, I managed to stand up. I had very limited vision, because the jacket was wrapped over my eyes. I walked over to the office door, which was locked. I turned my back to the door and, with my hands cuffed behind me, opened it.

Now I was in the corridor, and all the offices were closed except my neighbor Cathy's. I could hardly talk because the sleeve was still jammed in my mouth. I knocked on her door with my foot and tried to call her name. Eventually, she opened it slightly. When she saw me, she did not recognize me because there was blood all over my face. She got frightened, started screaming, and closed the door. I was left standing outside knocking at the door again. This time, she recognized that it was me. She opened the door, still screaming in fright. Shaking and crying, she removed the jacket from my head, gave me a glass of water, and called the police. I was still bleeding profusely all over my white suit.

The police arrived and had difficulty removing the handcuffs until Cathy gave them her hairpin. An ambulance was waiting downstairs to take me to the hospital. Cathy wanted to go with me, but I knew that Florence was waiting for me at the opera house. I asked Cathy to go to the opera and tell Florence that I was not coming.

When Florence saw Cathy, she immediately knew that something bad had happened to me. Cathy told her that I had been mugged, but that I was okay. They both rushed to the hospital and found me in the emergency room. Luckily, my injury was not serious. I got a few stitches on the side of my forehead and was sent home that night. I was quite shaken, but was mostly aggravated and upset that I had not been able to do anything about the situation. Florence wanted me to stay at home for several days, but I decided to go back to the office the next morning with a bandage on my head. For the next two weeks, I went to the police station and looked at mug shots. However, I could not recognize my mugger. Eventually, I had no choice but to give up looking.

For a while, I was very upset that I could not protect myself against the mugger. In order to relieve my anxiety, I took a karate class, which helped build my self-confidence. I enjoyed going to the karate school and kept going once a week for the next two years. I was awarded a 2nd degree green belt, which I still keep in my bedroom with great pride. What I enjoyed most about karate was that the form of the exercises extends the performance of your body and muscles. It not only teaches you how to protect yourself, but also shows you the best way to attack your enemy. I enjoyed practicing these exercises with the young men in my classes. Yet as time went by, I could not keep up with them, and had to give it up. I kept practicing my exercises for several years, which improved my confidence in myself.

Several years passed and I found that I was getting restless again, so I decided to buy a motorcycle. I went downtown and bought a nice, blue, shiny motorcycle. It was very exciting. It reminded me of the time when I had one in Israel and Abadan, Iran. Riding it made me feel like I was free. I rode it around town and, for the next two years, I rode it every morning to the office. I avoided riding it on the highway, because it was too dangerous. Florence did not like the idea of me riding it in town. However, she agreed to take several rides with me through Central Park. At times, she rode with me to the market downtown. She always carried a shopping bag in one hand and held me with the other.

One evening while I was riding my motorcycle home from the office, the traffic was very heavy. When the traffic stopped, I rode slowly as usual between the cars and the sidewalk. As I was slowly progressing along the street, a woman suddenly opened her car door. Before I could grip the brakes, I slammed into the open door, falling off the motorcycle and crashing onto the sidewalk. Despite the impact of the fall, I was able to get up quickly. The motorcycle engine was still running and several bystanders had rushed over to my aid. Fortunately, I was not hurt, but I was shaken up. I lifted the motorcycle, which had been slightly damaged from the collision, and rode it back home.

Florence had been waiting for me and was very upset that I was so late; we were supposed to have gone to the opera that evening. At first, she did not notice that I had a big bump on my head and that my jacket was torn. Of course, when she did see what had happened, we did not go to the opera. The accident made me realize that it was irresponsible for me to take such chances. I had huge responsibilities managing an office and had many employees who depended on me, not to mention a wife and son. Several weeks later, I decided to sell the motorcycle, and that was the end of my motorcycle adventures.

John Clark, His Life and Death

While expanding the agency, I always looked for capable personnel. For the agency, I constantly reviewed their ability to become a recruiter for me. Of course, the applicants never suspected this. My questions covered many aspects of their life. I asked personal questions about their family, children, etc. On the one hand, it fulfilled my natural curiosity and interest in the lives of others. On the other hand, I could feel whether the person I was interviewing was a good fit for the company.

The salary I offered was lower than the salary that the applicants could expect to get from a regular job, but working in the agency, in the long run, offered a greater potential for earning more money than a regular.

One of the applicants who came to my office was a man called John Clark. He was a manufacturing manager who had lost his job some months back. He was a tall, slim middle-aged gentleman. When I met him, he looked very tired and depressed. He was wearing an old suit which hung loosely on him. I gathered that he must have lost a lot of weight, and I was sorry for him because his chances of getting the job he had applied for was nil. But I did not want to cut the interview short and make him feel worse than he already felt. I thought that he could sense that he had no chance of getting a job with me.

Just as I was ready to conclude the interview, he looked at me intensely and said quietly, almost in a whisper, "Please, Mr. Margolin. Help me. My wife is sick. I have been out of work for a year already. I am broke and I am at my wits' end. I need any job you have. I don't care about the money. Any minimum wage job will do, but I have to do something. I have no one who can help me. I don't know what to do."

I felt sick. Suddenly, I saw myself sitting in his chair. I remembered how I had felt just a few years earlier and how desperate I had been. I had been in the same situation, with no help and no future. He had no idea how awful I felt, but I really felt like crying for him. Maybe he could see this on my face.

At first, I did not think of him as a potential recruiter, but then I thought that maybe I would give him a chance. I told John that I might have a job for him in my office, but that I could only pay him $75 per week and the hours would be long. If he did not mind, I would train him for the job.

For a minute, he did not say a word. He was just in shock. He could not believe that I had offered him a job. Then he grasped my hand and said "Mr. Margolin, you saved my life. This is a great moment in my life." His eyes were full of tears. He was ashamed to show me his feelings, and I felt the same way. I was not sure that I had done the right thing. It might turn out that John would not be able to do the job I had offered him, but at that moment I just felt that I needed to do it. The future would tell.

The next morning, John came to the office early. His shoes were shined, and he wore a white shirt with a nice tie. He had a big smile on his face and looked like a different person. I gave him a desk and asked Bob, my office manager, to start training him for his new job as a recruiter. As the day went on, I watched John from my desk. He was very attentive and followed instructions very carefully. In a very short time, he began to show results.

Six months later, he was already making $150 per week. He was happy and was always smiling, but he was very quiet and efficient. He always dressed nicely and was liked by the other employees in the office. In time, his wife recovered. Her illness had started after their 30-year-old son had been killed in an automobile accident.

At the next Christmas party, John brought his wife. She was stunning and was incredibly charming and pleasant. It made me feel so good that I had, by chance, saved the lives of these wonderful people.

Two years later, John was making $500 per week. He eventually moved to Long Island, bought a new car, and went to Florida on vacation during the winter. He was so happy and I was happy to see that he was succeeding and making money for himself and the agency.

One Monday morning, John did not come into the office as usual. Generally, he was very punctual, so I was surprised not to hear from him or his wife. I called his home and there was no answer. I left a message and was getting worried, because it was so unusual for John not to call if he was late. I thought that his wife might be sick again. They lived by themselves with no other relatives.

On Monday night, I received a call from John's wife, Rose. She was crying, and I could not understand what she was saying through her sobs. She told me that John had just died. He had been in a car accident the previous day. They had rushed him to the hospital, but he had died shortly thereafter.

I was in shock. Poor John. He had finally started his life over again and now he had been killed. It was not fair. I thought, "What will Rose do all alone?" She told me that the funeral would be on Wednesday. I asked her if I could come and help her, but she said that her cousin had come from Florida to be by her side.

On the Wednesday of John's funeral, Florence, Bob, and I went to the funeral on Long Island. There were only a few people there. We drove to the cemetery with Rose. Then she told me that while John was driving to the store from home on Sunday night, his car had been hit by a garbage truck. When he got to the hospital, there was not much that they could do. He died there five hours later.

I asked Rose what she would do now and she told me that she would move to Miami to live with her cousin. I still had money coming in from John's placements, so I sent Rose the money that John had earned.

I had a picture of John that was taken at the Christmas party in the office. I framed that picture and carried it with me from one office to another while the agency was growing. After years, John's picture still hangs in my office.

Joe Schwartz and Sons

I knew Joe Schwartz for years. He was one of my first customers, and I had provided him with production supervisors. He had a large factory in Brooklyn that manufactured plastic bottles. Through the years, I often met him at his plant. He was always talking about his three great sons. When we first met, they were young boys and he had great plans for them. When they were older, two of his boys graduated from M.I.T. and the other graduated from Columbia University. When they finished school, they started working for Joe in his factory. He always dreamed that he would retire, live in his second home in Florida, and leave the factory for his sons to manage.

From time to time, I spoke to Joe and heard about the wonderful progress his sons were making in the factory. When one of his sons got married, I was invited to his wedding. It was an elaborate wedding with several hundred of their family and friends.

Eventually, I lost contact with Joe. For some reason, I did not get along with his sons, and as a result, I was not placing any more personnel with their factory. Years later, Joe came back to my office. At first I could not recognize him. He had gotten so old that he had shrunk to half of his original size. Despite my disagreements with his sons, I was happy to see him. Sitting at my desk, I wondered why he had decided to visit me. I thought that he possibly needed some help in his factory. Maybe he wanted additional personnel. However, to my surprise, he asked me whether I could get him a job. He said that he needed one badly. I could not understand what had happened and then he started telling me his horrifying story.

After several years, when Joe's sons were running his factory and all was progressing well, he had decided to retire and move to Florida. He transferred the factory over to his three sons under the condition that they pay him $200,000 per year as a consultant for the rest of his life. Two years passed and all was going well. As a matter of fact, some of his grandchildren were spending their summer vacations down with him in Florida.

In the third year, his monthly payments started to diminish. When he asked his sons about the delay in his monthly payment, they explained that the business was not doing well. They assured him that as soon as things improved, they would catch up with their payments. However, a few months later, the monthly payments stopped altogether, and Joe's telephone calls were not been answered.

He knew something was wrong, so he rushed to New York to see his sons. The meeting took place in their factory in Brooklyn. Joe demanded an explanation. His sons told him that the business was doing poorly, so they did not have money to send him. Joe insisted on seeing the books in order verify his sons' claims, but he was told that he had no right to do so since they owned the company. The best they could do for him was send him $500 per week until things improved.

It dawned on Joe that his good intention to give his business to his sons had been a terrible mistake. He had trusted them so completely that he had given them the entire stock of the company. In doing so, he had totally lost control of the corporation. He no longer had any say in the company's affairs or how it was run. His lawyers told him that, unfortunately, he had made a mistake to trust his sons and there was nothing that could be done about it.

While Joe was telling me his story in my office, he was crying. It broke my heart to see him in this condition. Unfortunately, I could not help Joe find a job because of his age. After several months of trying to help him, I lost contact with him and never heard from him again. It was a lesson I have never forgotten.

Losing My Father

My father had been ill for a year. A heart attack had slightly paralyzed the left side of his body, but he could still walk without a cane. After working with the Kern Kaimet for 40 years, he decided that he and my mother should move to Holon, a suburb of Tel Aviv, because my mother was ill. They bought a small house with a small parcel of land where my mother planted a beautiful flower garden.

After relocating, my father was feeling better, and the mayor of the city of Holon asked him to join the municipality. He wanted my father to serve as the comptroller of the town. My father accepted and held this job until he fell ill.

It was becoming too difficult for my parents to take care of their small house, so they decided to sell it. They moved into a small two-room apartment on the first floor of a building in midtown. There, my mother kept a flourishing garden next to the windows of the apartment.

Since I had moved to the States, my visits to Israel were few. I was very busy building my business and my contact with my parents was limited mostly to correspondence with my father. My mother still had not mastered writing in Hebrew.

My associations with my sister and brother were likewise very limited. My sister had had a son and divorced her husband. He was a Canadian flier who had come to help fight in the Israeli War in 1948. Unfortunately, he had not been able to adjust to life in Israel, so they had decided to move to Canada. Later, after they got divorced, my sister returned to Israel with their son. Years later, when her son joined the army, she settled in Canada and became a Hebrew teacher for a large synagogue in Toronto.

My brother had two sons and lived near Tel Aviv. Over the years, he became the superintendent of the Water and Oil Drilling Company in Israel. He worked with this company for 35 years until he retired at 65. Both of his sons graduated with engineering degrees from Technion in Haifa.

My relationship with my sister and brother was very limited. Unfortunately, we did not have too much in common and living so far away from each other did not help. Most of our relationship was through correspondence or telephone conversations.

One morning, while sitting in my office, I received a telephone call from my mother. She called to tell me that my father had just passed away. For a minute, I was not sure if I could go to Israel and leave everything at the office, but that thought quickly disappeared. Because Jewish funerals take place no later than one day after death, I would have to leave immediately. I knew that I had to go; I was the eldest son in my family. I had loved my father very dearly and I could not even consider the idea of not going.

I left New York that evening with the only nice dark suit I had and arrived in Israel early the next morning. I had not been able to sleep much on the plane and arrived at my parent's home just before the funeral started. My parent's apartment was crowded with many of our relatives. My aunts and uncles were there with their children, whom I had not seen for years. They were all strangers to me.

It was very painful when I realized that I had lost my father; he was an icon of light for me. I always thought of him with great love and admiration. Unfortunately, I had not had the chance to spend much time with him after I had turned 14 and left for Haifa, but my feelings for him were still very deep, and I missed him.

My mother was devastated, but she kept herself under control, which helped keep all of us going. The funeral procession started at home. We drove pass the municipality building where the mayor gave my father's eulogy. Some close friends spoke to us about their memories of my father, and then we proceeded to the cemetery. At the entrance, I was approached by the rabbi's assistant. He told me that because it was a custom, they would have to cut part of my jacket lapel as a sign of bereavement. So he cut the lapel of my best suit. It was too late for me to stop him. He then asked me if I wanted to see my father before he was buried. I said, "No. I do not want to see my father dead." I wanted my memory of my father to be of him when he was alive.

We walked to the grave site and, before he was laid to rest, I said Kaddish, which is the prayer for the dead. When he was placed into the grave, I could not hold back my tears. It took me some time to come back to myself. This was the first family funeral I had ever attended.

When we returned to the apartment, I had the opportunity to meet and talk to my uncles and aunts and their children. I stayed with my mother for the rest of the week and helped her out as much as I could. I met with my brother and sister and got to spend some time with them and their families. They felt like new acquaintances. I had been away for all these years and had not been able to develop any relationship with them. Now, I had suddenly found them again. As the oldest, I felt that I should retain my relationship with them. I also found that they were very happy to find their older brother after all these years, and they were very respectful towards me.

I returned to New York and plunged back into my daily routine. Florence was busy with our son David, who was now in high school. He was taking photography and was still an active member of the Boy Scouts.

Moving To A New Apartment

For several years now, I had wanted to move to a larger apartment. I had been looking at apartments on Riverside Drive. Through the years, whenever I drove along Riverside Drive, I always hoped that I would live there one day. It had always been just a dream, because the rent was much too high for my limited income.

But now that my business was doing well and I could spend more money on rent, I looked through the paper every Sunday morning for apartments on Riverside Drive. As soon as I saw an advertisement for something on the river, I rushed to check it out. Most of the time, it was too expensive and I could not afford it. This process of searching went on for several years. My income was growing, but the rent simultaneously was increasing, and it was like a vicious cycle.

One Saturday morning, I saw that two apartments were being advertised on Riverside Drive. I rushed to see them early in the morning and met the agent, who knew me by this time well. He showed me both apartments. One belonged to an old woman who had lived there for 40 years. It was exactly what I had been looking for. It was on the sixth floor and had six rooms, most of them facing the river. However, the apartment was old, dirty, and unkempt. The floors were dark; the wooden cabinets were worn out. All of the appliances were 40 years old. Nevertheless, I could see the potential.

Overall, the apartment was great. The rent was somewhat over what I could afford, but I did not want to lose this opportunity, since I had been searching for an apartment like it for several years. I left a $500 deposit with the agent and told him that I wanted to bring Florence to see the apartment that afternoon.

For some reason, the old woman who rented the apartment did not like us and did not want us to be the new tenants. She did not own the apartment, But after living there for 40 years, she thought she owned it. Our agent forced her to let us see it again. When Florence looked over the apartment, it was dark because heavy drapes were covering the wonderful windows. Once she saw the dark, dirty floors and the dingy old kitchen her first remark was, "No. This apartment is too dirty. How could we live in such a place?" I told Florence not to worry; I said I would remove everything from the apartment. I would take out all of the appliances, remove the kitchen cabinets, scrape the floors, change the windows, and make it a great apartment. In my mind, I could see the change, but for Florence, it was difficult.

Eventually, Florence agreed that we would rent the apartment. The old woman did not let us in again until midnight when her lease was over. The day after she left, I called a contractor and instructed him to remove everything from the apartment. All of the appliances and cabinets were thrown out and the floor was scraped before I showed it to Florence again.

A day before we left on vacation, I ordered all new appliances and cabinets. When we returned, the apartment looked beautiful, and Florence realized how fortunate we were to have it. Most of the windows were facing the river and the park, so we could see the change of seasons. We could watch the rain pour in the spring, the leaves change color in the fall, the snow fall in the winter, and the large green trees blossom in the summer. We could always see the blue water from the Hudson River behind it all. My dream of living on Riverside Drive had finally come true.

We started to fill the apartment with all kinds of plants. We placed them all around the house, near the windows and the floors, but I realized that we needed some plant stands to keep them off the floors. My old knack for inventions came back to me, and I designed a plant stand. The model was flexible and could hold twelve plants. A friend of mine who owned a manufacturing facility built three of these stands. They were very practical, so I registered the plant stands as a patent. Friends who came to visit our home inquired where they could buy one. I thought that I could possibly make a good business manufacturing plant stands and selling them in the marketplace.

It happened that one of the plant managers, Ruben, whom I had interviewed for a job, was a very capable designer and engineer. I suggested that rather than getting a job, he could be my partner, build plant stands, and sell them with me. I was excited to get into a new business, which was a relatively small investment that I could afford at that time. We rented a small warehouse space on 29th Street near Sixth Avenue and began manufacturing.

Ruben was a very capable production manager. Together we developed the packaging. I recruited a young, Chinese graphic designer who made a catalog for us and, once we had all the parts ready, we started assembling the plant stands.

The first thing I did was place ads in the New York Times. To my pleasant surprise, orders started coming and the business began to grow. Ruben was responsible for the manufacturing, and I took care of the orders, financing, and administration. I was spending a lot of my time in the warehouse helping Ruben and things were moving fine.

The business was making money, and I planned to expand the operation. Two years had passed since we started the business. The warehouse was full of parts and packaging materials, and each day, shipments were made through the post office, which was near our warehouse. Ruben also had a helper to assist him with manufacturing.

Ruben, who had originally come from Israel, was going there on vacation for two weeks. During this time, I divided my time between working at the personnel agency and the warehouse. Florence and

David hardly saw me. I was busy for 16 hours a day and waited anxiously for Ruben to return.

When he finally came back, he informed me that his uncle had bought a large apartment house in New York and had offered him a job managing the house. He said that he was sorry, but he had to end our partnership. I was stunned. With everything that was going on, I knew that I could not manage both my agency and the plant stand business alone. I asked Ruben to stay with me for a few months to assemble and sell some of the plant stands which we had orders for, and he agreed.

I stopped advertising in the papers and magazines, and the orders practically ground to a halt. My warehouse was still full of parts and boxes, and after Ruben left, I still had orders to fulfill, so each Saturday morning I would spend several hours assembling plant stands and shipping them through the post office. It was hard work, but I could not pass up the additional income of five hundred dollars a week. My inventory was already paid for, so all my sales were now net income on my investment. For the next year, whenever I could spare some time, I went to the warehouse and made a few shipments until I ran out of my inventory. The warehouse rent was inexpensive, so I kept it as storage for many years for my personal effects and office files.

Chapter 8 – Developing my Business

Our First One Room Office - 1966

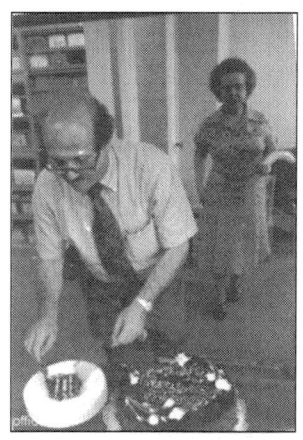

Cutting my Birthday Cake

Me in my Office - 1982

Chapter 8 – Developing my Business

Mr. Goodfriend, My Bookkeeper

Remembering Joe

Bob Lerner,
My Office Manager

Office Personnel

Chapter 8 – Developing my Business

**1982
Office Personnel**

CHAPTER NINE
SARAH CALDWELL
THE METHODIST ZIONIST;
DEVELOPING OPERA

Living With Opera With Sarah Caldwell

During all of the years of our marriage, Florence loved the opera and went as often as possible. She could now afford to spend the money, and in addition to having two subscriptions, she sometimes bought tickets for performances outside the opera house. I usually joined her and I started to love opera.

Florence had some friends who were associated with the opera in Israel. They invited us to join a small group that had fundraising meetings at which a singer would perform. The money collected was sent to the Israeli Opera. The group was like a small private club of older women, and the money collected was small--perhaps $50 per meeting. I could not see myself being associated with this pitiful group, so we stopped going to these meetings.

Some time later we were asked to come to a meeting in a hotel and meet the founder and general manager of the Israeli Opera Company, Ms. Edith Dephilip, who was visiting the U.S. to raise money for her opera. Besides being the general manager, she was also the singing star. She came to the meeting wearing a long mink coat, which spurred Florence to remark that at least 1,000 minks had died for her coat. She was beautiful and very impressive.

We were a group of ten interested opera friends, and she told us about the performances of the opera in Israel and the financial difficulties she was having. At that time, Placido Domingo was just starting his career, and he was singing in the Israeli Opera for her. (It is interesting that later on, after becoming the most successful singer in the opera world, Domingo never mentioned his experience in the Israeli

Opera Company.) I asked Ms. Dephilip how large her budget was and what sum of money she was looking for, and pointed out that it was important to have this information when looking for donors, including me. Her answer was very general, without any details. I concluded at the time that under these circumstances I was not ready to help her, and I left the meeting very disappointed.

A year later I heard that unfortunately Ms. Dephilip had died, and her husband had taken over the management of the Israeli Opera. We were approached again by the group to join them and help raise money for the opera. They offered me the opportunity to become the president of the group and expand its operation. Florence was very excited at the prospect that we could help the Israeli Opera Company.

Before committing myself to becoming president, I asked the group to give me the corporate checkbooks to review their previous activities. Looking at the books, I was shocked: they were a mess! In fact, the group did not even keep any real bookkeeping records. The money they raised was negligible, only $1,500 per year, and they transferred this money in cash when they visited Israel. I also checked up on the corporate registration paper with the state and found that they had never filed their income tax returns properly. I told the group that I couldn't be their president under these circumstances. However, I offered to register a brand-new corporation as a non-profit corporation and start the operation from scratch. I filed through my attorney for a new corporation and several months later received the approval.

Not knowing enough about the Israeli Opera Company, Florence and I decided to travel to Israel and see for ourselves how we could help them. Since we had not been to Israel for some years, we planned to make a tour of the country, spend some time with our family and friends, and at the same time learn more about the Israeli Opera Company.

After taking a trip around the country, we settled down in a hotel in Tel Aviv and contacted Mr. Even-Zohar, the husband of Ms. Dephilip, who was the general manager of the opera company. The opera house was in a dilapidated old building near the seashore. The office was in a small, dark, corner of the opera house. We had an official reception by Mr. Even-Zohar, the board of directors, the previous mayor of Tel Aviv, and another old gentleman.

Mr. Even-Zohar was a very impressive gentleman wearing a large brimmed hat and a long cape. The story about him was that he had a very important job in the labor union. He was the friend of the first Prime Minister of Israel, David Ben-Gurion, and he helped Ms. Dephilip raise money for the opera.

At the time, he had a wife and four children. He fell in love with Ms. Dephilip, left his family, and moved in to live with her. He left his important job with the union and dedicated himself to working with Ms. Dephilip. Seven years later, Ms. Dephilip died of cancer and he decided to continue to run the opera. Unfortunately, due to a shortage of funds, the opera could not support first-rate singers and the performers were mediocre.

My friends in Tel Aviv never attended the opera because of their poor performances. Most of the singers were new Russian immigrants, who looked for the opportunity to sing without much pay. However, with the little money they had, they kept performing every night for a small audience, mostly old retirees who got their tickets through their organizations.

The mayor of Tel Aviv at the time, Shlomo Lahat, wanted to close down the opera and was cutting down on her financial support. We were invited to attend a performance at the opera house and I convinced some of my friends to attend with us as guests of Mr. Even-Zohar. When the time came to start the performance, Mr. Even-Zohar came on the stage and informed the audience that unfortunately, because the major singer's wife was having a baby, he had left for the hospital, so the performance was postponed until the next day. It was very disappointing. We left the opera house and I invited my friends to dinner. The next day we returned and heard a very poor performance. We felt sorry for Mr. Even-Zohar; he kept his opera going against all odds.

For the next two days we were invited to join the opera singers and travel with them for an opera performance in Demona Town, 50 miles south of Tel Aviv. Demona's mayor was an avid opera lover and he invited the Israeli Opera Company to perform in his small concert hall several times a year. We joined the singers and Mr. Even-Zohar in a bus that evening for the trip to Demona. Before we left, we gathered at Mr. Even-Zohar's home, which was like a museum in memory of his wife Edith. All over the walls were large paintings of Edith dressed up in her various opera performance gowns. It was all very sad; it was obvious that he deeply missed his wife, whom he had adored.

The bus ride took us about an hour and a half, and when we arrived we attended a reception by the mayor and were invited to a delightful dinner before the performance. The concert hall was full of local residents who were all very excited, because the opera performance was the highlight of the season and it was a great celebration.

The performance of "The Merry Widow" was a delightful light opera, which the audience loved. We too enjoyed the Russian singers. Of course it was not a first class opera; however, they tried their best, and after all, it was the only opera company in Israel. We returned at midnight from Demona to Tel Aviv on a bus. The singers were singing all the way home, eating perushky pastry and drinking wine. We all had a wonderful time. Florence loved them all. It was a lovely day to remember.

The next day we went with Even-Zohar to discuss how we could help the Israeli Opera Company raise money back in the United States. While talking about our plans, Even-Zohar asked Florence and me if we could help him immediately, because he could not keep the opera going for his next performance without funds. We were sorry for him, and I wrote him a check for $5,000. He was so happy and appreciative that it embarrassed us. He reminded me of Don Quixote, tilting at windmills against all odds.

The mayor of Tel Aviv, Shlomo Lahat, was an opera lover. When he was a general in the Israeli Army, he ran the army's chorus, which had hundreds of singers. Ironically, it was the very fact that he loved opera that made him want to close up Even-Zohar's opera company: he felt it was a shame for the city of Tel Aviv to support such a poorly performing opera company.

Before we left to go back home, we stopped by Zohar's tiny office to say good-bye. His two board members were also there. While the members were talking to Florence, Even-Zohar took me aside and asked me if I could give him another $5,000 so that he could keep the opera house doors open for another month. I could not refuse him; I gave him another check for $5,000. The next morning we flew back to the States.

Several months later, Tel Aviv Mayor Shlomo Lahat discontinued his financial support to the opera and they had to close their doors. Florence was sick about this, claiming it was not fair. She said, "Israel must have an opera company and we have to do something about it!" For a while longer, even though the opera house was closed, Even-Zohar would still go to his office every morning and stay there all day to make sure that no one took over his opera house.

I reported my findings to the small group of opera supporters in New York and discussed how we could help raise money for the opera company in Israel. We succeeded in organizing a small concert in New York and raising $2,000. This was not enough money to help save the opera.

I realized at that time that the group of women I worked with would never be able to raise the amount of money needed, for them it was just a club, a hobby, a few women having a little fun together, and besides that, not one of them had any money to give. I resigned from the organization, and shortly thereafter they discontinued their meetings and their fundraising.

Florence was very unhappy and she felt very bad that Israel no longer had an opera company. Not knowing much about how to start or organize one, Florence came up with the idea that we should recruit some well-known opera person to help us. She mentioned to me that the greatest person in the opera world was Sarah Caldwell, the conductor and general manager of the Opera Company of Boston. Perhaps she could be the person to help us establish a new opera company in Israel. We attended several concerts and operas in New York conducted by Sarah Caldwell and were impressed. Florence was sure that if Ms. Caldwell would be our adviser, we could have a direction on how to establish an opera company in Israel. I told Florence that this was a great idea and that I would call for an appointment with Ms. Caldwell in Boston.

It happened that one of my secretaries was getting married and we were invited to attend her wedding in a town near Boston. I thought that this was a good opportunity to also have an appointment in Boston with Ms. Caldwell. I called the opera company several times until I reached her assistant, Jim Morgan. After I explained to him that I would like to have an appointment with Ms. Caldwell about the opera company in Israel, we scheduled a time to meet following my secretary's Sunday afternoon wedding.

We made a hotel reservation for that Sunday evening, and after the wedding we drove to the opera house, which was an old converted movie house located in the red district of Boston. From the unimpressive exterior, you could not imagine how beautiful the opera house was inside: all marble columns and stairs, glass mirrors, chandeliers all around. Although the red carpets and chairs were somewhat rundown, everything else was shiny and very impressive.

We were met by Jim Morgan, who ushered us into the first floor orchestra. A rehearsal was taking place, so the theater was dark; only the stage was lit. We sat up in the back row and were asked to be quiet. We noticed in the dark that Sarah, who was sitting in the middle of the orchestra floor in front of a large control panel, occasionally stopped the orchestra and singers to talk to them about the changes she wanted.

After about an hour, the rehearsal ended, and Sarah, whom I had never met before, walked over to us. After saying hello she said that she was going to change out of the large loose dress she was wearing and would see us in a few minutes.

We walked with Jim out to the foyer to wait for her. When she arrived I was surprised to see how large and heavy she was.

I asked her if she would like to come with us for dinner and she said, "Yes, let's go to a Greek restaurant." We got into my large Cadillac and drove with Jim and her to a nearby restaurant, which was on the second floor of an old building. She walked very slowly up the stairs. It was a very simple restaurant with several booths and some tables in the middle of the floor. I thought first that she would choose a table rather than a booth, but she walked over to a booth and squeezed herself into the small space between the table and the seat. Jim sat next to her and we sat across facing them.

We ordered some Greek food and while eating, I started telling Sarah about our experience with the Israeli Opera and the closing of the opera. I explained that we were committed to helping Israel start an opera company and we were looking for advice and guidance. Florence listened quietly through most of this, but just before the end of the meal she suddenly asked Sarah if she would like to come to Israel and help us set up a new opera company there. To my surprise Sarah said, "Yes, I would like to help you." She never told us at that time that she had been to Israel before. We found out later that some time back she had recruited an Israeli designer to design several stage sets for her opera in Boston.

We were elated to find out that Sarah was ready to help us. Florence was in seventh heaven. I could tell by her smile and shining eyes that she was delighted. She was in awe of Sarah. She thought of her as a goddess of the opera world and could not believe that she was so close to this opera titan. It was the start of a new exciting life for Florence, and I was happy to take part in this new venture.

We set up another meeting with Sarah and we were invited to attend her next opera performance in Boston. Later, on one of Tel Aviv Mayor Lahat's visits to New York, Florence and I were introduced to the mayor as opera lovers who were helping to restore the opera company in Israel. We invited the mayor for a lunch at the Russian Tea Room. During lunch we told him that there was an opportunity to recruit Sarah Caldwell to help launch a new opera company in Israel. As Mayor Lahat was a great opera lover, he was extremely interested.

During the next two months, we traveled to Boston nearly every week to attend Sarah's opera performances and stayed overnight at a hotel next to the opera house. Usually after the performance we invited Sarah and Jim to have dinner with us, and we had long talks about opera in Israel. With Sarah's help, we also started to put together a program and financial planning for the opera in Israel, conferring all night into the wee hours of the morning in the hotel to lay out the plans for the opera company's launch. While we talked, Florence would take notes, and when we returned to New York she transcribed her notes and typed them. It was pages and pages of information.

All this was very new to me. I had had no idea how an opera company operated and the costs involved, but through our planning meetings with Sarah, I began to get the idea of what was involved. We were also getting to know Sarah well. Unfortunately, she was sick, and her sickness sometimes made her fall asleep in the middle of her conversation. At first, it was embarrassing, but over time we got used to seeing her close her eyes for a few minutes at a time and then wake up.

Later we also met several members of the board of directors of the opera company and were invited to dinner with them from time to time. To them, Florence and I were an odd couple of Jews from New York. However, we were warmly received by all the members and eventually we were elected to the Board of Directors. Of course we paid our dues and became donors to the opera.

On several Saturdays we were invited to Sarah's home, which was a beautifully designed concrete structural house, built in the shape of the letter "S". All the beautiful wood furniture was built by a boat carpenter so as to fit the curved walls around the house. The house had been built by a contractor for himself. and when he moved out of town he sold it to Sarah. It was next to a pond with beautiful trees all around and through the windows, which were from floor to ceiling; you could see the beautiful view.

Jim, who was young and handsome, lived in the house too, and he helped Sarah at home as well as in the opera house. Her mother also lived with her. Unfortunately, when we met her mother, she already had Alzheimer's and could not communicate with us. Sarah had a full-time attendant for her and whenever she was away for a day, she never missed calling her mother to find how she was. She loved her mother dearly. Sarah also had a brother who unfortunately was mentally ill, and she took care of him financially. She also had two little dogs, which followed her around the house.

Florence was very happy to have this close association with Sarah and the opera people. During this period we met many opera singers as well as the staff and Sarah's dedicated office personnel, and we developed great friendships with them. Although we were invited to attend the opera performances as guests, we always paid for our tickets because the opera company was always short of funds and they were in debt most of the time. They owed money to the city, the state, the set builders, and the dressmakers, as well as to the singers and orchestra. Sarah managed the opera all by herself as well as conducting and fundraising. She had several dedicated office personnel who kept the opera running.

The opera performances which Sarah staged were outstanding. Although the stage was relatively small and not too deep, Sarah's genius in staging made it look much bigger than it was. Sarah was not a very sociable person: not too friendly, very reserved and in many ways very difficult and demanding. Opera was her life and her calling, and she was a perfectionist in her craft. She cared about nothing except her opera, but she was a genius and was considered the greatest female opera personality in the world.

For some unknown reason she took a liking to Florence and me. A great respect and friendship developed between us. For me, the association with this great personality gave me the opportunity to see a genius at work: the talent, the music, the know-how, her organizational capability of putting together all the elements of music, singing, staging, lighting, dressing, sound and hundreds of other details to make a performance on time. It was an unbelievably complex activity. The more I knew Sarah, the more I respected and appreciated her genius and I felt fortunate to have the opportunity of being her friend.

The outline of the plan to start a new opera company in Israel was taking shape. The first question that came up was: what was available in Israel for the local opera? What quality of singers were there? We concluded that before we finalized our plan, Sarah should go to Israel and investigate the potential and the availability of the singers there. We decided that the next time Tel Aviv Mayor Shlomo Lahat visited New York; we would arrange for a meeting with Sarah and see how we could progress with our plan. I knew that the first question that would come up would be money: how to finance such a trip to Israel. I suggested to Sarah that I would register a non-profit corporation in New York, which could raise money for such an operation. After reviewing several names, we named the corporation "The American Israel Opera Foundation." Sarah would be a member of the board, Florence the secretary, and I the president. For her part, Sarah would offer selected Israeli singers and directors the opportunity to be trained at the Opera Company of Boston, then perform in Boston, and then go back to Israel.

As our trips to Boston were becoming frequent, we made most of the trips by air, getting to Boston in the early afternoon and leaving after the opera performance on the last flight at midnight back to New York. We were getting used to this schedule. The office was running well. We added three more personnel managers and two clerical helpers. The business was expanding and I could afford to pay for our expenses to Boston.

the entrance to the store there were beautiful girls standing dressed in beautiful Japanese kimonos, bowing to the customers in appreciation of them coming to their store. Everything in the stores was exhibited beautifully, and it was easy to select whatever we wanted. We spent some time in several stores, browsing more than buying. Most prices were much higher than in the States, and we had to think of our luggage, which was already overloaded before we started our trip.

We visited several beautiful shrines, which were intricate structures. In most of them there were monkeys running loose on their plazas looking for a handout of peanuts, which visitors would buy beforehand. One of the shrines had several hundred statues of armed soldiers, all with their army gear on, looking extremely lifelike. Another shrine had a tremendous Buddha statue sitting in the center, and many of the Japanese visiting were kneeling in prayer around the Buddha. Other shrines had small written paper prayers hanging all around, which were left by visitors. It reminded me of the little paper notes which were written by men and women asking for God's help at the Wailing Wall in Jerusalem. However, at the Wailing Wall the notes were inserted between the cracks of the large stone wall. I understand that from time to time all of these paper notes at the Wailing Wall are removed and buried in a grave in the Mount of Olives in Jerusalem.

We took a bus to see the countryside. The bus driver wore white gloves and a nice clean uniform. Each bus had a woman attendant, also wearing white gloves, and a guide who spoke Japanese and English. The countryside was beautiful. Everything was set up as though in a picture: the field, the trees, and the small houses were all very clean and well laid out. Up on the mountain a light fog was hovering over some of the area and it added to the view. We stopped for lunch in a large Japanese restaurant and had meat soup with noodles. It was very tasty. We returned in the evening and after dinner stayed in our hotel room.

At about 3:00 a.m., we were awakened by a rumbling noise, and suddenly our beds were shaking. I realized that it must be an earthquake. I was just ready to step out into the corridor when the shaking stopped. Later I found out that small earthquakes happened often in Japan and most of the time they did not cause any damage, but it was a frightful experience.

Next we took a trip on the bullet train, which is the fastest train in the world, traveling at 110 miles per hour. The seats were very comfortable and there were white doilies on the back of each seat. Once the train started going it ran very quietly, and the only way we could tell how fast the train was traveling was to watch the large clocklike indicator showing the speed of the train. In one hour we were 110 miles out of Tokyo, in the country. Back in Tokyo, we visited several museums and the palace, which was located next to our hotel.

We spent an evening walking in the center of town, which was lighted with neon signs (even more than in New York's Times Square.) Most of the streets were crowded with people. Most men did not wear hats, and it was amazing to see all these thousands and thousands of people all with shining black hair everywhere we went. A lot of the women were dressed in beautiful kimonos while the men mostly wore black suits and black shiny shoes.

Our visit to Japan was coming to an end and we made our reservation to fly to Manila in the Philippines. We were sorry to leave Japan so soon. It was an unforgettable short visit, which we would never forget.

<u>Opera In The Philippines</u>

The flight to the Philippines was uneventful. When we arrived at the airport, we saw armed soldiers everywhere, making us feel as if we were in a war zone. It seemed that there was some unrest in the Philippines at the time and the army was stationed in the airport as protection against a possible terrorist attack.

The taxi brought us to a luxurious beautiful hotel owned by Mrs. Imelda Marcos, the wife of the president. Several members of the Opera Company of Boston were already there, as well as Sarah. It was early evening and the large outdoor pool looked very inviting, so we changed into our bathing suits and went for a swim. The weather was much warmer than in Japan, and the cool water of the pool was refreshing. Sarah left a note for us inviting us to have dinner with her. The dining room was next to the swimming pool, which was all in marble, enclosed, and well air-conditioned. We spent the evening having a wonderful dinner with Sarah and Ms. Kasilag, who was the head of the arts program, and listened to Sarah's plans. The opera they were planning for was "The Magic Flute" by Mozart, which they planned to perform seven times during the next three weeks. There was a lot of work to be done as well as rehearsals.

The next morning we had breakfast in the restaurant next to the swimming pool. It was an impressive feast: mangoes, papayas, oranges, bananas, and all kinds of other exotic fruits were set up on our table, as well as all kinds of eggs, hot rolls, bacon and sausages. Unfortunately, we had to pick and choose carefully because it was too much food to eat! After breakfast Ms. Kasilag drove us to the opera house. It was a beautiful new building, which was part of the performing arts center, containing a theater, concert hall, opera building and the administration offices.

Mrs. Marcos was the patron of this elaborate center. It was her concept and her idea to have a "New York Lincoln Center" in Manila. Sarah was invited by Ms. Kasilag under the auspices of Mrs. Marcos to start and organize an opera company in Manila. As mentioned, the company would be launched with seven performances of "The Magic Flute," sung in German. It was a very big undertaking. Before we arrived, some of Sarah's personnel such as the dress designers and makers, the set designer, the lighting and sound operators, assistant conductors, piano accompanist and music director -- had already been busy for the last two weeks preparing for the opera performance.

Sarah took us along to all her meetings, and at the rehearsals we had an opportunity to see how opera performances are put together and to meet and spend time with the opera personnel and all the singers. It was a special treat for Florence, and every day was more exciting than the last. Most dinners and breakfasts were spent with Sarah and sometimes also with Ms. Kasilag. After breakfast we were driven to the opera house, where we joined Sarah and observed her working with her artists, taking care of all the hundreds of details, and then rehearsing with the orchestra and the singers.

From time to time we skipped out of the hotel, took a taxi, and drove into town; It was an experience to remember. The air was so polluted that we could hardly breathe. The traffic was full of converted jeeps that were open with only a roof, and seats along the sides. There were people hanging and standing outside the jeeps, while the jeeps were driving. On top of the engine hood were all kinds of statues screwed onto it with different colors. The jeeps were painted with various colors and designs.

There was hardly room to cross the street. Small buses were also painted with all kinds of designs and colors and loaded with people hanging outside the bus, while the bus was driving. It was all very crowded with people, and the heat and the fumes mad it difficult to breathe. The stores were full of inexpensive goods, so we loaded up with gifts to take home with us. There were also many churches and cathedrals to visit. Each had its special characteristic. One in particular was one of the oldest churches with an enormous organ that was several hundred years old.

Besides preparing the opera performances, Ms. Kasilag also organized a program to introduce opera to the public schools around the city. A small children's opera was put together with several of Sarah's singers and a small four-piece orchestra, and during the day they performed at schools in various parts of the city. Most times Florence and I joined the troupe and spent time in the schools with them. It was very exciting to see the reception of the young children to the Western opera shows. Most were performed in the school auditorium and the children would sit on the floor, all very well behaved. The children all spoke English so they understood what it was all about, and they loved and enjoyed the operas. In every school we were received by the principal and the teachers and we had a small party at the end of the performance.

The opening night of "The Magic Flute" was coming soon. Besides the singers who came with Sarah from the States, Sarah had recruited several first class Filipino singers who practiced together with Sarah's singers and had an important part in the opera performance. It was a good training ground for the local singers who, after we left, continued performing in the Philippines. Sarah wanted Florence and me to see how she developed a new opera company so that we could do the same later on in Israel.

At the opening night of the opera, many dignitaries of the government and the city came. The women were all dressed in beautiful expensive gowns, the men were in tuxedos, and it was all very impressive. After a short introduction by the mayor, the curtain was raised on a beautiful stage, and the orchestra conducted by Sarah started the beautiful music of Mozart's "Magic Flute." The performance went very well; there were a few minor hitches here and there, but the audience did not notice them. After the performance we had a cocktail party with our friends, the local dignitaries, and their wives. Sarah kept Florence and me close by her, introducing us as Boston Opera Company board members, which we really were. It was a real glamorous occasion for Sarah.

We heard that there was an Israeli ambassador living in town and we decided to invite him to come to one of the opera performances. We found his address and phone number, and we called him for an appointment. It was Friday and the performance was on Sunday. The Israeli ambassador had an unimpressive second-floor office in mid-town Manila. He greeted us and asked us to wait because something urgent had come up, but he assured us that as soon as he had attended to the matter, he would see us. He was a very apologetic, nice, gentle young man, Israeli but with a hint of a German accent.

After about an hour, he returned and explained his problem to us. One of the Israeli Kibbutz members who was working in the Philippines helping the agricultural department grow avocados had died of a heart attack the previous day. The ambassador had to make arrangements to ship the body to Israel before Saturday because there was no refrigerated morgue available, and a special permit had to be made before the end of the day. Having completed the shipping arrangements, the ambassador was now free to join us, and we had a very pleasant conversation. He accepted our invitation to come to the opera on Sunday with his wife and his two young daughters. We were happy that he could make it on Sunday before the performance.

He arrived at the opera house with his beautiful young wife and two small daughters, who were about six years old and beautifully dressed with white gloves on. We ushered them to the blue room where Sarah was sitting before the performance and they had a nice chat. The little girls spoke English, German, Hebrew, and Filipino. Before they came, their father had played a record of "The Magic Flute" for them at home, so they knew the story of the opera.

The Israeli ambassador was originally from Germany, as was his wife, whom he had met in the Caribbean Islands where he was stationed before coming to the Philippines. Her family had settled in the Caribbean during the Second World War. She was quite a bit younger than her husband and very beautiful. We reserved good seats in the opera house for them. The performance was very successful, and afterwards we met them together with Sarah at the party in the blue room. We invited the ambassador and his family again for lunch in our hotel, and we spent a very pleasant afternoon with them. Florence corresponded with them for a while after we returned to the States.

On one of our days off we were invited to visit a music school up in the mountains, which had been built by Mrs. Marcos for especially talented students. It took us about two hours to ride to the school, which was in the most beautiful location. There we had lunch around a large rotating table on which plates of various foods were stationed and people could pick whatever food they liked as the large food plates passed by. Later we spent time listening to a performance by the young students, and some of our Boston opera singers also performed for the young Filipino group of singers. We returned back to our hotel full of beautiful memories.

On our next day off we arranged for a trip on small boats up the river to a waterfall. The only way to reach the falls was by having each small individual boat for each of us pushed by two boatmen on each side of the boat against the current between the rocks. Up the river it was quite a rocky drive but very unique. It took us about an hour to get to the waterfall. It was a beautiful view. Florence wanted to go for a swim under the waterfall, but I held her back. She never forgave me for this, and always reprimanded me for preventing her from this little adventure.

Each day before dinner we took a swim in the gorgeous swimming pool. On each floor in the hotel there was always a beautiful woman sitting near the elevator entrance. We assumed she was guarding the floor, but I found out later that she was there for other purposes. Once when Florence was in the pool, I went up to the room and the young woman, who knew us by this time, stopped me and said, "Your wife is downstairs. Why don't we have a quickie in your room?" I was embarrassed, not having realized before that she was a prostitute and not a guard on the floor. I told her politely, "Sorry, but I have to run back to the swimming pool. My wife is waiting." The prostitution business was flourishing in Manila and most of them were exceptionally beautiful woman. The woman at the elevator door always greeted Florence and me with an understanding smile.

On one occasion the American ambassador, who had attended one of the opera performances, invited Sarah and our group to a cocktail party at his home with many of the dignitaries and government officials in Manila. It was a very hot night and the party was held outside in the ambassador's garden, which was large and beautiful. A swimming pool was built partially into the house so that one could just step from the living room right into the swimming pool. The garden was surrounded by a high fence and outside there were stationed Filipino soldiers guarding the ambassador's home. We returned to the hotel late at night. It was a wonderful evening.

Since we were the guests of Mrs. Marcos, she followed our activities and was happy to see how well Sarah performed with her opera group. Mrs. Marcos arranged for an official dinner for the members of the opera, including all the American and local singers. Sarah was seated at a table with Mrs. Marcos and Ms. Kasilag and a few of Mrs. Marcos's friends. Next to her table we were sitting with the group of our singers. It was a very official dinner, beautifully arranged with big bouquets of flowers on each table, gold and silver utensils and plates.

Mrs. Marcos, who was a gorgeous tall woman, came to our table and shook hands with each of us, asking us where we came from and chatting with us. She told us how important our work was for the opera in the Philippines and she hoped that we would continue to come to the Philippines in the future.

Of course, as it turned out this could not happen, because she and her husband were deposed from the Philippines shortly thereafter, with the millions of dollars still in their possession.

One of the stories told about Mrs. Marcos was that she had 2,000 pairs of shoes in her closet, and this was in fact true. However, the reason was that she was a sponsor of various industries in the Philippines and many of the local manufacturers wanted her to have a sample of their shoes. Of course she could not turn them down, so she kept her shoes. The fact was that the quality of the shoes was not as good as the shoes Mrs. Marcos bought on her visits to Paris or London, and what she wore most of the time. However, on her local visits in the

Philippines, she wore local manufactured shoes to show her support for the local industry.

From what we observed during our visit to the Philippines, Mrs. Marcos had done a lot of good for the country. She worked hard to promote light industry, helped the arts (music and opera), built hospitals and performing art centers, and helped to improve education. However, she and her husband did take advantage of the poor population, which eventually revolted against them, although they did keep all the millions of dollars which they had amassed during the years they ruled the country.

Years later, on one of Mrs. Marcos' visits to New York to attend a Metropolitan Opera performance, Florence and I approached her and reminded her of our dinner with her and Sarah. She was very happy to be reminded of the dinner we had with her. We spent some time talking with her until the end of the intermission.

Visit To Hawaii

By this time we had heard seven performances of "The Magic Flute." After the last performance we had a big party at the opera house to say good-bye to our friends and the opera personnel and to thank Sarah for the wonderful time that we had.

The next morning we left on a flight to Hawaii. Most of the flight was over the great span of the ocean. We flew for six hours before ever seeing land. We had a reservation at one of the large hotels in the center of town on the main island. The weather was warm and pleasant and the swimming pool was inviting. We rented a car, and for the next two days we traveled all over the island. We visited the rain forest and drove through the great mountains, which were all very lush and green. The beaches were beautiful and there were palm trees everywhere. We just relaxed and enjoyed ourselves.

Next we took an island hopping trip, which is a short trip by plane from island to island. Some of the islands were small and visiting them took only a few hours, but on the larger islands we would rent a car and drive around the island and sleep there overnight. Some of the volcanoes on the island are still active and we saw them spouting hot red lava moving slowly towards the sea. Many parts of the island are blackened by the lava, which covered much of the land. Our guide explained that years ago there were many villages next to the volcano, and when it erupted, the hot lava spouting out moved at a speed of 50 miles per hour down the mountain. Before the villagers realized what was happening, the lava overran the village and they all perished, buried alive with no trace left of the villages. Traveling by car, we found this charred and blackened part of the island to be a very eerie and scary sight. It is all black rock with no vegetation anywhere. Part of the island has high black rocky mountains sticking up like fingers into the sky close to the beautiful blue sea. Other parts of the island are lush green with palm trees and beautiful large hotels next to the sandy black beaches. We drove on several of the islands and stayed at night in great hotels. We took hundreds of pictures and then returned to the main island.

While having lunch in the hotel one day we met one of our young singers, Ron, who had been with us in the Philippines. He and five other singers were also returning to the States. They had stopped in Hawaii for a week's vacation and rented a bungalow on the beach several miles out of the city. We were invited to spend an evening with them on the beach, but I was afraid to drive at night on the unknown roads on the island. Ron offered to take us with him in his car and he would drive us back later.

That night there was a full moon. We arrived at the bungalow on the beach at about 9:00 p.m. The singers had a large cooking stove with roasting chickens, potatoes and hamburgers -- a real picnic. Of course they were singing, drinking, and having a wonderful time together. The moon was shining with not a cloud in the sky. The weather was pleasant with a slight breeze and we enjoyed every moment with this wonderful crowd of singers. Ron was the only male singer among all the beautiful girls in the group; unfortunately, he was gay.

Years later we met the group in Boston at various opera performances and always remembered our wonderful evening in Hawaii. Ron eventually moved to New York and tried his luck singing in small parts in concerts and local operas, living off and on with his male lovers. We met him on occasion in the city and at his concerts. He was a lovely, large and handsome young black man with a beautiful voice.

Unfortunately, we eventually lost contact with him. Years later, we met a friend of his and asked about Ron. We were told that he was in a hospital in New York, sick with AIDS. We rushed to visit him.

The hospital was full of AIDS patients, all heartbreakingly young yet in their last days of their lives. We entered Ron's room and saw a few friends sitting next to his bed. We could not recognize him: he was just a skeleton laying in bed with pipes in his veins, hardly breathing and unconscious. As Florence stood in front of his bed, crying, he suddenly opened his eyes and said, "Hi Flo," and fell back into a coma. It was a terribly sad sight, which we never forgot.

Several days later Ron died. His memory will always remind us of the wonderful times we spent together in the Philippines, Hawaii, and New York and at his concerts. Two days after that wonderful evening on the moonlight beach we returned through Los Angeles to New York. It was a great wonderful three weeks of adventure.

Sarah Caldwell And The Opera In Israel

It was great to be back home and back to my office routine. To my pleasant surprise I found that the office had been managed well while I was away. Bob and his office staff were doing a good job.

Meanwhile, Sarah also returned to Boston, getting busy with her new opera season. For the next two months we traveled constantly to Boston to hear Sarah conduct her new operas and to discuss our plans on how to help start our Israeli opera in Israel. As previously mentioned we had decided that Sarah should go to Israel and investigate what opera talents were available there. I told Sarah that the next time Mayor Lahat visited New York, I would arrange for him to meet with her and plan our next activities in Israel.

We knew when Mayor Lahat was coming with his wife to New York because he always called Florence to arrange for some opera tickets for him; this was a pleasure that we always had to pay for. Florence once asked the mayor why he didn't ask some of his millionaire friends to buy his tickets for him, and his answer was that he loved to go with us to the opera or ballet. We were fortunate that we could pay and charge it to our new opera company, which we supported.

On Mayor Lahat's next visit to New York, I invited Sarah to have lunch with him at the Russian Tea Room, which Sarah loved. During the long pleasant meal we outlined an agreement by which the mayor would pay for Sarah's visit to Israel and our foundation would finance her flights, while I would pay my own expenses. I recruited two of my close friends in Israel, Moshe and Jacky, to help me arrange for auditions with Sarah. We placed advertisements in the local Israeli papers for auditions of singers and I flew to Israel to prepare the schedule as well as the theatre where the auditions would take place. The mayor gave me a space in his office as well as a secretary to help me organize the auditions. In one week we received over 120 applications for auditions.

Sarah arrived a week later, and after reviewing the location for the auditions, we selected a concert hall in mid-town Tel Aviv. It was early November and the concert hall was not heated, so we arranged for electrical heaters to be placed next to Sarah's seat. We set up a time schedule for each singer. Moshe and Jacky stayed in the theatre's entrance hall where Sarah and I were sitting. Sarah did not want to have anyone in the hall besides me while she was auditioning the singers. This made many of the mayor's personnel very unhappy. However, no one could overrule Sarah's decision. It took us three days to audition 120 singers. We never turned down any singer, even though many of the singers had no singing experience at all.

Although I had never been to any auditions before, while sitting next to Sarah and listening, I realized even with my limited knowledge that most of the singers were unfit to sing anywhere, much less in the technically demanding world of opera. Sarah told me that the fact is that after hearing just a few notes sung by a singer, she could immediately tell whether they were real singers or not. To be polite, in most of the cases she let even the worst singers sing at least four or five minutes before dismissing them.

As the auditions were progressing, Sarah told me that none of the singers she had heard so far were qualified to sing opera. It was indeed disappointing. There were only a few male Israeli singers and female Russian singers who were a possibility. However, they needed a great deal of training and improvement.

Once, while we were listening to a female Russian singer, Sarah suddenly turned to me and said, "Please leave the theater. I will see you later." I was very upset to be dismissed in such a manner, especially when I was doing so much for her, arranging for her to come to Israel and organizing the auditions. I walked out into the entrance hall to join Moshe and Jacky, who managed the crowd of singers waiting for their turn to be auditioned. I did not join Sarah for the rest of the afternoon.

After the audition, I took Sarah back to the hotel, but I did not feel like talking to her. As we drove, she turned to me and apologized for dismissing me so abruptly, and explained the reason. She said that the Russian singer whom she was auditioning needed some personal advice, and she did not want to make these remarks in front of me. The remarks were: "Young lady, you have a pretty good voice; however, your physical presentation is very poor. Your large bosoms are reaching your stomach and you are not wearing a bra. So why don't you go home, take care of yourself, and come back for another audition." Sarah said to me, "I realized that I hurt you and I am very sorry. Please let us be friends." Of course I forgave her. That is how Sarah was, abrupt and in most cases not very polite, but that was Sarah. She was known to be unsociable. The thing she cared for most was her opera and its successful performances. Unfortunately, she had her sleeping sickness, and from time to time, as embarrassing as it was to me, she would fall asleep for a minute or two in the middle of talking or an audition and I would touch her arm so as to shake her out of her sleep. She never wore a watch, she had great difficulty getting up in the morning, and most times she did not keep her appointments on time. As a result, I had a lot of trouble keeping up with her appointments and her schedules with Israeli conductors, singers, set designers and other dignitaries. If the appointments were arranged for 9:00 a.m., I started knocking on her door at 7:00 a.m., knowing that she had a hard time waking up. Unfortunately, she would finally appear only at 11:00 a.m. instead of 9:00 a.m. By that time I would have half a dozen visitors waiting for their appointments with her. It was very embarrassing for me to keep postponing all this appointments for hours, but that was Sarah, and in most cases she was forgiven. She was, after all, the greatest woman in the opera world, a genius, and as such, was not one of us simple mortals.

Sarah did much better in the evening, and on most evenings we were invited to dinners and parties in her honor. Once we were invited to a 6:00 p.m. party at the home of Israel's president in Jerusalem. Sarah did not feel too well that day, but I told her it was very important that she attend. I started knocking at her door at 3:00 p.m. Every time that she said she was coming but then didn't appear, I would get very nervous, because I knew that she must attend the President's party dead or alive. It took an hour to travel from Tel Aviv to Jerusalem, so we had to leave the hotel no later than 5:00 p.m.

At 4:30 p.m., I knocked on Sarah's door again and said that she must come out within fifteen minutes and I would never forgive her if she didn't. She did come out, wearing a simple loose dress. I rushed her to my car and took off to Jerusalem. On the way she said "I feel very sick, and if I die you'll be responsible for my death."

We reached the President's home just in time. There was a big crowd waiting for Sarah and she was greeted by the president and his wife. Everyone in the crowd was coming to shake her hand. As sick as she was, Sarah enjoyed the party…but while the president, was speaking I noticed that Sarah, who was sitting next to me, was falling asleep! I kept nudging her constantly so that no one would notice. All and all, however, it was a very successful evening, and Sarah thanked me for insisting on her coming to the party.

The next morning, we toured the city with some of the mayor's personnel to review the various buildings and theater spaces which could be used for opera performances. The best theater was the Habima Theater, which was the home of the Israeli Symphony Orchestra. However, it was limited because there was no backstage space for scenery, which has to be changed during intermissions. While Sarah was sitting at the theater discussing the situation with the group, she fell asleep again for a few minutes. It made me sick to my stomach, realizing that Sarah's sleeping sickness performance would not go over well with the eager beaver attitude of the Israelis, and it was very embarrassing to me. But I could do nothing but follow the events as they progressed.

Every evening we were invited to opera friends' homes for parties where we met many opera enthusiasts who knew of Sarah and were honored to be spending time with her. In contrast, although Sarah was polite, she never warmed up to the crowds. She always kept her distance, never acting too friendly except to a very few close friends, including Florence and me. I don't think that Sarah thought much of herself because she was so fat and cumbersome and could hardly walk. Yet even with all this physical difficulty and her sleeping sickness, she was still able to bring glorious opera performances to the world. She had no other interests in her life except for opera, so nothing stood in her way of attaining this goal. Managing an opera company is an unbelievably difficult undertaking, yet she always managed to succeed in coming up with great innovative opera performances which were appreciated by her loving audiences. Despite her impressive background, the Israelis were disappointed by her physical weakness. But they never showed it, and treated Sarah with respect for her greatness in the opera world.

Having completed the auditions, we had a meeting at the mayor's office with representatives of the city arts and music department, and there Sarah reported the results. Her conclusion was very disappointing: none of the singers who auditioned were qualified to sing in a good quality opera. There were, however, a few who had some talent and experience, so Sarah therefore suggested starting a summer opera workshop to train some of these potential singers. Sarah agreed to come back again to Israel next summer to start this opera workshop. The mayor approved a small budget for Sarah and her group, and they selected a local Israeli manager to coordinate the activities of the workshop. For the next two days Sarah, the manager, and I sat and outlined the program and the number of singers, teachers, lighting, sound, and set designers and other opera personnel who would come with Sarah from Boston for the workshop. Florence and I would join them and pay our own expenses. Mayor Lahat was very enthusiastic about this project and promised to do his best to help us.

Before returning to the States, I took Sarah for a buying spree in Jaffa, Jerusalem, and Hebron. Sarah loved to shop, and she quickly learned how to negotiate prices down with the local shopkeepers. In Hebron she bought a great number of local green glass tumblers and plates, and in the bazaar in Jerusalem she bought various gifts for her friends in the States. In Jaffa we went to a small brass shop where she spent a lot of time selecting lamps, candlestick holders, and a Russian tea samovar. She negotiated every item down in price, and the owner of the shop appreciated her talent in selecting the best items in his shop. We found out later that the tea samovar she bought was a real antique which had belonged to the Russian Tsar, stamped and dated by the Russian Court. She knew what she was buying. I helped her package all her gifts, and carried most of them back to Boston for her. Some of the glass items we packaged and shipped via the postal service. Unfortunately many of the glasses arrived broken in Boston.

The day came for us to go back to the States. Sarah was very tired and could hardly walk. She asked me to pack her luggage. I was somewhat embarrassed to pack her personal belongings, but complied. I started to fold each item properly, but Sarah told me not to bother, saying "Just push it all in the valise." After I finished packing I found two more pairs of her shoes. I asked her where I should pack them, and she said, "In the valise." The valise was already packed full, and when I opened it and put the shoes in, I had a hard time closing it. Sarah said, "Let me help you." She sat on the valise and her ample weight sure helped in closing the valise! One thing about Sarah: she had a good sense of humor.

Flying back to the States, Sarah's seat was next to mine, and unfortunately, because of her size she was half spilling over into my seat and I was very uncomfortable. She, on the other hand, fell asleep as soon as the plane took off. We stopped in London for several hours, and since she could not walk much, I got a wheelchair for her and pushed her around in the terminal. She loved going shopping in the duty-free shops. She also bought me a gift: a watch with two time zones so that I would know the time difference between the United States and Israel.

On our flight from London to New York, knowing that I was uncomfortable in my seat, she suggested that I talk to the stewardess and tell her that it was difficult for me to sit squeezed in my seat because of Sarah, and hopefully she would get me another seat. I took Sarah's suggestion: as soon as the flight took off I told the stewardess my difficulty, and sure enough, she moved me to the first class cabin. I had a wonderfully pleasant flight to New York, thanks to Sarah's thoughtfulness. When we arrived in New York I booked her on a flight to Boston, and once again I got her a wheelchair and wheeled her to her plane to Boston.

The trip to Israel with Sarah opened a new chapter in my life. Getting to know such a great person and learn about the life of the opera world firsthand was an exciting and wonderful opportunity for me. I managed to overlook the problem of dealing with someone as difficult as Sarah. I realized that she was not one of us average human beings. She stood head and shoulders above us. I respected her genius and I felt lucky to be so close to her. I learned a great deal from her: her strength of character, her perseverance, and her ability to overcome difficulties against all odds and come out with great opera performances.

I admired her knowledge of the art of opera, which includes orchestration, singing, set designing, lighting, sound and hundreds of other elements, which when put together produce a great performance. Working with her added another dimension to Florence's and my life.

For Florence, her close relationship with the singers and the opera personnel brought great emotional fulfillment. To her, Sarah was a god of opera, whereas for me she was just a great exceptional woman with whom I had the fortune to be closely associated.

Opera Workshop In Israel

For the next two months we traveled frequently to Boston to recruit and prepare the personnel for the opera workshop in Israel. Avrom Roseman, the workshop's Israeli representative, was preparing the location of the workshop in Tel Aviv, and we were in communication with him daily.

Mayor Lahat visited New York again, and we met with him and finalized the plan for the workshop. A budget was approved for a three-week workshop. It included eleven members of Sarah's opera personnel: singers, music teachers, piano accompanist, conductor, and light designer. Details of the workshop classes were made and the money was allocated for each of the activities.

Florence and I left for Israel in order to be there a few days before Sarah and her troupe arrived. We helped arrange for the location of the workshop and make the hotel reservations. Mr. Roseman, who was appointed by the mayor to be the Israeli coordinator of the workshop, came from the Israeli orchestra management. When I met him, I was not particularly impressed. He was a fast, slippery talker. Yet he was supposed to be the budget manager of the workshop, and that worried me. Unfortunately, my instincts were correct. We found out later that Mr. Roseman was known to be unreliable on matters of finance with his previous organizations, and he turned out to be no more trustworthy in handling our budget.

The space for the workshop was set up in a large hall in the center of Tel Aviv, which included several classrooms. Sarah and her troupe arrived and settled down in the hotel. Many of the singers who had auditioned previously for Sarah were invited to participate.

I noticed that Mr. Roseman was busy setting up an office for himself with new furniture, a typewriter, a secretary and a new car. I asked him why he needed the office for the short time our workshop would run. He said that it was necessary for the future. The fact was that he took all these expenses out of the workshop's budget without consulting Sarah and me, as well as setting himself up with a fat salary that also came out of our budget. Before long, we found out that we were short of money for our workshop activity.

Mr. Roseman's shady accounting came out later in the season, unfortunately. At the beginning, as far as we knew, the workshop was progressing nicely. The sound of singing and music was always coming out of the various classrooms and Sarah was busy lecturing.

In the evening we were meeting with groups of local opera supporters and friends and were invited to local homes to meet the various opera groups who were happy to spend time with Sarah.

On our day off, Saturday, we rented cars and our entire opera group took off for trips around the country. We visited the old city of Jerusalem, where Sarah spent much of the time bargaining in the bazaar for purchases she was making. She learned quickly how to talk to the merchants and negotiate with them. The Arabs loved to bargain and Sarah provided them with that pleasure.

We visited Nazareth, the beautiful New Church of the Nativity. I remember the church years back when it was the small original building with steps going down to the cave where Jesus lived. The new church above the old building is a beautiful marble structure, but in my opinion it had lost its originality.

For whatever reason, Sarah did not go into the church. She sat outside while we visited the church. We continued our trip to Tiberius.

It is always a beautiful drive over the mountain, and then you suddenly see the blue Sea of Galilee spread out in front of you, surrounded by mountain all around. We stopped in Tiberius at a restaurant at the water's edge and had of course a fresh fish lunch with pita, humus, and French fries. Afterwards, we continued to the church next to the seashore where Jesus walked on the water and then visited the ruins of the synagogue and church where Jesus preached. We all had a wonderful time and returned late at night to Tel Aviv.

The workshop was progressing very well. Sarah selected three singers and two directors to come for their training with her opera company in Boston. Later in the season, just before we left, we found out that Roseman had spent most of the money, and the last payment due to Sarah could not be paid. It was very aggravating for her. She left with a promise to be paid later after she returned to Boston.

On our final night in Israel, we had a very touching farewell party with all the singers taking part in the ceremony. Mayor Lahat was very pleased with Sarah's accomplishments, and a plan was made for Sarah to return next year to stage a new opera performance with the local Israeli singers and directors who would spend time training with Sarah's Opera Company of Boston.

Unfortunately, several months after our return to the States, the war in Lebanon started. Our plans to perform opera in Israel had to be cancelled, and our dream of starting a new opera company there was shattered. Notwithstanding this disappointment, Sarah brought two of the Israeli singers and two directors to Boston, and we paid their expenses out of our foundation money. Two of the Israeli directors who were trained by Sarah in time became famous directors in Israel and personal friends of ours.

Although Sarah was always short of money for her opera company, she always managed to put on outstanding performances. Many sets were designed by our friend Sharir in Israel and built by an Israeli company named Irgonit. The cost of building the sets in Israel was much lower than in the States. Most of the time, I was the negotiator between Sarah and Irgonit. Unfortunately Sarah was always short of money and payment to Irgonit was postponed for years, which left me embarrassed.

Despite all the difficulties Sarah faced, nothing could stop her from staging outstanding original operas. She was a world-class opera genius. I remember one of the performances of "The Mass," composed by Leonard Bernstein. She had Leonard Bernstein himself sitting with us in the first row in the orchestra. When the performance was over, Bernstein was so excited that he walked onto the stage while Sarah was receiving her ovations, knelt down next to her, and kissed her hand. It was a very touching gesture on his part. He loved her performance. Sarah adored Leonard Bernstein, whom she knew from the time they were students together with famed conductor Dr. Sergei Koussevitzky, and no one could ever say a bad word about "Lenny" to her.

The next evening at a dinner party for Sarah, Bernstein arrived wearing a cape and a large brimmed hat. He had three young men with him. He was drunk and could hardly stand on his feet, wobbling from side to side embarrassing everyone. Eventually he sat down next to Sarah and Rosalie Levine, the wife of the famous Joe Levine movie mogul. She was wearing a beautiful feather dress like a large bird. He was picking at her feathers, drinking and singing aloud. While our entertainer was singing, accompanied by her pianist, Lenny was drunkenly singing along, mimicking the singer, who was brave enough to continue singing. What a sorry sight it was to see the deterioration of this great outstanding genius, world-renowned composer, conductor, and musician, who had become such a drunk. I was sorry for him.

The next evening we were invited to the wedding of Linda Cabbot Lodge, who was a member of the opera company's board of directors. She had grown children and the wedding was taking place at Princeton University in her family-established Cabbot Hall. Linda came from very famous old Boston families, the Cabbots and the Lodges. The ceremony was very simple. The son and daughter read poems about the mother and their love. Linda wore her mother's original lace wedding dress. Roger, her new husband, was a professor at the university, a wonderful gentleman. After the ceremony came dinner and dancing. It was a lovely evening.

The next day, we had a big party under a very large tent at the top of the mountain resort. Except for Florence and me, everyone was dressed in costume. Rosalie Levine came dressed as a cowgirl with boots, a hat, and all. That outfit must have cost her a fortune, but she could well afford it. Most friends of the opera and members of the board were there and we had a great day together.

Through the years we had many parties and dinners with Sarah and the opera crowd. For unknown reasons, Sarah was always giving Florence and me special attention and befriended us more than many of her rich friends. After dinners or parties she always left early with us, spending a few hours with us in a small restaurant or hotel lobby having coffee and dessert.

She never let us get too friendly with the singers we loved because she felt that they only wanted to get friendly with us because of our close relationship with her. She always kept her distance from her singers. However, at the same time she could recognize talent, and through the years she started the careers of many of the world's most renowned singers, who started singing in her Opera Company of Boston. For all the years I knew her she never badmouthed any singer or person she associated with, and never complained about anything. As for myself, I always felt that I was privileged to be associated with this great personality. With all her faults, and all the difficulties of keeping up with her, and as rough and abrasive a personality as she had, in a strange way I admired and liked her.

Visit With Sarah Caldwell To London

Our plan to have an opera company in Israel had been placed on a back burner. However, since recruiting top opera singers requires a year's worth of advance planning, Sarah continued to search for potential singers for opening night of the performance of "Aida" in Israel. One morning while I was working in my office I received a call from Sarah. In her usual abrupt voice, she said, "Rafa" (that is what she calls me); "we are flying to London tonight at 9:00 p.m. to recruit two singers for the opera in Israel. I have the tickets already and I will wait for you in the airport in Boston at 8:00 p.m. Our flight is with United Airlines, Flight No. 211 at 9:00. See you soon." Then she hung up the phone.

It took me several minutes to digest the meaning of this call. I was in the middle of an important meeting and a trip to London was hardly included in my plans. I called Florence and told her that I was going to London with Sarah that night and that I would be home shortly to pack and fly that evening to Boston. Florence thought at first that I was joking. But knowing Sarah, we were not surprised, because that is how she was.

I arrived in Boston at 7:00 p.m., picked up my ticket, and waited for her. By 8:00 she had not arrived, so I called her home and was told by Jimmy, her assistant that she had just left for the airport. The flight to London was on time and I was getting jittery. By 8:30 p.m. the waiting passengers started boarding the plane and there was still no sign of Sarah. By this time I was shaken up and worried that we would miss our flight. At five minutes to 9:00, when the last passengers were boarding, Sarah finally arrived with a small valise.

We were rushed to our seats, but Sarah had difficulty walking and it took her some time to walk through the aisle. I was seated next to her in the middle row and since she was so heavy, I was squeezed in between her and the next passenger and I could hardly move.

Sarah told me that in London we would meet Shirley Verrett and Sherrill Milnes, two famous singers who had started their careers with Sarah's opera company in Boston. As soon as the jet engine started and before we took off, Sarah already fell asleep. The perfume she used was very irritating. When I had to go to the bathroom I did not want to wake Sarah up, but after several hours, I could not wait any longer. I tried several times to wake her up. Eventually she woke up and I rushed to the bathroom. For a while I stood in the back of the plane, not wanting to wake her again, but eventually I did and again sat squeezed between her and my other neighbor. I could not fall asleep through the whole flight, and by the time we arrived in London at 3:00 a.m. I was a real wreck.

When we got off the plane I got a wheelchair for Sarah and pushed her through the airport to a taxi. We arrived at the Ritz Hotel at 4:00 a.m. We planned to have breakfast at 9:00 a.m. I helped her to her room and left for my room next to hers. I tried to sleep, but I was so exhausted that I couldn't.

I got out of bed at 7:00 a.m. and took a luxurious warm bath for an hour and a half. That relaxed me and made my exhaustion disappear; even though I had not slept all night I was fully awake and felt much better. I called Sarah at a quarter to nine to see if she was ready for breakfast. After several rings, Sarah answered and told me that I had just woken her up and that she would be ready in half an hour.

From my previous experience with her in Israel, I knew that she had a hard time waking up in the morning. I called her again at 9:30, but got no answer. I called again at 10:00 and she answered and said she would be ready at 10:30. I called again at 10:30. Finally, at 10:45, she met me for breakfast in the beautiful restaurant of the Ritz Hotel. The food was great and after several cups of coffee I was fully awake. Sarah told me that Shirley Verrett was also staying at the hotel with her husband and daughter, and Sarah planned to meet with her some time during the day.

After breakfast we sat in the lobby and Sarah asked me to call Shirley Verrett and tell her that she was in the hotel and wanted to meet her. I had never met or seen Shirley, but I had heard that she was a beautiful woman. There were several glass telephone booths at the lobby and I went in one of them to call Shirley Verrett's room. As I was standing in my booth I saw a gorgeous, tall black woman in the next booth. She was on the phone and her phone booth door was open. When I asked the telephone operator for Shirley Verrett's room, the gorgeous woman next to my booth turned to me and said, "I heard you calling for Ms. Verrett. That's me. Can I help you?" I was shocked and terribly embarrassed that I hadn't known that Ms. Verrett was a black woman. I told her that Sarah Caldwell was in the lobby and would like to talk to her. She was delighted and left the booth with me to meet Sarah, who was sitting on the sofa in the lobby.

Ms. Verrett was very happy to see Sarah again. She knew Sarah very well, having sung in many operas in Boston under Sarah's direction and conducting. Sarah told Shirley of her association with the Israeli Opera and asked her if she could come to Israel for the opening night of the Israeli opera season for the "Aida" performance. Shirley said that she would be happy to, but that it would have to be some time the following year because she was currently busy singing in Paris and London. She promised to check her schedule with her agent. Shirley and Sarah talked for an hour about various opera performances and their old times together in Boston. I sat there listening and looking with admiration at this beautiful singer with a wonderful personality. Ms. Verrett asked me what I did and where I came from. When I told her I lived in

Manhattan, I found out that we were neighbors. She lived just one block away from my apartment, and when she heard that I was in the personnel business, she said that she wanted her husband to meet me because he needed help in his lithography printing business. While talking to Shirley I was thinking how impressed Florence would be to hear that I had met Shirley Verrett.

After Shirley left, Sarah told me that she also wanted to meet Sherrill Milnes, who was also in London, and see if she could also recruit him for the opening night of "Aida" in Israel. Sarah's plan was that he would sing with Shirley Verrett in "Aida" as he had done before in Boston with Sarah directing. I called Sherrill Milnes in his hotel and Sarah got on the phone and told him that she was in London and wanted to speak with him. She set up a meeting with him for that afternoon. After a pleasant lunch in the hotel we took a taxi to Sherill's hotel.

Sherrill was waiting for us. He was a tall, handsome man with a great baritone voice. Like Shirley Verrett, he was delighted to see Sarah again, having sung in her operas many times. He shook my hand warmly and we sat down in his hotel living room. Sarah told him of her work in Israel and told him that she would like him to sing with Shirley Verrett in "Aida." Sherrill immediately said that he was interested and that he would like Sarah to meet his agent, who was staying at the same hotel. A few minutes later his agent joined us. We had a drink together and a discussion started. First we reviewed the schedule to see when Sherrill would be available, and then the discussion moved onto the financial cost of having him sing in Israel.

Although I knew the limits of our budget, I never negotiated with singers or their agents; Sarah took care of those details. We were planning to have six performances as well as four master classes. Sherrill wanted to bring his wife along, fly first class, stay in a five-star hotel in Israel, and get paid $5,000 per performance. While Sarah was discussing these details, I was trying to figure out how all these expenses could be paid out of our limited budget of $35,000. As I sat quietly listening to the discussion, suddenly Sarah got up and said that she had to leave. She said that she would be back in an hour and that I should conclude the negotiations while she was away. I was dumbfounded. I had no idea how to negotiate with an agent or a singer.

I started by telling Sherrill and his agent how difficult things were in Israel, the limited budget we had, and how important it was to have such a great singer like him come to Israel to sing there. I planned to have El-Al Airlines give us free tickets as their donation, and have the hotel in Israel do the same. If Sherrill would agree to give us seven master classes instead of four, the sale of the tickets would enable us to cover our budget of $35,000. Sherrill's agent wrote an outline of our negotiations, and by the time Sarah came back, we had it all complete. Sarah looked over the outline and was very pleased with my accomplishments. The date for opening night had to wait until we could review Shirley Verrett's schedule. We left Sherrill with the copy of our agreement. Sarah was very happy and complimented me on my negotiating skill.

The next morning we left for the airport.

Unfortunately with all the effort we spent on this project it did not go through. The war between Israel and Lebanon was raging and no funds were available for the opera and the project was scrapped.

American Israel Opera Foundation

Even though our project of starting an opera company in Israel was discontinued, Florence felt that we should continue with our activities and raise funds to help Israeli singers and opera directors. Sarah could train them in her opera company in Boston, and when they returned to Israel they could help Israel establish an opera company some time in the future. Sarah's concept was that Israel should have an Israeli Opera with Israeli singers, not imported talent, and her Opera Company of Boston could be the source of this training for the future company in Israel.

Our first goal for our opera foundation was to raise money. Florence and I recruited several new members of the board who were willing to help us find donors. Sarah was always ready to travel with us and speak to various groups helping raise funds for the foundation. As the president of the foundation, I could not escape speaking at such meetings, which unfortunately was a torturous experience for me. Sarah was a wonderful speaker and a great enthusiastic supporter of Israel. She always said in her speeches that she was "Methodist Zionist." and she meant it. In contrast, for each of my speeches I spent many hours of preparation, but when I finally stood up to speak, my heart was pounding, I would get short of breath, and I would sweat profusely. However, I had no choice, because as the president of our small organization, I had to speak if I wanted to raise money for the foundation.

At the same time I was getting very busy in my own business, which was growing and expanding.

One of our friends, Mira Berman, who had a prosperous public relations company, approached me and told me that while she was out of the country on a business trip, her partner had stolen all her money. She was left without a penny to her name. She had lost all she had, including her business and her clients, and she was destitute. She said, "Efraim, you must give me a job, any job, with any salary. Please help me." It occurred to me at the time that Mira could help me fundraise for our foundation. However, I did not have much money to offer her. I told Mira that I could offer her only $250 per week, if she was interested. She haggled with me and thanked me for helping her, and she started working for me the next day. She closed her office and sold all her furniture except for her personal large desk, which she brought along to my office. Although Mira only worked for me for two years, that desk remained with me for the next 20 years, moving from one office to the next.

With Mira running our fundraising activities, things began to move quickly. Mira was a first class public relations person who knew hundreds of people. With her help, we started raising substantial amounts of money. Our plan was to have a gala dinner with the hope of raising over $100,000 as a start, and then to spend some of the money training singers in the States. At the same time, we would help various groups in Israel start small opera performances and introduce opera to schoolchildren around the country. For this purpose we decided to visit Israel with Mira and Sarah.

For the next several months Mira arranged various meetings in Israel to introduce our plans. Mira traveled to Israel a week before we did and set up many meetings for us. For the next two weeks Florence, Sarah, and I participated in many small parties, mostly around Tel Aviv. We met many executives of government agencies, heads of departments in the performing arts, and private individuals interested in promoting opera, concerts, and choruses. We met many local conductors, singers, and composers. We visited several small orchestras and music schools. We were busy 14 hours each day, and we found a great enthusiasm for our plans.

Before we returned to the States, I called Mayor Lahat to tell him of our visit, and we met with him one evening at the municipality. He had several of the city's officials with him. Sarah, Florence, Mira, and I sat with the mayor and discussed our foundation's fundraising activities in the States. The mayor said that the money we raised belonged to him, and he would decide where the money should be spent. He insisted that the money raised by us should be sent to him and not spent by us. I was shocked to hear his attack. I told the mayor that it seemed that he did not understand that our American Israel Opera Foundation was an American corporation and was free to act as it wished to dispose of its funds at the direction of its board. He could not dictate to us what we should do with our funds. Of course we did not mind helping the mayor with some of the funds, but it was our decision, not his.

The discussion was getting ugly. Florence was so upset that she started to cry and left the meeting. Mira and Sarah did not say a word. I stood up to leave. The mayor's last words to us were that he would report us to the Internal Revenue Service to look into this matter. My last words to the mayor were, "I am sorry that you forget that we are American citizens representing American corporations, and you have no jurisdiction over our activities. I am sorry that you have to spoil a good relationship between us," and we all left. It was the ugliest meeting I ever had in my life.

However, this unpleasant experience did not stop us from proceeding with our plans in preparing our fundraising dinner, which took eight months. Mira, Florence and I did most of the work. We planned to have 500 guests. We rented a hall at The Lincoln Library of the Performing Arts and decorated it with scenery and sets from the opera house in Boston. It was a black tie dinner. The date was Saturday, October 17, 1987. We chose the best caterer in town, as well as a first class orchestra. Most of my female employees were recruited to help us at the dinner. Sara brought along several singers from the Opera Company of Boston who sang before and during dinner. We had six ambassadors and several consulates from various countries. It was a chic, plush and elegant dinner. Most of the woman dressed in long gowns and jewels, and all the men wore tuxedoes. The tables had silver utensils with crystal glasses around the table. Sarah was the guest speaker, and as usual she charmed the guests. Some of the invited guests were Kitty Carlisle Hart, Telly Savalas, composer Lukas Foss, singer Anna Moffo, the actor Topol, and others. Three of the winners of our singing competition sang. One in particular was the outstanding Markella Hatziana. Sarah had discovered her, and she went on to have an outstanding career as mezzo-soprano. We heard her sing in Philadelphia and the Metropolitan Opera.

The gala dinner was an outstanding success and everyone was very happy. We had over $100,000 of pledges committed and we looked forward to a successful year. After dinner, we left exhausted. Sarah flew back to Boston. The next morning we dismantled all the stage sets and shipped them back to Boston.

That evening, we heard of the market collapse and its unbelievable financial losses. To our misfortune, most of the pledges committed were not paid, and in the end, we barely had enough money to pay for the dinner. It was very discouraging and heartbreaking. The financial market continued to drop and it also affected our agency's business, as well as the Opera Company of Boston, which had been running in the red all along. This never fazed Sarah. She always put together sufficient funds to stage a performance. She owed money to everyone: the singers, directors, orchestra, and stage builders. The board of directors had a difficult time keeping up with Sarah's commitment. However with all the difficulties Sarah succeeded in staging a marvelous performance.

To help promote peace between the United States and Russia, Sarah started a program of music exchange with Russia. She called it "Let's Make Music Together." She received a grant from the U.S. government to start this program. She brought a group of singers and musicians to Russia and held opera and concert performances there. Unfortunately, at this time I was having difficulties with my various business ventures, and I could not join Sarah in her visit to Russia.

While she was in Moscow, Sarah stayed at the home of Ambassador Matlock and his wife at the American Embassy. They formed a close relationship which continued after the ambassador finished his tenure in Russia and settled down in New York. We had the opportunity to meet them with Sarah in New York several times, once when the ambassador's book was published and the second time at his birthday party. The ambassador and his wife are a charming couple, very simple and pleasant.

Sarah is never impressed with people and never mentions her important friends and her meetings with them. I remember that she was once invited to meet with President Clinton and his wife at the White House. When we met Sarah the next day, she never mentioned the meeting; we only learned about it from the New York Times. Through the years when we spent time with Sarah in public places, many opera enthusiasts approached her and told her how much they loved her operas and appreciated her performances. She would just nod and thank them, never continuing a conversation. It was always embarrassing to see all this enthusiasm rebuffed by her.

One of the great performances Sarah was going to stage was "Turandot." This was a very big undertaking during this period. We were visiting Boston often to see the rehearsals. Sarah had the idea to have the costumes made in China so that they would be authentic. Some years previously she had performed in China with the Opera Company of Beijing and had known some of the directors and personnel in China. Sarah invited a group of the Chinese costume designers and dressmakers to Boston to plan and measure the various costumes needed for the singers and actors on the stage.

Several months later, the costumes arrived with several of the designers. They were gorgeously made of beautiful Chinese material, and to our surprise all the costumes were lined with fine cloth at no additional cost because the Chinese did not want the singers to have the material of the costume worn directly on their bodies, so as not to damage the beautiful cloth.

One morning I had a call from Sarah telling me that two of the Chinese designers were on their way to New York and would arrive that afternoon, and she would like Florence and me to meet them at the airport and bring them to the Chinese Embassy. She also added that they did not speak English. We waited at the gate for the flight to arrive and eventually we saw two middle-aged Chinese carrying small valises, looking lost in the big crowd. We approached them and said "Hello." They smiled and shook hands with us, but when we asked them how the flight was, they just smiled and said something in Chinese.

We guided them out of the airport and I left Florence and them at the curb while I went to get my car from the parking lot. As Florence stood waiting with them, they pulled some boxes out of their valises and gave her several small gifts. While they did this they talked to her in Chinese -- not a word of English was spoken between them. Even the words "yes" and "no" could not be conveyed to them. We got them into our car and drove to Manhattan. On the way Florence talked and they also talked, neither party understanding what the other was saying.

Eventually we reached the embassy, which was on 43rd Street and 12th Avenue, across from the 42nd Street Piers. It seemed that the embassy also served as a hotel for important Chinese officials. We stopped at the entrance, and as we were looking for someone to speak to, a beautifully-dressed Chinese woman asked us in perfect English if she could help us. We explained to the young woman that we were with two Chinese designers whom we had brought from Boston. She knew of their visit, And there was a pleasant meeting between our passengers and the young woman. She thanked us profusely for helping her comrades and invited us into the embassy for a cup of tea.

The young lady was in fact a singer, a graduate of the Julliard School of Music in New York, and was head of the cultural department at the embassy. Florence suggested to her that she might like to join our two new Chinese friends on a tour of New York to see some of the museums and possibly an opera performance. She accepted our invitation and for the next two days we all enjoyed New York, visiting the Metropolitan Museum, the Guggenheim Museum, and the Natural Museum of Art.

The two designers were mesmerized. They had never visited a foreign country before and had never been to a museum such as the Met. They looked at each painting closely, studying the brush strokes, and we could see how excited they were. In the evening we invited them for a Chinese dinner, and our singer friend suggested a restaurant she knew. When we got to the restaurant, we were greeted with a royal reception by the owner, and we had a Chinese meal, which we had never had before. The next day we took them to the Metropolitan Opera and we had a wonderful evening with them.

Unfortunately, we could not talk to them directly. Our singer was our translator, and with her help, we learned a great deal about their life and their work in China. It seemed that the designers were very famous designers in Communist China and had never have been out of the country before. They appreciated our spending our time with them. In turn, they learned that Florence had a broken elbow and had continuous pain, and invited her to come to China, where, they assured her, they had a guaranteed, traditional Chinese cure for her pain.

The singer, too, told us of her life experience. She was a singer in the Opera of China. However, during the revolutionary period, most artists and educated people were sent to work on the land as farmers and workers, and she was on a farm for four years before a change took place. Her husband, whom she did not see during those four years, was working for the Chinese embassy in Egypt, and she also lost contact with her daughter. In the last several years, things had changed, and now she was in the United States working for the embassy. Before the return of our two Chinese friends to China, we were invited to the Chinese embassy for a reception and we had a very pleasant evening with our new friends.

The rehearsals for "Turandot" were progressing nicely. Sarah recruited a whole group of Korean martial artists to act in one of the scenes. She also recruited a jazz band. Both were very original ideas. The costumes arrived from China with a group of Chinese dressmakers and designers who worked on fitting the costumes for each of the singers on the stage. The staging was a grandiose undertaking and Sarah was much over her budget, but this never bothered her. As she once said to me, "Who pays?" She was ruthless with no boundaries when it came to making her performances possible. Her promises to pay meant nothing to her. She always ran over her budget and she drove the board of directors crazy. However once you attended her opera performance you were mesmerized by her genius, forgave her, again fell under her spell, and continued to raise money to pay for her next performance.

The opening night of "Turandot" was a great success. Our Chinese friends were also very impressed. After the performance we had a cocktail party on the main entrance hall. The marble floors, pillars, and hall mirrors shone. The large chandeliers were lit and it was all in all a great night. We stayed in Boston for two days so as to hear the opera again the following night. When we arrived at the opera house on the second night, we were called in by our Chinese friends to a room on the second floor, and there to our surprise was the whole group of our Chinese friends waiting for us with a table of fruits and all kinds of sweets and drinks. When Florence and I came in they gave us a standing ovation. The manager of the group, through an interpreter, told us how appreciative they were for the help and attention that we had given their friends when they were in New York. Then they pulled out two rolls of beautiful embroidered Chinese cloth, a gift to us to remember them by. It was all very touching and wonderful. On our part we never thought that we had done that much to deserve all this attention. The rolls of beautiful material are still in our closet. Florence never made a dress out of the cloth, but we look at it from time to time and remember the wonderful time we had with our Chinese friends.

Sarah's project with Russia, "Making Music Together," was also progressing well. Sarah traveled to Russia several times a month while still running her opera company in Boston. But her health was failing, and at one point she was rushed to the hospital with double pneumonia. We heard of her illness while we were visiting Israel and we kept in touch, following her condition every day on the phone with Jimmy, her assistant. She was very sick and at times we feared that we might lose her. She stayed in the hospital for several months, during which time she was cared for by her personal friend, Dr. Joe Gardella, who was very devoted to her, as was his wife. Without his help, I don't think Sarah would have survived.

We met Dr. Gardella and his wife several more times though the years at the opera house as well as in their home. They were wonderful people and great friends. On one of our visits to Boston at the Gardellas' home, we met their son, Charles, and his wife. Charles was a sculptor who lived in the Netherlands.

At that time, Sarah was preparing the Greek opera "Medea", and in her staging she planned to have a large white sculptured horse on the stage. Sarah wanted to help Charles, and she discussed with me the possibility of having Charles design and build the horse in Israel with our friends at Irgonit, who had built several stage sets for Sarah. Irgonit would work with Charles to build that large horse statue in Israel and then ship it to the opera house in Boston. I negotiated a contract with Irgonit and Charles went to Israel with his wife.

For the next six months Charles worked in Israel. When the large white horse was completed, it was dismantled and shipped to Boston. Of course it took some time for Sarah to pay Irgonit for their work, and unfortunately I was involved in taking care of this debt on Sarah's behalf. For the "Medea" opera, Sarah imported Greek performers and singers. The large white horse was hanging over the stage, very impressively. Again the opera was a very original work of Sarah's and very successful.

Sarah never forgot her commitment to help Israel, and she invited two of the young Israeli directors whom she had met named Chanan Snir and Micha Levinson, to come to Boston and learn how to direct an opera. Our foundation allocated the money and each of the directors spent several months in Boston.

Sarah spent a great deal of her time with them and in fact gave them the opportunity to participate in directing two of her operas. Sarah's uncanny intuition of selecting talent eventually paid off. The young directors, Chanan Snir and Micha Levinson, eventually were the most successful directors of several festivals and theater performances in Israel. She also invited Robin Risel Capsota, one of the singers she had met in Israel, to sing in one of her "Madame Butterfly" opera performances, and paid for her under the auspice of our foundation.

Florence and I were participating in many of the board meetings of the opera, and many times when we could not attend, I was called on the phone during their meeting to cast my vote on some important decision. Of course I always voted as Sarah wanted me too. My commitment to Sarah was without reservation.

Through the years the financial difficulties of the opera were piling up. Sarah sometimes paid for opera expenses out of her own salary so as to be able to perform. These payments were in fact loans to the corporation against the mortgage of the opera house, and in time it piled up to a point that Sarah owned the property of the house and she thought that it might be her retirement fund. Unfortunately it did not work out that way. The opera house was deteriorating and there was not enough money for repairs of the building. The opera house also owed a great deal of money for city and state taxes. The president, Laszlo Bonis, who was a committed friend to Sarah, was always busy juggling the little money he had to pay the bills and keep the creditors away.

Eventually the city inspectors found the opera house to be unsafe, and since the opera had no money to spend on repairs, the group was forced to discontinue their performances. Although by this time Sarah owned most of the property of the house, the debts to the city, state, and federal government did not leave much for her, so her plan to have a retirement fund did not materialize. One of her major financial supporters, Miss Timken, heiress of the Timken Bearing Company, unfortunately died, and several members of the board who were unhappy with her through the years quit, and the great Opera Company of Boston discontinued its operation.

For a while we lost contact with Sarah. Meanwhile I had troubles of my own. Several of my managers in the personnel agency were retiring. The country's economy was slowing down and I had to start retrenching. Our business with Israel was also affected, and to cut my losses I moved our offices to a smaller space across the street on Madison Avenue.

Sarah Caldwell's Auditions In Santa Fe

For some time we did not hear from Sarah. We heard that she had moved to Fayetteville, Arkansas, where she was teaching music at Fayetteville University. Apparently she had gone to her college reunion, and while she was there, she was asked whether she would like to join the faculty and teach opera classes at the music school. As much as she did not have any commitments in Boston and no plans of employment, she accepted the job in Fayetteville. She bought a little house next to a small pond, and from her description, it was nice and cozy. Her health was deteriorating, and the health insurance provided by her new job was very important to her.

Florence and I had not seen her for a while and we wondered how she was doing. Then one day she called and she told us that she was going to Santa Fe during the opera season to audition young singers for her small school opera performance in Fayetteville. She said that she was going to stay with one of her friends in Santa Fe, and she would love to meet us if we might be in Santa Fe at the same time. We actually did have plans to spend a week in Santa Fe and we had our reservations to fly there, but our plans did not coincide with Sarah's schedule. So we decided to change our schedule. It took us several days to have our flight reservations changed, but we did it. Sarah told us that she was bringing along two of her assistants to help her.

We had reservations at The Eldorado Hotel. Sarah told us that she could not stay too long at her friend's house, and she would love to stay with us in our hotel. Fortunately we could afford the additional expense of having her as our guest, so we added her to our reservation and she moved to the hotel with us. For the opera tickets Sarah suggested that we should call her good friend Julie Wheeler, the box office manager of the opera company in Santa Fe, and she would help us get the tickets. So I did and bought three sets of tickets for four opera performances.

After we settled down in the hotel, Sarah arrived with a walker and her two assistants. She had great difficulty walking. We felt sorry for her. But her mood was good and she was happy to see us. We, too, were delighted to spend time with her. Her two assistants were staying in a small motel, not to far from our hotel, and most days they joined us for breakfast in our hotel. The Eldorado Hotel is beautiful and it is the best hotel in town. Sarah loved the atmosphere and her accommodations. Most of the time she had to use her walker and from time to time needed to use her oxygen bottle. But she was in a very good mood, enjoying every minute of her stay in Santa Fe. It made Florence very happy to spend time with Sarah. We made arrangements to have the auditions in the administration building of the opera house, which are next door to the theatre. Several young singers were chosen for the auditions and a schedule was set up to hear them over the next few days. We spent mornings listening to several young singers, most of whom were excellent. Sarah sat Florence next to her and wanted to hear her honest opinion about each singer's voice. Sarah kept saying that Florence had heard more operas than anyone she knew, and she valued Florence's opinion. Florence was embarrassed by this compliment. However, whatever comment she made about the singers, Sarah agreed with. Several of the singers were selected by Sarah for her opera school performances in Fayetteville.

We spent most of the days with Sarah, and in the evenings we went to the opera. Sarah's two assistants helped her walk from the hotel to the opera house and back. The high altitude in Santa Fe made breathing difficult for Sarah. During one of the intermissions we walked over to see her, but we could not find her at her seat.

We eventually found her in the emergency room attended by a doctor and lying down on the sofa with a bottle of oxygen. At the end of the intermission her two assistants drove her back to the hotel, but we stayed on to hear the rest of the performance. The next day Sarah felt better and we spent the day visiting Santa Fe museums and the stores around town. My brother-in-law Irving and his wife Louise invited us one evening for a dinner with Sarah at one of the exclusive restaurants in town. They had never met Sarah, but knew all about her from our stories about her through the years. Both Irving and Louise were very much impressed, and Irving spent most of the evening talking to her. Later we all went together for a performance at the Opera House.

All along we were very worried about Sarah's health. Each evening we went with her for a performance, and several times, she had to return to the hotel before the end. But her mood was good and we spent a great deal of time together, especially during meals. At the end of our stay, Sarah left to go back to Fayetteville, and we moved to Albuquerque for a few days to spend with my brother and sister-in-law before returning to New York.

Sarah Caldwell's Visit To Seattle, WA

The following summer we made reservations for six opera performances in Santa Fe and four performances of Wagner's Ring Cycle in Seattle. When Florence told Sarah of our opera schedule, Sarah asked her if she could join us. Not knowing Sarah's health condition, we called Jim Morgan, who assured us that Sarah was well and we should not worry. The high price of the opera tickets in Seattle and Santa Fe combined with the cost of the hotel reservations added up to a considerable expense. However, we felt that as long as Sarah could still travel and participate, she should join us, because who knew if she would be able to make it another year. Florence in particular felt that we owed Sarah for all the wonderful times she had given us over the years.

For Sarah's tickets in Seattle, I called Speight Jenkins, the general director of the Seattle Opera Company, who was an old friend of Sarah's, and he was delighted to reserve the tickets for her. For the opera tickets in Santa Fe, I called our friend Julie Wheeler, the box office manager, and a few days later, she reserved the tickets for Sarah. We made hotel reservations for Sarah at the Hilton Hotel in Seattle and the Eldorado Hotel in Santa Fe.

We flew to Seattle and arrived there late at night. Sarah was not there yet. At 2:00 a.m., we heard some commotion in the corridor of the hotel, but we were so tired that we did not bother to find out what was happening. The next morning we checked to see if Sarah had arrived, and we were informed that she had arrived in a taxi from the airport at about 1:00 a.m., entering the hotel in a wheelchair with an oxygen bottle on her lap. We were dumbfounded. We realized that we had a very sick woman on our hands. Jimmy had never told us Sarah's real health condition.

We called Sarah at 10:00 a.m. and she told us she was ready to go out for breakfast. Her room was across the hall from ours. I knocked at her door, which was unlocked, and found her smiling, sitting in a wheelchair, with oxygen tubes attached to her nose, but happy to see me. I was happy to see her, too, and sorry to see this great opera mogul in this unfortunate condition.

Although she could not walk and had tubes in her nose, she was in high spirits, ready to go out and have some fun. Despite the hardships she was going through health-wise and her demeaning position as a teacher in a small school in Fayetteville, Arkansas, she was still cheerful. I never saw her depressed, even when she was sick. She was still in command, like a general ready for battle. I admired her strength and resolve, and I learned a great deal from her about how to cope with and overcome difficulties.

The moment I saw her condition, I knew that at this time she needed me. It was time to pay her back for all the great times she had given Florence and me through the years, and make her as happy as I could. I knew that whatever I had to do for her, I would do, because this was possibly the last great adventure she would have away from her small teaching job in Arkansas.

Each morning Sarah was waiting for me, sitting in her room in the wheelchair with the bottle of oxygen on her lap and the tube in her nose, ready to go for breakfast on the top floor of the Hilton Hotel. The hotel restaurant had large windows facing the city and the harbor of Seattle, and Sarah loved sitting there and having breakfast with Florence and me.

Wheeling Sarah was not too difficult for me; I considered it part of my daily exercise, which I missed while I was in Seattle. The difficulty started when I had to move her to my car in the garage. Once she stepped from the wheelchair to the front seat of the car, I had to fold the wheel chair and lift it into the trunk of the car. The chair was oversized and very heavy to lift and place in the trunk of the car properly, so it was quite an undertaking. Sometimes I felt that I could not do it, but fortunately, I managed it without hurting my back. The procedure of taking Sarah out of the car and helping her into the wheelchair was even more difficult than placing it in. However, I survived. It was a situation, which I had to manage. There was no one else to take care of her. She was my responsibility and I had to do the best I could.

Florence was very worried for me, afraid that I would hurt myself lifting the wheelchair and pushing it all over town. If I got sick, what would happen to her and Sarah? Florence herself had a difficult time with continuous back pain and had to walk with a cane. Fortunately, I was in good shape, and I kept my spirits high.

Sitting through four Wagnerian opera performances for the first time was an unforgettable experience for me. Frankly, I am not one who understands Wagner's music, which for me has no melody that I can follow. However, the stories were interesting, and as long as I was with Sarah and Florence, who were very excited and happy to be there, I made a great effort to sit and attentively listen to the music and follow the developing story. I enjoyed seeing Florence so happy.

Our daily schedule was simple: breakfast, lunch, and dinner together, visiting the sights and the stores during the day, buying small items with Sarah such as sneakers, socks, scarves, and other small gifts for her friends. Before dinner, we would rest. Then, after a light dinner, we would drive to the opera house. During the intermissions, Sarah was often surrounded by admirers who recognized her and told her how much they enjoyed her performances in Boston. I was happy for Sarah, but at the same time, I was sad because I knew that due to her declining health, these would be among her last happy exposures to her admirers. Florence and I felt fortunate to have the opportunity to spend the time with her.

Back To Santa Fe

Right after the last Wagner performance, we planned to continue with our opera schedule in Santa Fe. Flying Sarah to Santa Fe was not an easy task. She needed oxygen during her flight, and that required special arrangements at her seat. In addition, getting her into and out of the plane without a wheelchair was quite difficult. Even with all this happening, Sarah's mood was good, and she even seemed to enjoy all this commotion around her.

At the Eldorado, Sarah insisted on paying for her room, which was next to ours. A supply of oxygen bottles was delivered to Sarah's room and I took over the technicians' job of connecting and disconnecting the various valves and the plastic tubes, which were attached to her nose. She could hardly walk, and the high altitude of Santa Fe made it difficult for her to breathe, but she was happy and in a very jolly mood.

The weather was wonderful and I was kept busy pushing Sarah in her wheelchair all around Santa Fe, back and forth from the hotel to the opera house. I kept the oxygen bottle next to Sarah while she was in the wheelchair, in the hotel, in the car, and in the opera house. Each day we started with a great breakfast in the beautiful Eldorado hotel dining room. Sarah loved her breakfast. Later we would take a walk in town with Sarah in her wheelchair, visiting gift shops and bookstores, and then we would have lunch at a local restaurant.

All this time, during this visit and through the years that followed, I never heard Sarah complain of pain or hardship, despite the wheelchair and oxygen bottle on her lap and plastic tube in her nose. I never minded taking care of her, whether it meant pushing her wheelchair, or keeping her oxygen bottle near, or helping her buy shoes and socks, or helping her put her shoes on her feet, or taking her to the hair salon or dress shop. Of course, Florence was always there too, watching and attending to Sarah's personal needs.

Every evening before the performance, Florence helped Sarah dress and always kept her hair groomed. During some of the opera performances, Sarah got ill and we rushed her into the opera emergency room, but she insisted that we remain in the opera house and pick her up from the emergency room after the performance was over.

After six wonderful opera performances in Santa Fe, the time came to say goodbye. We made arrangements for Sarah to fly back to Fayetteville, and we drove back to Albuquerque to spend few days with Florence's brother Irving and his family and later flew back home to New York. It was a wonderful time that we cherished and remembered fondly.

Sarah's Last Days

Two years had passed. We were busy in New York and had not heard from Sarah or Jim in a while, and we were wondering what had happened to Sarah. Then a call from Freeport, Maine came into in my office, I was on the phone at that time, so my secretary took the call and told me afterward that "Jim" had called. At first, I did not connect the call to Sarah, but when I called back, I was pleasantly surprised to discover that the caller was Jim Morgan. I wondered what Jim was doing in Freeport, Maine.

Jim told me that after years of struggling to receive money owed to Sarah from selling the Opera House, she had finally received the payment, and had used some of the money to buy a house in Freeport, Maine. The house contained several rooms, enough for two live-in staffers as well as for Jim and Brian. It was heartwarming good news, knowing that Sarah was living close by rather than in Fayetteville, which was too far away for us to visit her.

Time passed, and we often spoke to Sarah on the phone. Sarah's 80th birthday on March 6 was approaching, and Jim invited us to come and celebrate this occasion together with some of Sarah's closest friends. Florence was very excited and looking forward to spending some time with her old friend. Since the party was taking place at noon, we decided to drive to Freeport a day early and spend the night in a hotel. Knowing that we had a free evening, Jim called us and invited us to have dinner with Sarah at their home. Their house was just a few streets away from our hotel.

Jim picked us up and we received a warm reception from Sarah, who was connected to a long plastic tube that let her walk around without carrying the oxygen bottle with her. Sarah, Jim, Brian, Florence, and I had dinner at a small table set with lovely china and a beautiful flower centerpiece. Jim and Brian cooked a delicious meal and we had a great time together.

The next morning, we went to an excellent seafood restaurant facing the ocean for Sarah's birthday celebration. Also in attendance were Jim, Brian, Bob Green and his wife Phyllis, close friends and supporters of Sarah, and Mrs. Gardella, the wife of Dr. Gardella, who had saved Sarah's life. Small red and blue helium balloons were attached to Sarah's wheelchair, and each of us placed his gift at Sarah's place. Sarah was excited, opening every present and admiring her gifts. Wine was served and a delicious seafood meal followed.

Looking around the table, I felt saddened to see just a few of Sarah's closest friends attending. Despite all the hundreds of thousands of people who knew Sarah and had enjoyed her operas through the years, there were only a few of us left to celebrate her 80th birthday. How ironic and unfair it was--Sarah had devoted all her life to opera, making so many people happy, but in the end, it meant nothing.

We remained in touch with Sarah, checking up on her health from time to time on the phone. She had difficulty breathing and her health was deteriorating. On March 26, 2006, we received a call from Jim telling us that Sarah had passed away and he wished us to come to her memorial service, which would take place in a cathedral in Boston. Florence was devastated; we had lost a great friend who had added so much pleasure to our lives.

The memorial service was a grand musical affair. Jim and Noel Velasco, along with several singers and friends, had planned every detail. We met many of our old friends and reminisced about the good old times we had spent with Sarah through the years. Following the service and the reception at the Ritz Hotel, we spent the afternoon with hundreds of Sarah's friends, members of the Opera Board, and some of the singers in Sarah's opera performances. Later in the evening, we went for dinner with a few of our friends, and the next morning drove back to New York.

It was difficult for me to close this chapter because Sarah is very much alive in our memory, and her friendship enriched our lives. We were fortunate to have had the opportunity to be friends with the greatest woman personality who had left a historical mark on the opera world.

Chapter 9 – Sarah Caldwell in Israel

Sarah Planting a Tree in
Margolin Peace Forest

Sarah and Me at the
Margolin Peace Forest

At the Forest
with Friends

Chapter 9 – Sarah Caldwell in Israel

Sarah at the Entrance to
The Church of Nativity in Bethlehem

Sarah and Florence
at the Z.O.A. House

Sarah in Bethlehem Glass
Factory

Sarah with me at
the Z.O.A. House

295

Chapter 9 – Sarah Caldwell in Israel

Signing Agreement with
Tel – Aviv Mayor
Shlomo Lahat

Lunch with Mayor Shlomo Lahat

Conference with the Mayor

Auditioning Singers in
Tel Aviv Theater

Looking for
Theater Locations

Chapter 9 – Sarah Caldwell in Israel

THE TEL AVIV FOUNDATION

March 17, 1983

Music & Theatre, Inc.
for the Services of Sarah Caldwell
Lincoln Center Post Office
Western Road
Lincoln, Mass.

Gentlemen:

This is to confirm our understanding that Miss Sarah Caldwell is appointed as Artistic Director of the new Israel Opera program for the purpose of developing a new Israel Opera Company to be inaugurated with two productions between August 10 to September 22, 1983.

We will provide for these porductions a production budget of $500,000 (not including the use of performance houses and local Israeli administrative expenses). She is authorized to negotiate and make commitments on our behalf for this budget. Her appointment as Artistic Director is for two years at a fee of $1 per year and out-of-pocket expenses.

In the first year as an administrator, stage director and conductor (conducting up to five performances) the fee for her services will be $50,000 to be paid from the authorized production budget according to her instructions.

For the second year fees for these services will be nogotiaged on mutually agreeable terms by August 1, 1983.

Miss Caldwell also agrees to advise in the development of operatic training and appreciation programs.

If this is acceptable to you please sign and it will constitute a binding contract between us.

Accepted: Accepted:

_____   President
Tel Aviv Development Fund   Music & Theatre, Inc.

Mayor Shlomo Lahat   Sarah Caldwell

Hanan Ben Yehuda

Chapter 9 – Sarah Caldwell in Israel

To
FLORENCE and EFRAIM
MARGOLIN
Founders of the
TEL-AVIV
FOUNDATION
In deepest gratitude
and friendship
SHLOMO LAHAT
Mayor
1986

עיריית תל־אביב־יפו
Municipality of Tel-Aviv-Yafo
March 31, 1983

Mr.& Mrs. Ephraim Margolin

NEW YORK, N.Y.
U.S.A

Dear Florence and Ephraim,

I would like to express my appreciation, also on behalf of Hanan and David, for the warmth and courtesy extended to us on our recent visit to New York.

I do not have to stress to you of all people, the significance of the Opera Project in Israel, and I am delighted to discover over and over again, how you keep the wheels rolling, as the saying goes, and how through your efforts we are able to implement our plan in bringing about the realisation of a long-awaited dream, namely The New Opera in Israel.

I was happy to meet again with Ms. Sara Caldwell, and was amazed once more, with her abilities and her talents. I am hopeful that she will be able to find and select the best possible artists for our premiere productions this year so that they may turn out to be most successful. I have also thoroughly enjoyed all the meetings you have arranged with opera lovers in the U.S.A., and the beautiful dinner in Boston. I am aware and grateful for your effort to help our cause through other means, as having arranged our meeting with Mr. Elyashar.

We shall keep in close contact, and I am positive, that with such dedication and devotion as you have shown, we shall attain our goal in creating an extraordinary and successful Opera in Israel.

Sincerely Yours,

Shlomo Lahat
MAYOR

Chapter 9 – Sarah Caldwell in Philippines

Manila Opera House

Opera Performance for Children

Cultural Center

Performance for Children

Chapter 9 – Sarah Caldwell in Philippines

Israeli Ambassador Family with Sarah

Florence with the Israeli Ambassor and his wife

Party at the American Ambassador Home

Sarah with a Bouquet of Flowers after the Performance

Chapter 9 – Sarah Caldwell 80th Birthday

Sarah 80th Birthday with Friends

Me and Sarah

Florence and Sarah

CHAPTER TEN
ISRAEL ADVENTURES

Developing New Business With Israel

In addition to all the attention I was giving to the opera, I was also very busy with my business, training new personnel and expanding our office. Our personnel agency was becoming known in the city for its successful placing of top personnel in various industries in and around New York. Our name also reached some Israeli companies, who needed sales managers capable of selling their products in the U.S. Since our agency specialized in this area, we were approached by several of the Israeli companies to help them recruit sales managers. It was difficult for the Israelis at first to get used to the idea that they had to pay a high price for such a service, but after long negotiations, we settled on a price.

Recruiting sales managers requires a high level of expertise and knowledge. By recruiting the best salesmen, companies can increase their sales and out-perform their competitors. Every company knows its competitors and who their best salesmen are. Our job as recruiters was to get this list and then approach the salesmen and offer them a better opportunity. It is a simple formula in theory, but difficult to achieve in practice. I found that in our free market system, most intelligent employees whom I approached with an offer of a better job were willing to talk to me, especially when I told them that they had nothing to lose by simply listening to the opportunity I had for them.

Most of the Israeli companies who were looking for sales managers were representing kibbutz manufacturers. They were sent to the States to manage their New York offices, but unfortunately, they had no experience on how to handle an American sales manager. In most cases, after I successfully recruited sales managers for these Israeli companies (and was paid for my services), the sales managers would end up quitting their jobs because the Israeli kibbutzes did not know how to work with American employees. But this consequence was beyond my control.

Recognizing the shortcomings of this type of management failure, I had an idea: drawing on my experience in finding the best sales managers for selling Israeli products, I could set up my own marketing company representing Israeli products and recruit my own sales managers, importing and marketing Israeli products in the U.S. Although I did not forget my previous failure with Israel, I now felt that by having my own strong, well-financed organization, I could undertake a new venture and help Israeli companies expand the sale of their products in U.S. markets.

On my next visit with Florence to Israel, I engaged a public relations company, which advertised my visit to Israel and set up appointments for me with Israeli manufacturers interested in marketing their products in the U.S. I had several group meetings in the Hilton Hotel in Tel Aviv, and had more than 100 private meetings with representatives of various manufacturers. I was busy with meetings from 8:00 a.m. to midnight. As a result, I ended up with more than ten companies who were interested having me represent them in the U.S.

Next Visit To Israel

I had a little time left to visit with my family before we left. We made a quick trip around the country and visited Beer Sheva, which by this time had grown into a big bustling city. I called David Tuviyahu, the former mayor of Beer Sheva, who was now the president of The New University of Ben Gurion. I expected to see him for only a short visit, but he insisted that we stay overnight at the motel because he wanted to spend some time with us. It was too late to return to Tel Aviv, so we stayed in this new large motel without a change of clothes. We just bought a pair of toothbrushes and a tube of toothpaste.

After breakfast we drove to David Tuviyahu's home, which was a simple little house built during our time in Beer Sheva with a little cactus garden. We met his wife, a very small, lovely woman, and she asked us to come back after our visit in town. We got into my car, and for the next three hours, Tuviyahu took us around town. First, he showed us the industrial area. We stopped at the ceramic factory, which I had built many years previously, with its thousands of toilet bowls, bathtubs, and ceramic tiles stored over a large area. I could see the old water tower with the steel tank on top, which I had removed from the old Turkish Railroad Station moved to its new location at the factory. Tuviyahu said to me, "If you had not returned to the States, you would have been the first general manager of this factory." For a minute, my heart skipped a beat. True, I thought how much more exciting it could have been running this large factory, rather than sitting in an office in New York, just making money.

We continued our drive through the new city, seeing large buildings six to eight stories high, a shopping center, movie houses, flourishing gardens, and wide streets crisscrossing the town. Tuviyahu also took us to see the first housing project of the town, which I had built in 1949. I could not recognize the original houses; they all had additional extensions built on them, with trees and gardens surrounding them and beautiful tiled streets next to them. Only a few of the buildings remained the same as they had been when I built them.

At the end of our visit, Tuviyahu took us to see the large new university building and dormitories. He took us through each floor, showing us the classrooms with beautiful furniture for the students, the various laboratories and computer rooms. Down in the basement where the air conditioning and power plants were located, he stopped again and said to me, "Just think, Efraim: if you had been with me, you would have been the man responsible for all this great construction." For a minute, I felt sick to my stomach. It was so true. I sure missed the time when I had worked for Tuviyahu…but that was in another lifetime.

We returned to Tuviyahu's home, where his wife prepared tea and cookies for us, and we spent an hour reminiscing about old times in Beer Sheva. I insisted on taking several pictures of Tuviyahu and his wife sitting on the veranda. Before we left, Tuviyahu gave us a small cactus plant to take with us as a gift. It was so very touching. I loved this great man and I always thought of him fondly.

When we returned to the States, I sent Tuviyahu the pictures, but I did not receive any acknowledgement, which surprised me. About three months later, I received a letter from his daughter together with his original letter, which I had not received previously because of the wrong address he had on the letter. His daughter's letter told me that he wrote to me after he received my pictures. Shortly after we left Israel, his wife had died, and he kept the pictures on his night table. These were the only pictures he had to remember her by. He had written me a letter of thanks, which unfortunately I had not received because the letter was returned to him. Two months later, Tuviyahu died of a heart attack. It was a great shock to me. He always remained alive in my memory and I think of this great man often.

New Ventures With Israel

In 1985, back in the States, I registered a new company called Isratech Marketing Corporation for the purpose of marketing Israeli products in the U.S. The products included envelopes, stationery supplies, plastic-coated fabrics, white chalk, and surgical gloves. I rented a large warehouse in New Jersey and I added four additional desks in our office, which was getting crowded, to accommodate a manager and three salesmen. Except for the surgical gloves, most of the products came from kibbutzim in Israel.

My first undertaking was to recruit a sales manager for the sale of coated fabric. The best place to recruit a sales manager is at an industrial show, where exhibitors show their products and usually their sales managers manage their booths. The next textile coated material show was down in New Orleans. I decided to take several days off and take Florence with me, and spend some time at the show and the rest having a good time in town.

After settling down in the hotel, I went with Florence to visit the exhibits. There were hundreds of exhibitors and many were direct competitors to our Israeli products. My first goal at the show was to select the best companies to approach for my recruiting. We made the rounds of the show, and in the evening, we toured the town and had a very good dinner.

The next morning at breakfast in a noisy restaurant, I noticed several salesmen, whom I presumed were attending the show. I told Florence that I would try talking to one in particular who was busy looking at a resume. Against Florence's objection, I approached the salesman and said, "I noticed that you are looking at a resume. I would like to introduce myself: I am a headhunter from New York looking for a sales manager. Do you mind if I sit next to you?" The salesman was surprised but was pleased to talk to me. I described to him what I was looking for. He told me that his specialty was not a good fit for my needs. My next question to him was, "Who is the best salesman in the show that you know who can fill the position I have?" Without hesitation, he replied, "Ed Johnson, who works for Dratis Corporation, but I don't think you can recruit him. He is very well known in the industry." I thanked him and returned to join Florence to finish my breakfast. Florence was not very happy with my performance because it was embarrassing to her, but to me it was my daily routine, which she had not had the opportunity to see before.

After breakfast, we went into the exhibit hall, and I searched for Ed Johnson's booth. When I found it, I circled around his booth until I saw him standing alone. I approached him and said, "Ed, my name is Efraim Margolin, and I am a headhunter from New York. I was told that you are the best salesman in this show, and I have a great opportunity which I would like to talk to you about." I gave him my card and he gave me his.

As I was talking to him, another salesman joined us. Ed turned to him and introduced him to me as his sales manager. Ed told the sales manager that I was trying to recruit him for another job. The sales manager turned to me and said, "Why don't you recruit me? I'm a better salesman than Ed!" We all laughed as though it was all a joke. We talked about my company and its products. I left without a resolution to our discussion.

The next day at the show, I met several good prospects, but I still liked Ed the best. At that time, Ed had already spent more than fourteen years representing one of the best American manufacturers of coated fabric material, which is used to cover the back of trucks, tents, swimming pool covers, and has many other industrial and agricultural uses. He was one of the most respected salesmen in his field. I knew I wanted him on my team.

I circled Ed's booth several times until I saw him alone in the booth and approached him again. I asked him to have a cup of coffee with me. He agreed and we went to the coffee shop together. While having coffee, I outlined to Ed the opportunity I had for him to work for me representing an Israeli manufacturer who manufactured similar products to his own. Of course, the salary would be much higher than his current pay. In addition, he would not have to relocate; he could work from his home in Alabama. I invited Ed to visit me in New York, see my operation, and meet the Israeli factory manager. Ed listened to my offer and said he would think it over and let me know.

For a while, I did not hear from Ed, and I thought that he was not interested. Two months passed. Then I suddenly received a call from Ed, saying that he was accepting my offer and was coming to New York to finalize an agreement with me. I was elated.

After his visit to New York, I traveled with Ed around the country, mostly in the South, to introduce our Israeli products to his old customers. His customers loved and respected him, and everywhere he went he received orders for our Israeli coated fabric material. In ten days, he achieved over $250,000 in orders. It was just amazing, and it was a great success in my effort to sell Israeli products in the States.

One evening during our trip, I asked Ed what had made him change his mind and accept the job with me. He told me that he had discussed the offer with his wife for some time, but could not make up his mind. He and his wife were very devout religious Baptists, and each morning they would pray together and read the Bible. One morning, his wife said to him that they should try to see what the Bible had to say on their question about taking a job with the Israelis. So the next time they read the Bible, she asked Ed to close his eyes. She opened the Bible randomly and told him to place his finger on the page. When he opened his eyes, his finger was pointing on the word "Israel." They knew then that the Lord had made the decision for them, and that is how he decided to accept the job to work for Israel.

During my association with Ed, Florence and I met Ed's wife, Ann, several times. She was a beautiful, tall Southern woman. She had married Ed after losing her first husband, a famous racecar driver who had died in an accident. Years later, I heard that her son, who also was a racecar driver, also died in a car accident. We spent many evenings together during various trade shows around the country, and we learned a lot about life in the South, their close relationship to the Bible, and their love for Israel. Ed worked for me for the next four years, producing over $2 million worth of orders per year. It was very beneficial to him as well as for our company.

The sale of our Israeli chalk took a different avenue. After searching the market, we found that one of the biggest users of chalk was the New York City school system. The idea of having the schools use Israeli chalk appealed to me, and I put a great deal of effort into winning a two-year bid for the supply of chalk to the New York schools. We finalized the price with the Israeli kibbutz manufacturer to make sure that we would have a continuous supply of chalk for the next two years. We leased a small truck and had our warehouse driver deliver the packages of chalk to several schools each day. I was pleased to know that each of the 1,000 schools in the city of New York used Israeli chalk as a promotion for Israel.

The first year, everything went well. But the second year, the kibbutz raised the price of the chalk, reneging on the agreement we had with them. Since I had an ironclad agreement with the city for a set price for the second year, I found myself in a bind. I had to pay the kibbutz the increase in price and lose on each shipment I made to the schools. Six months into the second year, the kibbutz advised me that they had had a machinery breakdown in the factory and they could not continue their shipment. My contract with the city was such that if I did not deliver the chalk on time, they would buy the chalk in the open market, which would cost double the price they were paying me, and send me the bills to pay.

This was a real catastrophe for our company. I set up a meeting with the schools' management and explained my situation. I told them that I would find another source of chalk for them and pay the difference in price, which would reduce my loss, rather than buying in the open market. They were very understanding and cooperative. Of course, we lost a lot of money on this venture. A year later the kibbutz approached me again asking me to continue our business with them. Of courses, I turned them down, disgusted with their chutzpah.

In one of my visits to Israel, I was introduced to a surgical glove manufacturer in Hertzelia, near Tel Aviv. This was a large company that sold most of their gloves in Israel. Their prices were competitive and their quality was first class. The owners were an Israeli family originally from Germany. While I was negotiating with them for representation in the States, the company was sold to American investors, and their plant manager was appointed to become the operations manager. Daniel was young, ambitious, smart, and a very tough negotiator. At that time, the AIDS epidemic was sweeping the U.S., and the demand for surgical gloves was growing rapidly. I agreed with Daniel's suggestion to set up a special department in our office, which would exclusively sell the Israeli-made gloves in the U.S. I recruited two salesmen and a warehouse manager to run the new operation. Our main buyers were hospitals all over the country. The single largest buyer of gloves was the U.S. Department of Health. However, there we had to officially bid for a contract, which required FDA approval. This approval required an inspection of our manufacturing facilities in Israel and the setting up of a documentation program that could identity and follow each glove and box of gloves from the factory production line until the delivery of the gloves to the hospital. This method ensured that if there was a problem with a glove during a surgical operation, the glove could be traced back to its source, where inspectors could find the reason for its failure. The inspectors from the FDA visited the factory in Israel and we received their approval. Our bidding price was competitive, and after four months, we received our first order of $2 million for a two-year supply of gloves to U.S. government hospitals all over the country.

In addition to the government contract, our salesmen were selling the gloves to private and public hospitals. By this time, we were receiving a shipment of gloves from Israel every week, and this required us to enlarge our warehouse and have several more men working in the shipping department. The gloves were of excellent quality and we were making good money.

Of course, from time to time we had problems. On one occasion, we received a telephone call from one of the hospitals complaining that the boxes of gloves they had received smelled fishy and could not be used in the operating room. We were shocked and dismayed about this occurrence. I went myself to visit the hospital to check the boxes and the gloves, and they indeed smelled of fish. We started investigating the shipment from its source, starting in the factory and tracing its journey until its delivery to the hospital. Eventually we found the container it came from, which by this time was back on its way to Israel. The inspection in Israel found that the container indeed was contaminated by previous shipments of fish from the Netherlands, and had not been washed and cleaned properly before loading the gloves in Israel for shipment to the U.S. We had to remove the fishy gloves from the hospital and discard them. We placed a claim of $50,000 on the value of the gloves with the insurance company and eventually we were paid for our loss.

Our next large sale of Israeli products was envelopes made in Israel. The supplier was a kibbutz, which I had visited on my previous visit to Israel. I was impressed with their ability to produce envelopes for the U.S. market. We placed an order with the kibbutz for several million envelopes to be shipped to our warehouse. I recruited another salesman who specialized in the sales of envelopes. The envelopes required additional space in the warehouse. By this time, our warehouse in New Jersey had expanded to over 100,000 square feet of space. Our warehouse manager now had six men working for him. We now had approximately thirty employees, including our personnel agency, and we were getting to be too crowded in our office. After an intensive search for additional space, we found a large office space on 35th Street and Madison Avenue, which could accommodate our expanding operations.

Although I was getting very busy, I was very happy to see my business growing and prospering. The move to our new office took us three months. We had several private offices and large space for most of our employees. As for myself, I did not believe in sitting in a private office; I preferred to sit together with my employees. I liked to see and feel the action, and I also believed that with this method of management I could increase the efficiency of the office.

Coincidentally, the building that housed our office was bought out by the deposed president, Marcos family, after they left the Philippines. We met Madam Marcos one evening at the Metropolitan Opera and had a short pleasant conversation with her, reminiscing about old times in the Philippines, and of course, she remembered Sarah Caldwell.

Although we were very busy, I was always open to additional business opportunities. I felt that since we knew many companies in the field, we could offer a merger and acquisition service to our customers. For this purpose, I recruited one of the applicants who came to our office for a job to manage our new merger and acquisition department. During the next two years, we were successful in merging three companies, which provided us with considerable additional income.

While we were becoming known in Israel through our success in the U.S. markets, several Israeli kibbutzim who were looking to establish new industries in their kibbutzim came to the U.S. for help. I was very enthusiastic about this opportunity. I wanted Israel to expand into the manufacturing industries. For some unknown reason, my unfortunate unsuccessful previous experience with Israel was forgotten. I felt the way that I had years back in Beer Sheva, when I was involved in building Israel. This time I would build not a housing project, but new industries for Israel's growing economy. My pioneering spirit for Israel had awakened in me. It was not only the business aspect, which was involved; it was that the bottom line was that I was committed to helping Israel.

One of the kibbutzim who came to me for help was Kibbutz Mizra, not far from the town of Afola and Neer, where I had spent summers in my uncle's kibbutz when I was a child. The kibbutz had a small metal factory for producing material handling equipment, and they also produced pork meat and sold it in their supermarket and restaurant. It was very much against the Jewish laws of kosher, which forbade eating pork, but that did not apply to the kibbutz life, which was not religious. The manager for the project from the kibbutz was Micha, who was from a German-Jewish family, which had immigrated to Israel and settled in the kibbutz. He was an exceptional man: educated, very well-mannered, and a real gentleman. I liked him from the start. After making an agreement with him to search for a new manufacturing enterprise for the kibbutz, I selected one of my top researchers, Lorraine, to run this project.

Micha was interested in the manufacturing of products by the powder metallurgy process, which makes hard metal parts for various industries. Our search was to find an American manufacturer who would provide the kibbutz with the know-how under license.

Lorraine started her search, and for the next nine months of our search, we investigated over 100 companies without success. Lorraine was ready to give up. However, I insisted we continue, and fortunately, by the end of the year we found one company in California, which had a new process of manufacturing plastic with powder metal injection molding. This was a new experimental process, which had just started to develop in the U.S. The factory was in San Francisco and the owner was a Swiss engineer. Micha and I visited him several times. We were very impressed with his process, but negotiations with him were very difficult. He knew what he wanted and never gave in on any point. Before even discussing licenses, he wanted us to invest $100,000, and it was very difficult to get such a large sum approved by the kibbutz. The Swiss engineer promised that once he was paid, he would guarantee the success of the transfer of the know-how and make it a success for the kibbutz. Micha had a difficult time convincing the kibbutz to invest $100,000 before seeing any results. However eventually, they approved and paid the $100,000.

Before long, the kibbutz sent several of their technicians, metallurgists, and engineers to the plant in San Francisco to study the process, and they remained there for one year. We found that the Swiss engineer was very serious about his training and his transfer of his know-how. He wanted to make sure that the kibbutz would be successful. When the time came to buy the equipment, he insisted that the new equipment would be first installed in his plant and operated there first before shipping it to the kibbutz, so as to make sure it all worked well. The plant was transferred into a new building in the kibbutz and the results were outstanding. On my last visit to the kibbutz, I saw more than fifty workers in the factory producing excellent products, which were sold all over the world. There were only a few such manufacturing companies around the world producing these licensed parts. To my pleasant surprise, I found that all the financial commitments to me by Micha were also fulfilled. Every time I visited Israel, I made it my business to visit the factory and spend time with Micha in the Kibbutz.

The third successful venture was with another kibbutz in the south of Israel not far from Beer Sheva, where I had built the new town in 1949. That kibbutz was looking for a manufacturing plant for plastic film fabrication. After searching for the type of plastic they wanted, we found that there was a need for plastic film material for the production of diapers in Israel. At that time, the film was important and there was a ready market for a local manufacturer. In addition, with some modifications, the same products could also be used in agriculture.

Our next step was to find a company in the States. I found two companies who were ready to negotiate with us. I brought two of the kibbutz members to the States and we spent several weeks visiting the various facilities around the country. Eventually we settled on one manufacturer who was ready to provide the kibbutz with the know-how and sell us the equipment, which cost over $1.5 million. I visited the kibbutz while the building was erected and later when it was completed and operating. I was very proud of my accomplishment. I was fulfilling my dream of helping Israel establish new industries and at the same time being paid for my effort.

ADDENDUM

My Mother's Funeral And Rabbi Pollak

After my father died, my mother's health deteriorated quickly. Her rheumatism limited her activities and her heart was weakened. From time to time, I called her to find out how she was. I missed her, but I kept postponing my visit to see her because of the daily problems I had in my office. I always hoped and planned to see her one day, before she died, but unfortunately, it was not to be One night, my brother called me, and before he said a word, I knew that my mother had died. I felt terrible for not taking the time to see her before her death, and that feeling of guilt has remained with me all my days.

I took the first available flight to Israel and arrived there the next evening. My brother was waiting for me at the airport and he drove me to the hotel. After I changed, we went together to my mother's empty apartment. My sister and most of my uncles and aunts whom I had not seen for years were there. I was very saddened because I had not visited my mother before she died.

The next morning at the funeral, I saw many old family friends from Beth Habocharim or Mekor Chaim whom I had known since I was a child, such as my friend Jackie from kindergarten. My mother's grave was next to my father's so they could be close to each other: as they were in life, so they were in death. Being the oldest son, I said the Kaddish, which is the prayer for the dead. I could hardly read the Kaddish because of the tears streaming from my eyes. I missed my mother terribly. She was a wonderful mother. Although I spent only 14 years of my life at home with her and my father, my attachment to them and love for them was always very strong. The years that I spent at home with them will always be in my memory.

After the funeral, we returned to my mother's apartment, and my sister Mira and my sister-in-law Nitza prepared the food and drinks for the family returning from the cemetery. We spent most of the afternoon together getting to know all my uncles, aunts and their children. In the evening, I had dinner with my sister at my brother's home and returned late at night to the hotel exhausted.

The next morning my brother came for breakfast in the hotel, and then we walked out to search for a synagogue in which to say our prayers. In our Jewish religion, we sit "Shiva", meaning we are sitting in mourning at home for seven days, only going out twice a day for prayers. Since my brother and I had not attended a synagogue since our bar mitzvah at the age of 13, finding a synagogue where we could say our prayers was a real undertaking. My brother and I drove around in his car that morning looking for a synagogue around the hotel. While driving slowly, we noticed a young man walking with a bundle of tefillim under his arm and realized that he must be walking to a synagogue for his morning prayers. We stopped him and asked him if he could guide us to a synagogue. He said, "Yes" and we offered to drive him there with us. As we drove, he asked us about our search for the synagogue, and we told him of our mother's funeral and our need to find a synagogue for the seven days of prayers. He was very understanding, and directed us to a synagogue not too far from the hotel.

My brother and I were very uncomfortable in the synagogue because we had not been there for many years. However, our newly acquired friend realized this and kept close to us. One of the necessary rituals before the prayers is to tie up the tefillim on the left arm and place the other on the forehead. Our young friend realized that we did not know how to use the tefillim, and to spare us embarrassment he said that he would show us how the tefillim are used in Israel. He found two pairs of tefillim and after close inspection helped us to put them on. He also stopped the praying crowd from praying so as to give my brother and me time to say our Kaddish for my mother. In the evening, we met the young man again and went together with him to the synagogue.

This routine of going to the synagogue was kept for seven days. At this time, I still did not know the young man's name. On the seventh day, I mentioned to him that I was going to Jerusalem before my return to New York. He told me that he also was going to Jerusalem because he lived there. I invited him to join me, and we left together early on Friday morning.

On the way to Jerusalem, the young man introduced himself as Mr. Jakob Pollak, a teacher in a school in Jerusalem. Knowing that my brother and I had no tefillim of our own, he suggested that we buy some at his friend's store in Measharim, which is the religious section of

Jerusalem. When we arrived in the store, the owner was very excited. He said, "Rabbi Pollak! What an honor and pleasure having you in my store. What can I do for you?" This was the first I came to know that the young man was a rabbi. Rabbi Pollak said to the storekeeper that he wanted him to find two pairs of tefillim for his friends, my brother and me. He wanted the tefillim to have special written prayers inserted in them by an old, well-known rabbi in Jerusalem. The storekeeper explained to Rabbi Pollak that it is very difficult to find such tefillim. However, Rabbi Pollak told him that he must find them that day, Friday, because I had to return to Tel Aviv before the Sabbath. Rabbi Pollak then left for his home.

After he left, the storekeeper asked me how I came to be a friend of the great Rabbi Pollak, who in his opinion was the greatest man in the city of Jerusalem. Rabbi Pollak was the principal of the largest religious school in Jerusalem, the Chorev School, which had over 500 students. In fact, two of the storekeeper's daughters studied in this school, and he felt it was the best school in the country. He told me that I was very fortunate to have a friend like Rabbi Pollak. I was astonished to find out that this young man I had met, who had helped me so much and never mentioned to me who he really was, had turned out to be such an important person.

The storekeeper asked me to return to the store in a couple of hours. When I came back, he had a pair of beautiful shiny tefillim ready, one for me and one for my brother. When I asked him the price, he told me $100 a pair. I did not show it, but I was surprised because I had not expected it to cost that much. I had expected a price of $25 a pair at the most. I paid the $200 dollars and left in a hurry to go to the old city to pray at the Wailing Wall of Jerusalem with my new tefillim, thinking to myself that I was taken advantage by the storekeeper by paying that much money for the tefillim.

Arriving at the wall, I placed my new shining tefillim on my arm and forehead and stood at the wall reading my prayers. Before long, I noticed several young men looking me over and talking among themselves. I thought that possibly I had placed my tefillim incorrectly on my head or arm. Before the end of my prayers, the young crowd surrounded me, looking at my tefillim closely and asking me where I had gotten such great tefillim, which were very hard to get. They were sure I must have paid a great deal of money for them, probably $400. I said, "Yes," and I felt sick to my stomach at having thought wrongly that the storekeeper had cheated me and overcharged me for the tefillim. In fact, I could sell the tefillim for $400 and have $300 profit. I was ashamed of thinking that possibly Rabbi Pollak and the storekeeper had swindled me. I never overcame this feeling of guilt.

Before I left to go back to Tel Aviv, I stopped to say good-bye to Rabbi Pollak, and met his wife and two of his daughters. They lived in a very small, third-floor apartment. I was served tea and cake, and left for Tel Aviv with my two new pairs of tefillim. The next day I left for New York with very pleasant memories of my meeting with my new friend Rabbi Pollak.

A year later, on a business trip to Israel with Florence, I went to visit Rabbi Pollak in his Chorev School. I was surprised to see hundreds of boys and girls playing in the yard, boys and girls separately, all well-dressed in uniforms. We were directed to Rabbi Pollak's office. There we found him surrounded by a small group of children, all talking to him and complaining about each other, and he patiently took care of their complaints. His principal's office door was always open and any child in school could enter to talk to the rabbi without an appointment. What a lovely sight.

Rabbi Pollak showed us around the school. All the classrooms were very clean and in good order. We passed by a ping-pong table and the rabbi asked me if I wished to play with him. Of course, I said, "Yes," because years back I was a very good player. Before long, I found myself playing with the rabbi, who was a real champion. All the kids surrounded us, and of course, they were rooting for the rabbi. I tried my best, but he won, delighting the children around him.

Some of the children came from very poor families, so Florence and I decided to help the school with a donation. I told Rabbi Pollak that I would send him some money from time to time to be spent directly and personally by him for children and families in need and especially before the holidays. For some time the rabbi wrote to me about the cases of the needy students whom he was helping, and I received letters of thanks from the children and their families. It was embarrassing to me. I told Rabbi Pollak that it was not necessary: I trusted his judgment, and all the giving should be anonymous.

I corresponded with the rabbi often. He wrote in exceptional Hebrew with wonderful handwriting. I always looked forward to his letters telling me about the school and conditions in Israel.

Several years later, Rabbi Pollak wrote me that he was coming to New York for the wedding of one of his nieces. I was looking forward to his visit, but when I met him, he did not look well. He told me that he was having heart trouble, and that when he returned from his trip to New York, he would be going for open-heart surgery in Israel. A friend of his had suggested that while he was in New York, he should see a famous heart specialist in Boston by the name of Dr. Loue. Rabbi Pollak asked me if I could find out if he could see Dr. Loue. I checked around with some of my friends and I found that Dr. Loue is one of the most famous heart specialists in the world, and it would take two to three months to schedule an appointment with him. Rabbi Pollak called his friend, the chief rabbi in Boston, and to my surprise the Bostonian rabbi made an appointment for him with Dr. Loue for the next day. It seemed that the Bostonian rabbi knew Dr. Loue very well and was a good friend of his.

Since Rabbi Pollak did not speak English and could not go to Boston alone, I offered to fly him there the next day and spend the day with him visiting Dr. Loue at Boston University Hospital. The next morning we took an early flight to Boston and were in the hospital by 8:00 a.m. For the next five hours, Rabbi Pollak was moved from room to room for various tests, while I acted as his translator.

When all the tests were completed, we were ushered to a small room where Dr. Loue was seated. He was a small, quiet man with a big smile, and he shook hands warmly with Rabbi Pollak and myself. He told us that he was a good friend of the Bostonian Rabbi and was happy to help Rabbi Pollak. Dr. Loue spent some time looking over Rabbi Pollak's x-rays and lab reports, as well as the x-rays from Israel, which Rabbi Pollak had brought with him. Then he said, "Rabbi Pollak, I am pleased tell you that nothing is wrong with your heart. You are well and I don't understand why the doctors in Israel want to operate on you." When Rabbi Pollak told Dr. Loue the felt weak and could not walk much, Dr. Loue said, "The reason is because you are not exercising enough and you are worrying too much about your heart, because you've been frightened by your doctors in Israel. In fact, I have had several patients come to me after being operated on in Israel, and I felt their operations were not necessary. I do not recommend you, Rabbi, to be operated on your return to Israel." Rabbi Pollak was in shock and could not believe his luck. I, too, was very happy to learn that Rabbi Pollak was well.

Before leaving Boston, we went to visit the Bostonian rabbi, who lived in a small two-story house. We talked in a second-floor room that was filled with books. The rabbi was a relatively young man. For the next hour, both rabbis talked about matters, which I did not know much about. At the end of the meeting, the Bostonian rabbi thanked me for helping Rabbi Pollak by bringing him to Boston and gave me his blessing, which made me feel good.

That afternoon we flew back to New York. During our flight Rabbi Pollak kept talking about how fortunate he was, finding out that he was well and did not need an operation after all. As a matter of fact, he told me that in Israel, his mentor had told him not to go for an operation, and Dr. Loue's conclusion confirmed Rabbi Pollak's mentor's opinion. I was very happy for the opportunity to help Rabbi Pollak be saved from the heart operation.

Ten years passed before Rabbi Pollak eventually did have to go for a heart operation, but meanwhile he had ten good years of normal life activity and a productive life. On my last visit to Israel, I found Rabbi Pollak at home recuperating from heart surgery. He was very frail and weak. I felt bad seeing him in this condition. I left him with the hope that he would recuperate by my next visit to Israel.

Bernice Korsavitzky Fisher

While we were active in recruiting members for the Israeli opera, we met many new friends. One of them was Bernice Korsavitzky Fisher. It began when she invited us for a Friday dinner in her small apartment in Manhattan. She set up a beautiful table for eight of her friends with a large bouquet of flowers, a silver setting with dishes that belonged some time back to Queen Elizabeth, and a superb meal she cooked herself. We spent a wonderful evening with her and her friends.

After that, we were invited to her home every second Friday of the month for Friday night dinner with her old friends as well as new ones. Bernice was a widow, a petite, beautiful, fascinating woman, a great entertainer, and a wonderful cook. We came to love her.

Her personal life was filled with great loves and tragedies. The more we got to know her the more we realized how great a person she was. Bernice's father had twelve brothers and sisters. He married Rose, his wife, in Russia and had two children, Bernice and Gershon. He immigrated on his own to Detroit, and eight years later brought his wife and two children there. At the time, Bernice was 15 years old. Among the immigrating crowds, she looked like a beautiful flower: small, petite, with the face of an angel.

At the age of 18, she met Philip Pasach Stolman, who was 26 years old, and ran away with him. They lived together for a year. By that time she was not sure she loved Philip. However, they got married, moved to Jackson, Michigan, and had two children, a boy and a girl. After ten years, they moved back to Detroit and had two more girls. By this time, her brother Gershon had emigrated to Israel. In time, Philip Pasach Stolman and his brother developed a very substantial real estate business, and Philip and Bernice lived in a beautiful home.

Bernice's husband was a religious man and a very committed Zionist, and was always very supportive of Jewish causes. With his donations, he helped establish the Bar Ilan University in Israel, which is one of the most outstanding universities in the country.

Although Bernice was a very good mother, she was unhappy with her marriage. She was a great entertainer in her Jewish community, and had many guests coming to her home. One of her guests was the famous Chazan singer, Korsavitzky, who had four children. After his wife passed away, he and Bernice fell in love without anybody's knowledge. Out of the blue, Bernice suddenly went to visit relatives in Florida and stayed with them. While she was away, her husband received papers from her asking for a divorce. It was such a shock for her husband and her children. At that time, the oldest child was 23 and the youngest was 12.

Stolman, who was crazy in love with his wife, had a nervous breakdown. The family tried to patch things up and to bring Bernice back, but to no avail: she loved Korsavitzky and wanted to marry him. Eventually Stolman gave Bernice her divorce with a considerable settlement. The oldest daughter kept up a relationship with her mother, and in a way understood her. The other three children were hurt to see their mother abandon them, and in the Jewish community, it was the scandal of the age. Her husband never recovered from the divorce and never married again, but Bernice got married to Korsavitzky and was very happy. These were the best years of her life. Most of the time they traveled around the world. Korsavitzky sang in concerts and at synagogues, and recorded and produced record albums.

Although they were both shunned by their families and lived alone together, they were very much in love with each other and very happy. Unfortunately, after seven gorgeous, lovely years, Korsavitzky got throat cancer and shortly thereafter died. Bernice was devastated and had a nervous breakdown. Korsavitzky left her his home in Long Island, but his will was contested by his children, and as a result, Bernice was left with very little money to live on. The Jewish community had never forgiven her for leaving her husband and four children and marrying Korsavitzky. It took her several years to recover from this tragedy.

Her close friends tried to help her find a new husband. At that time, there was a very important man in the Jewish community named Mr. Fisher. For years, he was the executive director of the Jewish National Fund, an organization which raised money in the U.S. for forestation in Israel, reclaiming the land and planting trees all over Israel. Coincidentally, it was the same organization for which my father worked as assistant controller for over 40 years in Israel. Mr. Fisher was a very rough and tough person and a great achiever for his organization.

Mr. Fisher was much older than Bernice and had lost his wife, and he and Bernice got married. For Bernice, who needed a home, it was just a marriage of convenience. Fisher's family resented that marriage because of Bernice's previous marriage to Korsavitzky and her unforgivable abandonment of her husband and children.

Five years later, Fisher also got cancer. For the next two years, Bernice had to take care of him. He was in and out of the hospital and she nursed him at home. Fisher's family did not help her. They hated Bernice. Eventually Fisher died and Bernice was left a widow for the second time. Fisher left Bernice very little money. Most of it he left to his children, although Bernice was the one who had taken care of him.

This was the period during which we met Bernice. She introduced us to two Jewish organizations. One was the Jewish National

Fund, with which she was associated while Fisher was alive, and the second was the Zionist Organization of America, a political supporter of Israel. By this time, I was able to donate money to these organizations, and Florence and I became active members, all due to Bernice's influence. We became very close friends with her.

By this time, four of her children had grown up and had families of their own. As time passed they understood the tragedies which had befallen their mother and came back to love her, forgiving her for what she did when they were children. Her first husband, however, never forgave her, and she never saw him again. He became one of the wealthiest men in the city of Cleveland and a great supporter of Israel, and donated a large sum of money to establishing Bar Ilan University in Israel. The children were all professionals and all were well taken care of by their father. Bernice now found herself surrounded by the love of her children and grandchildren. They all cared for her and helped her financially.

Bernice wanted to settle in Israel, and her children helped her settle in a small beautiful apartment in Tel Aviv. They provided her income so she could have a comfortable life in her new home. In no time, Bernice's home became a center of artists' lives. She was a great cook and great entertainer. She was surrounded by many new young Israeli friends, who loved to spend time with her, eating her great food that she cooked. She helped many painters and singers from America and Canada who came to Israel and had a difficult time adjusting in the new land. She was a second mother to them. She loved her life in Israel and on occasion, she had a young lover attracted to her. She was young and adventurous in spirit, and men fell in love with her despite her age. One middle-aged writer, who was married with three grown children, fell in love with her, and a long-term relationship developed between them. She helped the writer publish his books. The writer's wife knew of the romance and went along with it, not objecting, which was strange in a way.

Our Forest In Israel

In New York, we were busy with meetings and dinners with the Jewish National Fund. Each year they organized trips to Israel for their potential donors. We were invited to participate in one of these trips. At first, I objected to the idea of touring Israel with a group, because I felt that as an Israeli, I did not need anyone to show me around the country in which I had grown up. But Florence persuaded me to go anyway.

To my surprise, this visit turned out to be one of the best I have ever made. Each day, two busloads of our members were taken to see the work of the Jewish National Fund, the beautiful forest with millions of trees planted on the barren rocky hills of the country. We traveled north up to the Lebanon border, the hilly part of the country, visiting Nazareth, Tiberius, Haifa, and the beautiful Jesrael valley. We passed by my uncle's kibbutz where I spent my summer when I was seven years old, and passed through Haifa, where Florence and I lived before moving to Beer Sheva. Each evening we ate dinner with the group and listened to local speakers, learning a great deal about the work of the Jewish National Fund.

We traveled through Beer Sheva; the town that I helped to build, and stopped there for lunch. It was now a town of over 100,000 inhabitants, bustling with buses, cars, and heavy traffic. It made me very proud to see the result of my pioneering days. We stopped at the Solomon Mines where King Solomon had his copper mines, and stopped at a small lagoon, built by the Jewish National Fund with donations from one of the members traveling with us. At nightfall, we had dinner out near the lagoon. The moon was full, shining brightly, and the sight of the water between the wild rocky mountains by the Solomon Mines was a sight that one could not forget.

We continued after dinner to Eilat, passing through the Egyptian border to the Hilton Hotel. This was unexpected because just the previous week, Israel had returned that part of Eilat to Egypt, and our reservation to the hotel had been made before the transfer of that part of the land to Egypt. It took us some time to go through the border because it was an all-new experience to the border police on both sides of the border. The hotel was a great hotel, but the service with the new Egyptian personnel was not too efficient.

The next morning we found ourselves on the most beautiful beach with a great swimming pool and we spent the day relaxing. That evening we were entertained by a group of singers and dancers who came through the border from Eilat, and we had a great time.

The next morning we left to return to Jerusalem, passing by several large water reservoirs, built by the Jewish National Fund with donations from its members. The purpose of our trip was of course to promote the donations from the participants in the trip.

Florence and I were impressed, and we decided to donate money for a small forest of 10,000 trees. When we returned to Jerusalem, we discussed it with Sam, the executive director of the Jewish National Fund, and it was decided that we would be taken around the country the next morning to choose the site of our forest.

Our guide was, surprisingly, a former German S.S. member who had converted to Judaism, settled in Israel after the war, married an Israeli Sabra girl, and had three children. Getroia drove us to the northern part of the country and showed us various forests, suggesting that we should have our forest of 10,000 trees incorporated into a larger forest. This idea did not sit well with Florence. She insisted that she wanted a forest all of her own, separate from any other. Getroia told us that this was impossible. We had already deposited $5,000 as a down payment on our forest. When we returned to Jerusalem, we told our friend Sam Cohen that there were no hard feelings, but since we could not have our own forest, we would like to have our $5,000 deposit back, because we knew of other organizations to whom we could donate it.

Sam was quite upset. Not wanting to lose our deposit, he told Getroia that he must find a forest for us. The next morning, Getroia grudgingly took us again for a trip to see various sites, this time down south. Some of the forests were too small, some were too large, but Florence did like some locations. Eventually we passed a beautiful forest near the town of Keriat Gat. It was a lovely hill full of trees standing all by themselves. We stopped there, walked around, and Florence said, "This is the forest I want." Getroia turned to her and said, "But Mrs. Margolin, this forest has 40,000 trees, four times the size of the forest you were looking for, and your donation will have to be four times larger." We told Getroia that we would like to talk it over. We left Getroia and walked around the forest, discussing the matter between us.

The donation involved was much greater than we wanted to commit ourselves for; however, if we could pay for it over the course of ten years, we could undertake this commitment.

We told Getroia that we were interested and we would discuss the matter with Sam when we returned to Jerusalem. When Sam heard of our interest he was delighted, and when we returned to New York, we signed up an agreement to have the forest of 40,000 trees near Keriat Gat named "Margolin Peace Forest," because at the time, Israel had just signed a peace agreement with Egypt. Our forest was the first to be called Peace Forest. Florence and I were very happy with our new acquisition. For years to come many new donors, who saw our forest donated additional funds into our forest and had their names added to our memorial stone, which was standing next to our forest.

Each time we visited Israel we traveled to Keriat Gat to see and inspect our forest. Since the forest was close to the town of Keriat Gat, it became a picnic area visited by young families during the summers who left garbage all around the forest. It also must have been a lovers' nest, for many left their condoms spread around the forest ground. When we returned to New York we complained to Sam about it, and in time the forest was cleaned, the trees were trimmed, and the forest became a beautiful site again. Many of our friends who visited Israel traveled also to see our forest and bring back pictures of their visit there. To promote additional donation to the forest we printed a small brochure describing our forest as follows:

Whenever I think about the forest, or visit there, I always think about how interesting life is and how full of unexpected connections: my father's settlement in Israel, working for the Jewish National Fund for 40 years in Israel, and me in the U.S., working and establishing a forest in memory of our family in the land of Israel. How fortunate I am to be able to make this possible.

325

Selected Photos

Rabbi Jakob Pollack and his wife in Jerusalem
Deceased 2006

My Friend, Rabbi Sholom Duchman
Executive Director of Colel Chabad

326

Selected Photos

With Israel Chief Ashkehazi
Rabbi Yisrael Meir Lau

With The Lubaritche
Rabbi Menachem Mendel Schneerson

Selected Photos

Yakov Wachtel with my
sister, brother and me

My Kindergarten Friend,
Yakov Wachtel in my office
in New York - 75 years later

Nancy, who for 15 years
was my devoted secretary
Deceased 2008

Selected Photos

President Shimon Peres with Eilat Mayor, Rafi Hoffman

Members of Eilat Foundation Board with President Shimon Peres

Mayor Shlomo Lahat with Mayor of Boston

Selected Photos

**Bernice Fisher Korsavitzky
At the Israeli President's Home**

**Sarah Caldwell Received a Citation from
Jewish National Fund
with Kitty Carlisle Hart and Sam Choen**

330

Selected Photos

David Hachoen

**Hilton Hotel in Beer Sheva
1994**

Selected Photos

Selected Photos

333

Selected Photos

Florence and I visiting our Forest

334

Selected Photos

Florence and David
(Current Picture)

David and I
(Current Picture)

Florence and I on Our 60th Anniversary

Selected Photos

Yakov Lior,
My High School Friend

Avigdor and me
Baharien/ Beer Sheva

Moshe Kaufman, Elementary School Friend, Architect,
Writer, Painter, and Archaeologist and his wife, Mila
www.holy-land-landscapes.com

Selected Photos

Speaking at President Yizhak Navon's home

Florence and my sister, Mira

My Brother, Maza, his grandson, Guy and his wife, Nitza

Selected Photos

1950. Finance Minister Eliezer Kaplan's visit to the Negev for developing the Mining Industries including: Horowitz, Finkelstein, Givon, Hillel, Hachoen and Tuviyahu

Index

*(Page Number in *Italics* are Pictures)

A

Abadan, Iran 64, 65, 74-92, *93-96*, 101, *109*, 111, 112, 146, 153, 154, 200, 227
Abraham (Bible, Beer Sheva) 146
Achashverosh (Old Persian Monarch) 32
Adamas Carbide Company 183
Aegean Sea 24
Afula (Town in Israel) 47
Ahmad, also known as Little Ahmad (Beer Sheva) 154
"Aida" (Opera) 271, 273, 274
Alice Chambers (tractors) 113
Aliyah (Immigration) 25
American Air Force 100, 120, 130
American Association of the Construction Equipment Association 113
American Farber (kitchen pots) 65
American Jews 114
American Israel Opera Foundation 249, 275-284
American Technion Society 64, 180-188
Amtis Corporation (USA) 188
Anglo Persian Oil Company Refinery 75, 78
Ariali School (Haifa) 55
Aushiskin (J.N.F. Founder) 28
Avigdor (Solel-Boneh) 66, 97, 98, 148, *335*

B

Baghdad 77, 78, 98
Baharien Island 64-66, 97-108, *109*, *110*, 111, 112, 146, 148, 200
Baksheesh (money) 85
Baranoff Family (Mekor Chaim) 40-43
Barbar Green (tractor company) 113

Bardin, Ruth 57-61, *71*, 111, 136, *140*
Baroque style 25
Bosmat (Technion High School) 53, 61, *71*
Bazaar (Jerusalem) 52, 165, 265, 268
Beer Sheva 66, 142-167, *168-172*, 176, 177, 302, 303, 310, 311, *330*
Beit Safafa (Arab-Jerusalem Village) 36, 40, 43
Ben Gurion, David 112, 145, 147, 149, 153, 160, 161, *170*, *171*, 243
Berman, Mira (Opera) 276
Bernstein, Leonard 270
Beth Habocharim Housing Center (Jerusalem) 25-30, 31, 33, 43, 313
Bethlehem *294*
Bet Sefer Miktzue Tichoni (Technical High School in Haifa) 53
Bible 34, 35, 146, 306
Black, Ed (my underground Operator's name) 130
Black, Florence (Florida presumed name) 132
Black Sea 24
Bloch Publishing Co. 60
Bob (office) 211, 212
Bonis, Laszlo (Opera Company of Boston President) 284
Boy Scouts of America 187
Brandeis, Louis (judge) 60
Brigadier General of the British Mechanical Engineers 79
Brisk, Lithuania 36
British Administration 29
British Air Force 97, 98, 100, 107
British Army 40, 42, 69, 70, 91
British Authority 30, 74
British Foreign Management 89
British High Commissioner 29, 30
British Institute of Engineering 68
British Iranian club 91
British Israel Army 91
British Social Club 88
Brooklyn 60, 135, 192, 213, 230, 231
Brooklyn Chamber of Commerce 60
Brooklyn College 60
Brooklyn Jewish Hospital 60

Brooklyn Ethical Culture Society 60
Buckhara 25
Bullet Train (Japan) 253

C

Caftan (robe) 154
Caldwell, Sarah 241-292, *293-300*, 309, *329*
Campanelo, Gaspar (personnel agency manager) 199-202, 205
Canary Islands 137
Carmel Mountain 55
Caterpillar Tractors 63, 100, 113
Cathy (our next door office neighbor) 226
Central Park West 115
Chabad girls (religious) 26
Chaim (my father's first name) 19
Chorev School (Jerusalem) 315, 316
Clark, John (employee) 228-230
Clark, Rose (John Clark's wife) 229, 230
Claustrophobia 33
Columbia University 15, 60, 111, 113, 114, 118
Columbia University Teachers College 60
Communist government 19, 20
Cossacks (Ukraine) 20-22
Czar (Russia) 19

D

Dalia (Florence's friend) 115, 116, *160*
Damascus 76
Dan, Hiller (Solel-Boneh founder) 144, 145, 147, 177, 178
David (office employee) 221, 222
Dead Sea 68
Demona (Town South of Israel) 243, 244
Denmark 60
Dephilip, Edith (Israel Opera Company Founder) 241-243
Dewitt Clinton (Boat) 136

Dina (Uncle Moshe's friend) 49
Dinaborg, Avraham (old friend) 44
Domingo, Placido (singer) 241
Dov (English boy in Beer Sheva) 154, 155
Drafting 54, 174-176
Dr. Aharony (Bosmat Principal) 61
Dr. Bardin, Shlomo 56-61, 67, *71*, 111
Dr. Gardella, Joe (Sarah's Doctor in Boston University Hospital) 282, 291
Dr. Loue (Boston University Hospital) 317, 318
Dr. Yedidia (Beer Sheva Hadasa Hospital) 154, 155, 162

E

Egen (Hungarian word "yes") 156
Eilat (Town South of Israel) 164, 322, 323, *328*
Emek Israel (Jesrael Valley) 45
Empire Hotel (NYC) 112
Esterka (Uncle Moshe's Wife) 49
Esther (my mother) 19
Ethiopian church 34
Etzel (Underground Jewish Organization) 26
Euphrates River (Iran) 78
Even-Vesid Stone Company 179
Ezra Street (Jerusalem) 26

F

Feldman, Sam (my attorney) 203
Fishman, Jay (office) 217
Fisher, Bernice Korsavitzky 318-321, *329*
foot-loom weaving (Ruth Bardin) 60
French Hospital 43

G

Gangrene 162, 210

Geola (Street in Jerusalem) 31, 33
George (department manager) 223, 224
General Motors 63, 126
German Army 19
German Air Force 91
Germany 29, 39, 65, 116, 185, 256, 307
Ginigar (Kibbutz in Jesrael Valley) 45
Ginsberg, Baron (Russia) 19, 28
German colony (Haifa) 55
Goodfriend, Sidney (my Bookkeeper) 210, 211, 214-216, *239*
Greek Orthodox Church 36

H

Habima Theater (Tel Aviv) 264
Hach'sha'rat Ha'ye'shuv (settlement development) 36
Hachoen, David (Solel-Boneh) 45, 74-76, *330, 337*
Hachoen, Ruth 45
Hadar Hacarmel (Haifa) 55
Hadassah Hospital (Jerusalem) 150, 162
Hagalila (Boat) 136
Haganah (Jewish underground organization) 40, 42, 62, 82, 83, 117, 124, 142
Haifa 49, 52-57, 61-63, 65, 75, 76, 90, 91, 107, 108, 126, 142, 143, 146, 147, 149, 152, 165, 179-182, 185, 187, 233, 322
Haredim 35
Haman (Purim Festival Jew Hater) 32
Hanna (Florence's Mother) 173, 174
Harsa (Ceramic factory in Beer Sheva) 166
Hatziana, Markella (Singer) 278
Hebron (Israel town) 43, 69, 70, *72, 73*, 265
Hebrew 28, 31, 33, 34, 38, 57, 60, 77, 125, 150, 232, 248, 317
Hefetz (Buckarian Family) 25
Hertzel Street (Haifa) 55
Histadrut (Labor Organization) 144
Holocaust 116, 135, 136
Holon (Israel town) 232

Hovala (Dead Sea Trucking Co.) 68
Hudson River 128, 136, 236

I

Irgonit (Israel Opera scenery Mfg.) 269, 282, 283
Immigration Department 183
Industrial School of Engineering at Columbia University 113
International Commerce and Shipping 117
Isphan (City in Iran) 88
Israel 16, 19, 23-26, 28-31, 33, 34, 40, 44, 45, 47, 52, 60, 62-66, 74, 79-81, 83, 88, 89, 91, 92, 97-99, 111, 112, 114-116, 118-120, 123-126, 128-130, 132, 133, 135, 136, 138, 142-148, 150, 151, 155, 157, 160, 162-164, 167, 174-194, 200, 227, 232, 236, 241-247, 149, 250, 255, 256, 261-267, 269, 271, 273-277, 282-284, 302-304, 306-314, 316-324
Israel Defense Forces 62
Israel Defense Industries Equipment and Machinery 64
Israeli Army 43, 117, 128, 129, 146, 161, 244
Israeli Flying Club (Beer Sheva) 158
Israeli landscapes 25
Israeli Opera 246, 261, 273, 275
Israeli Opera Company 241-244
Israeli Symphony Orchestra 264
Isratech Marketing Corporation (NYC) 304
Istanbul, Turkey 24

J

Jaffa (City) 24-27, 37, 265
Jaffa Road 44
Jenkins, Speight (Seattle Opera Co.) 287
Jesrael Valley (Israel Valley) 322
Jerusalem 25-29, 31, 35-37, 39, 40, 43, 49, *51*, 52-54, 57, 66-70, *72*, 89, 90, 115, 116, 142, 146, 150 ,151, 162, 179, 193, 252, 264, 265, 268, 314, 315, 323, 324, *325*
Jesus (Messiah) 127, 268, 269
Jewish 19, 20, 23, 26, 33, 35, 39, 40, 63, 74, 114, 120, 129, 181, 320

Jewish Agency 74, 81
Jewish Cemetery 22
Jewish Families 25, 60, 88, 217
Jewish immigrants 16, 55
Jewish National Fund 28, 45, 57, 146, 320, 322-324, *329*
Jewish paramilitary organization 62
Jewish Theological Seminary 115, 128, 136
Jews 35, 40, 43, 81, 114, 120, 129, 133, 248
Joe 121, 122, *239*
Johnson, Ed 305, 306
Jonas, Nathan S. 60
Jonas, Ralph 60
Jones Beach 208
Jordan River 80, 164
Julliard School of Music (NYC) 280

K

Kaolin Rock (quarry in the Negev) 164
Kaddish (prayer for the dead) 234, 313, 314
Kashan (Iranian carpet) 88
Katzenelson, Zeev (Dead Sea Trucking Manager) 68
Kaufman, Moshe *335*
Kav-Venaki (Director) 179
Keren Hakeimet Leisrael (Jewish National Fund) 28, 29, 90
Keriat Gat (Israel Town in the Negev) 323, 324
Kfar Saba (small town north of Tel Aviv) 62
Kibbutz 37, 44-49, 63, 90, 118, 119, 147, 162, 301, 307, 310-312, 322
Kibbutz Mizra 310
Kibbutzniks 46, 118, 124, 125, 156
Kibbutzim 34, 47, 64, 90, 304, 309, 310
Kinert (Sea of Galilee) 80, 164
Kiev (Ukraine) 19
Knappen Tibbetts Abbett McKarthy Engineers 175
Korsavitzky (Chazan) 319-320
Kosher 310
Koussevitzky, Dr. Sergei 270

Krogliak, Moshe (my uncle) 25, 44, 45, 47-49, 118
Ku Klux Klan 113

L

Lahat, Shlomo (Mayor of Tel Aviv) 243-245, 247, 249, 261, 262, 265, 267, 269, 277, *295, 328*
Lake George (NY) 184
Landsman, Amos (Port of Haifa) 143
Lerner, Bob (Manager) 220, 221, *239*
Let's Make Music Together (Sarah Caldwell) 278
LeTourneau (Construction Equipment Co.) 113, 147, 161
Levine, Rosalie (wife of Joseph Levine, movie mogul) 270
Levinson, Micha (theater director) 283
Levy, David (My partner in Israel) 187, 188, 190-193
Lichnstein, Yakov (Yakov Lior, my friend) 62
Lida Airport 97
Lior, Sara 65
Lior, Yakov 62-66, *335*
Lodge, Linda Cabbot (Boston Opera) 270
London University 60, 68
Long Island University 60
Lubashevsky, Berle (my friend) 85

M

Macklef (Israeli General) 43
Makabi group 61
Manhama (town in Baharien Island) 100
Manila (City in Philippines) 253-259, *298*
Manufacturers Trust Company of Brooklyn 60
Mapay party (Israel) 158
Marcos, Madam Imelda (wife of President Marcos of the Philippines) 250
Margolin Personnel Agency 194-203, 205-237, *238-240*
Margolin, David 64, 174-180, 184, 187, 194, 201, 202, *204*, 206, 234, 237, *334*

Margolin, Florence 17, 49, 65, 66, 115, 116, 122-125, 128, 129, 132-136, *140*, *141*, 142-157, 161-167, 173, 174, 176-180, 182, 184-188, 190, 191, 193, 194, 196, 197, 200-203, 205, 206, 209, 218, 219, 222, 224, 226, 227, 230, 234-236, 241, 242, 244-250, 254-259, 261, 265, 267, 270-272, 274-277, 279-291, 294, *299*, *300*, 302, 304-306, 316, 321-324, *333*, *334*
Margolin, Maza (brother) 39, 89, *336*
Margolin, Mira (sister) 39, 314, *336*
Margolin Peace Forest (Keriat Gat, Israel) *293*, 322-324, *333*
Margolin Products (patented in the US) 177, *204*, 236
Maria (secretary) 211-216
Max (my father-in-law) 173
Mediterranean Sea (Coast) 24, 57, 58, 111, 128, 130
Meir, Golda (Meirson, Golda) 98, 153, 160, 162, 163, *170*
Meirson, Morris (Golda Meir's husband) 98, 99
Mekor Chaim (Jerusalem Village) 35-43, *51*, 313
Messiah 25, 26
Metropolitan Museum of Art 180, 181, 199, 280
Metropolitan Opera 259, 278, 281, 309
Methodist Zionist (Sarah) 241, 275
Micha (Kibbutz Mizra) 310, 311
Michael (Young Yemenite) 39
Mikve Israel (Agricultural School) 44
Milims (Pennies) 35
Milnes, Sherrill (Opera Singer) 272-274
Mira (Agency Employee) 217, 218
Miriam (English woman in Beer Sheva) 157
Miss Timken (Opera Co. of Boston) 284
Morgan, Jim (Opera Co. of Boston) 245-248, 272, 282, 286, 287, 290, 291
Moshav (settlement) 45
Moshe (Baharien Cook) 99, 100
Moshe (my best friend) 53
Moshe and Jacky (my best old friends in Israel) 262, 263
Mosque 147, 148, 158
Mount Carmel (Haifa) 54, 56, 57, 63, 111, 143, 181, 182
Mount of Olives (Jerusalem) 252
Mrs. Ben Gurion 112

Mrs. Bininfeld (Window Glass Distributor) 193
Mrs. Sokenic (mother of General Yegal Yadin and famous archeologist) 31
Mrs. Schwartz (Pension house owner in Haifa) 53, 54, 59, 62
Mr. Even-Zohar (Director of Israel Opera Company) 242-245
Mr. Fisher (Jewish National Fund) 318-321, *329*
Mr. Ilani (Jerusalem School Principal) 34
Mr. Korless (Abadan Iran Manager) 78, 79, 81, 82, 84, 85, 88, 90, 91
Mr. LeTourneau (Long View, Texas) 113
Mr. Weissberg (Solcoor employee) 177
Ms. Kasilag (Minister of Arts and Culture in the Philippines) 254, 255, 258
Muktar (Arab Chieftain) 42

N

Nahalal Settlement (Jesrael Valley) 45
Nameri, Davidka (Hagana Underground Operator) 117-130, 133, 135, *139*, 142
Navchan (my dog) 38
Nazareth 45, 48, 164, 166, 268, 322
Negev (south of Israel) 158, 162
Neta (Moshe's daughter) 49
New Church of the Nativity 268
New York 15, 42, 64, 66, 112, 114-116, 119, 122, 127, 128, 130, 132, 133, 135, 136, 142, 145, 146, 148, 150, 167, 173, 177, 178, 180, 184, 187, 188, 190, 193, 194, 207, 210, 211, 221, 231, 233, 234, 237, 245, 247-251, 259-262, 266, 267, 279, 280, 282, 286, 290, 292, 301, 303-307, 314, 316-318, 322, 324, *327*
New York City Board of Higher Education 59
New York Lincoln Center 254
New York Times *139*, 194, 196-198, 200-202, 206, 207, 210, 236, 279

O

Old City (of Jerusalem) 25, 36, 42, 43, 52, 79, 268, 315
Old Margolin (Solel-Boneh Founder, Director) 179

Olga (mother's friend in Mekor Chaim) 40
Opera Company of Boston 245, 249, 250, 253, 269, 271, 275, 277, 278, 284
Opera Company of Beijing (China) 279

P

Palestine 55, 60, 62-64, 74-76, 78, 81, 97, 98, 103, 107, 108, 114, 120, 121, 129, 144, 145
Palestinian Railroad Authority 40
Panamanian Consulate 135
Persia, Iran 64, 73, 75, 80
Philippines 250, 253-259, 260, 261, *298, 299*, 309
Physics 54
Pogroms (Russian riots against Jews) 19, 23
Police Department 30, 75
Professor Kaplasky (Past President of Technion in Israel) 60
Professor Ollendorf (Technion head of Electric Engineering Dept.) 185
Purim (Jewish Festival) 32, *50*

R

Rabbi Ha'im Cohen (Mekor Chaim) 36
Rabbi Jakob Pollak (Principal of Chorev School in Jerusalem) 313-318, *325*
Rabinovitz, Yudka (Hagana Undercover agent) 81, *96*
Rafa (My Russian name) 48, 271
Ramat Yochanan (Uncle Moshe's kibbutz) 49
Rebecca (office employee) 222
Red Army 19
Richon Letzion (town in Israel) 153
River Volga (Russia) 22
Riverside Drive 257, 234, 236
Riverside Park 128
Romania 20, 22-24, 28
Ron (singer) 260, 261
Rosa (my aunt) 23

Roseman Avrom (Israel Opera) 267-269
Ruben (office employee) 236, 237
Russia 19, 23, 25, 28, 40, 43, 44, 57, 74, 278, 279, 282, 319
Russian Orthodox Church 30
Russian Revolution 19
Russian Tea Room (NYC) 247, 262
Russian Tsar 266
Rusty (Florence's brother) 156

S

Saloma (Opera) 156
Saloniki (Greece) 55
Santa Fe 284-287, 289, 290
Sarah (office employee, Florence's friend) 218-220
Saudi Arabia Peninsula 101
Seattle Opera Company 287
Schneller (Jerusalem Neighborhood) 26, 35, 43, 44
Schwartz, Bill (American Technion Society) 181
Schwartz, Joe (manufacturer) 230-232
Sea of Galilee 163, 164, 269
Sharir (Israeli Artist-Painter) 269
Sheik (Muslim Religious Leader) 105, 106, 154
Sheila (Boston) 222-224
Shomer (kibbutz dog) 46, 47
Sieden, Norman (Technion Founder) 189, 190
Sea of Marmara (Mediterranean) 24
Sikh tribe (Indian) 83, 84
Snir, Chanan (Artistic Director) 283
Solcoor (NY Corporation) 180, 181
Solel-Boneh 45, 74, 80, 91, 97, 107, 108, 111, 143-145, 147, 149, 155, 157, 158, *171*, 177-181
Soviet Union 19
Steiglitz, Joe (Margolin office) 208
Stolman, Philip Pasach (Bar-Ilan University founder, Israel) 319
Sumeramis Hotel (Cairo) 112
Swoop, Girard (GM President, Retired) 184

Synagogue 25, 26, 38, 42, 88, 232, 269, 314, 320
Syria 76

T

Tachkimony Public School (Jerusalem) 34, *51*
Techina Chomos 48
Technion High School 53, 55, 60, 62, 65, 180, 185
Technion Israel Institute of Technology 60, 180
Tefillim (Religious articles) 314-316
Tel Aviv, City of 25, 40, 62, 65, 116, 126, 148, 149, 152, 155, 158, 159, 164, 165, 193, 232, 233, 242-245, 247, 249, 262, 264, 267-269, 276, *295*, 302, 307, 315, 316, 321
The house of the Messiah 25
"The Magic Flute" (Opera) 254-256, 259
"The Merry Widow" (Opera) 244
The New University of Ben Gurion 302-304
Tnuva (Dairy Food Co., Israel) 34
Tiberius (town near Sea Galilee) 164, 268, 269, 322
Times Square (New York) 253
Tokyo, Japan 250-253
Torah school 26
Tower of David (Jerusalem) 43
Trattoria (restaurant) 214
"Turandot" (Opera) 279, 281
Turkish Town Hall 158
Tulin, Mr. Abraham (Attorney, Technion founder) 184
Tuviyahu David (First Mayor of Beer Sheva) 145-148, 158, 160, 164, 166, 167, *171*, 302-304, *337*

U

Ukraine 19, 20, 28
United Nations 114
Upper West Side 114
Uvganin (Mekor Chaim, Jerusalem) 40
Uzbekistan 25

Uzi (automatic gun) 64

V

Vagman (Beer Sheva) 157
Verrett, Shirley (Opera singer) 272-275
Virginia Key (Florida) 126

W

Wachtel family (Beth Habocharim) 29, 30
Wachtel, Jackie (Yakov Wachtel) 29, 31, 33, 34, 313 *327*
Wadi 163
Wailing Wall in Jerusalem 252, 315
War of Independence 43
Water and Oil Drilling Company 233
Wertheimer Company 183
Wertheimer, Seth 183
West End Avenue 64, 178
Wheeler Julie (Santa Fe Opera) 285, 287
White Army 19
Woolworth (chain of stores) 191, 192
World War I (WWI) 26, 36, 136
World War II (WWII) 36, 119, 126, 257

Y

Yadin, Yegal (Israeli General and Famous Archeologist) 31
Yavitz, Boris *139, 140*
Yokinoam (Israel) 66
Yehudaiof (Jerusalem) 25
Yehudaiof, Elisha (Jerusalem) 26
Yemenite 39, 160
Yesacharov, Chay (Abadan Manager) 80, 81
Yezhak (my friend) 53
Yulish, Moshe (Solel-Boneh Manager) 98, 100, 103, 107, *110*

Z

Zhitomir (Russia) 60
Zionist 23, 30, 44, 60, 148, 241, 275, 319
Zionist Organization of America 321
Zionist Women's Organization 29